By Fire into Light

The Fiery Arrow Collection

Editors: Hein Blommestijn and Jos Huls of Titus Brandsma Institute

Advisory Board:

Elizabeth Dreyer, Silver Spring, U.S.A.
Chritopher O'Donnell, Dublin, Ireland
Helen Rolfson, Collegeville, U.S.A.
V.F. Vineeth, Bangalore, India
John Welch, Washington, U.S.A.

The *Fiery Arrow series* aims at the publication of books which connect their readers with the legacy of great teachers of spirituality from the distant and more recent past. Readers are offered a language and conceptual framework which can lead them to a deepened understanding of the spiritual life. The treasures of the spiritual tradition form a veritable "school of love", which is accessible to all who in contemplation desire to be touched by the fire of divine love. In 1270 A.D. Nicholas of France, former prior general of the Carmelites, wrote a letter bearing the title *Fiery Arrow* to his fellow brothers to urge them to call to mind again the fire of the beginning in which, in silence and solitude, they were consumed by the inescapable claim of the One. Based on the Carmelite tradition, this series seeks to share this spiritual legacy – which presents itself in a multiplicity of cultures and traditions – with all those who in a great variety of ways are in search of interior life and the fire of love. The series, which is grounded in scientific research, is aimed at a broad public interested in spirituality.

The Titus Brandsma Institute is an academic center of research in spirituality founded in 1968 by the Catholic University of Nijmegen and the Carmelite Order. Titus Brandsma, who from 1923 on was a professor of philosophy and the history of mysticism, especially that of the Low Countries, died in 1942 as a martyr in the Nazi death camp of Dachau and was beatified in 1985. The Institute continues his research in spirituality and mysticism with a staff of assistants and in collaboration with other researchers. In addition to this and other series, the Institute publishes the international periodical *Studies in Spirituality* and the series *Studies in Spirituality Supplement* (Peeters, Louvain).

Already published in this series:

1. Kees Waaijman
   The Mystical Space of Carmel
   An Interpretation of the Carmelite Rule
2. E.A. Van den Goorbergh, T.H. Zweerman
   Light Shining Through a Veil
   On Saint Clare's Letters to Saint Agnes of Prague
3. H. Blommestijn, J. Huls, K. Waaijman
   The Footprints of Love
   John of the Cross as Guide in the Wilderness

BY FIRE
INTO LIGHT

Four Catholic Martyrs of the Nazi Camps

by
JOSEPH M. MALHAM

PEETERS
LEUVEN – PARIS – DUDLEY, MA
2002

Library of Congress Cataloging – in – Publication Data

Malham, Joseph M.
  By fire into light : four Catholic martyrs of the Nazi camps / by Joseph M. Malham.
    p. cm. -- (The fiery arrow collection ; 4)
  Includes bibliographical references.
  ISBN 904291162X (alk. paper)
    1. Christian martyrs--Germany--Biography. 2. World War, 1939-1945--Atrocities.
  3. Stein, Edith, Saint, 1891-1942 4. Leisner, Karl, 1915-1945. I. Title. II. Series.

BX4659.G3 .M35 2002
272'.9'0922--dc21
[B]

                                                                2002066222

ISBN 90-429-1162-X
D. 2002/0602/83

© 2002 – Peeters, Bondgenotenlaan 153, B-3000 Leuven

Table of Contents

Acknowledgments

Writing a book such as this relies not so much on the intelligence of the author as it does upon the kindness of others. The list of those who helped and prayed this labor of love into fruition is endless, especially since the idea of writing a book about Catholic martyrs of the Nazi era had been simmering inside of me for several years. Unfortunately it is not possible to name everyone who assisted me with their hands and their hearts, but I will try to acknowledge as many as I can.

For their generosity, support and unconditional love for me as I struggled to find these 'Quatro Coronati', I would like to thank the following. Aside from my parents and my brothers and sisters, Reverend Christopher R. Armstrong of Cincinnati, Ohio and Reverend Bruno Healy of the Archdiocese of Westminster gave me encouragement and spiritual support during the entire process. Reverend Daniel C. O'Connell, S.J. of Loyola University of Chicago not only suggested including Blessed Karl Leisner in this book, but remained a spiritual beacon and stalwart friend during the long months of search and research. Loving support and encouragement was likewise given to me by Meltem Aktas, Joseph Luis Ramirez, Reverend Augustin Milon, OFM and Jim and Joan Lynch.

Sister Waltraud Herbstrith, OCD – whose writings on the life of Edith Stein enriched and inspired me on the way – gave generously of her time and wealth of knowledge during several days of interviews at the Edith-Stein-Karmel in Tübingen, Germany. Reverend Hein Blommestijn, O.Carm. of the Titus Brandsma Institute in Nijmegen, the Netherlands, has not only been a model of fraternal charity, but he also opened many doors that allowed an unknown author access to records and historical documents that helped to put the life and spirituality of Blessed Titus Brandsma into sharper focus. I would also like to express thanks to Reverend Constant Dölle, O.Carm., as well as to the Carmelites at the novitiate in Boxmeer, The Netherlands – some of whom knew Blessed Titus – for their generous hospitality and insights into the life of their brother Carmelite.

Herr Wilhelm Leisner of Berlin Germany graciously took me into his home and shared with me a wealth of facts, documents and stories on the life of his older brother Blessed Karl Leisner. Fellow author Suzanne Batzdorff gave me kind words of support and encouragement as I endeavored to reveal something new about the life of her aunt, Edith Stein. I would also like to thank Abbot Roger Corpus, OSB, Reverend Marion Balsavich, OSB, Reverend Claude Peifer, OSB, Reverend Joseph Heyd, OSB and all the monks at Saint Bede Abbey in Peru, Illinois, who in the great Bene-dictine traditions of hospitality, prayer and work, gave me infinite support and encouragement as I struggled to construct my book in their guestrooms and library.

For the monumental task of editing this manuscript as well as that of translating numerous documents into English, I would like to express profound gratitude to the following: Reverend Marion Balsavich, OSB, Reverend Hein Blommestijn, O.Carm., Reverend Daniel C. O'Connell, SJ, Sister Vivian Wilson, BVM, and the Carmelite Nuns of the Carmel of Saint Joseph in Des Plaines, IL. Without them the miracle of bringing polished order to chaos could never have been accomplished.

While I have utilized many numerous and secondary sources as well as interviews for the writing of this book, as the author I accept full responsibility for any errors, oversights and omissions.

Joseph M. Malham
Chicago, IL
January 2, 2001

Foreword

Why do books get written? Well, in the present instance, I am partially responsible insofar as I encouraged the author to undertake this project. More of that later. But a question ultimately of even more importance is why people read books once they are written. My hope is that many will read this book because it adds an historical dimension to many things that were happening in Europe toward the end of the first half of the twentieth century in conjunction with the Second World War. More importantly, this dimension has to do with the overarching Providence of our loving heavenly Father in our lives. And so, in the present case the writing and the reading have the same finality: the realization of the Lord's own master plan in a little corner of the human family. That is no mere abstraction or pious formulation; it happens to concern the day-to-day working out of our eternal destiny.

So let's look at some of the reasons why this book got written.

Cynicism is the middle name of modernity. To say that nothing is sacred anymore is to voice a commonplace. Hero worship is quaint and outmoded; innocence is nonexistent; reverence is hypocritical; sincerity is suspect; altruism is psychologically sick, if not inconceivable to the behaviorist; the only virtue is pragmatic self-seeking; prayer is a private monologue before a mirror. The twentieth century is now irretrievable in its tragedies, among which are two World Wars, the 'me' generation, the sexual revolution, the canonization of wealth, the irresponsible consumption and destruction of the world's natural resources, the affluence of the First World, and the starvation, sickness and strangulation of the Third World.

Do we need a few heroes along the way? Very definitely! Each one of us can consider it a singular blessing if someone comes across our path who is simply good, someone who leads an exemplary life – the simpler the better. And they are out there, today as in every age of the Church. But genuine heroism is not at all melodramatic,

not showy, not self-important. Much of the sanctity in our midst
goes literally unheralded until the Last Judgment vindicates the
good in the sight of the entire people of God.

Meanwhile, good people must be spotlighted somehow. And
since self-advertisement is repugnant to holiness, their goodness
must be otherwise chronicled, archived, pulled together and nar-
rated for our edification and rejoicing. The difference between the
stories told in this volume and the novels, epics, sagas, myths and
(yes) television sitcoms where many of us seek the unusual is that
these narratives are simply true. They are chronicles of the lives of
a small selection of people, all of whom have in common that they
died in the same decade in the same cause – the defense of the
Faith. And so, the gist of their edification is simply that they teach
us how to live the Faith.

But there is more. They teach us not only how to live the Faith,
but how to die for the Faith. For all of them were Christian martyrs of the Nazi era. Each of them chose: not death itself, but a way
of life for Christ which led them ineluctably to death in His Holy
Name. Still their lives were the path to Him, not their deaths; their
deaths were rather the culmination of their lives, their homecom-
ing with Him. And again, the message is one which the postmod-
ern world will not hear: "Take up you cross and follow Me."
Instead we seek out a cool Christianity, a comfortable, First World
Christianity, where the cross of Christ does not belong. Not only do
we need the antidote of martyr's lives in our midst, we need to
freely expose our souls to their stories, to immerse ourselves in their
experiences of Christ in the very Holocaust itself. For that was the
venue of their deepest personal experience of Christ. There it was
that they learned of His love for all His children, there that they
learned to suffer with Him for the salvation of the human family,
and to forgive their persecutors as He did. It is precisely the whole
burnt offering which defines the very concept of sacrifice.

But this small volume is only a tiny sample from the dedicated
lives snuffed out in the mid-twentieth-century by evil forces in
central Europe. Literally thousand of other innocent people went
quietly to their deaths for Christ in the midst of this orgy of hate.

Why select these few?

It is hardly an accident that all the chapters in this book are about priests and/or religious. Some might see in this an ominous bias against the laity. I think not. There are good reasons to select precisely the lives represented here. Priests and religious represent the public life of the Church in a far more visible and official way then do laypersons. Their lives are also typically better chronicles and certified by public milestones than are those of the laity. And when all is said and done, written and oral records are the source-book of biography. Some level of notoriety is a necessary prerequisite for a written story.

Having said all that, one must hastily add that the Unknown Soldiers of Christ who lay buried under the rubble of Europe at the end of the Second World War are truly the Church Triumphant whom we should be and are celebrating in these pages. Christians do not love the Lord by virtue of their public roles in the Mystical Body, but through His Grace hidden in their hearts. The lives selected in these pages are far more the representative of God's people than of His shepherds – chosen ones from among His people.

And just as appropriately, it is a layman who has undertaken this project. Joseph Malham has quite obviously done his homework well. He is already remarkably well read in Catholic spiritual literature. He has traveled throughout Europe to interview people who have known these martyrs of Christ, has visited their homelands and the places where they worked, were persecuted, imprisoned and died. He has read everything he could lay his hands on about them. And it shows in sensitive biographical essays which accurately and reverently – and humanly – depict the lives of these heroes for Christ. History's great virtue is precisely afterthought, and it is only there that clarity finally emerges. This is what Joseph Malham has succeeded in producing in his retrospective narratives of these few among many Christian martyrs of the Nazi era. He has truly entered into the spirit of dedication of their lives in order to breathe life into them for us.

Central Europe is no stranger to me; I am very much at home there. And I smugly thought, before reading these essays, that I was as well informed as I was ever going to be about what happened to these Christian martyrs. Not only have I been richly educated, but moved to tears by these narratives. They are not theological reflections, and they are certainly not intended as scholarly, professional history. They are intended precisely for the edification of Christ's Mystical Body. I am deeply grateful for the privilege to have been one of the first to read them and to be moved to a deeper love of Christ and His people.

Over a year ago, Joseph Malham proposed this project and asked my advice about taking leave of his usual work commitments to do the needed research in Europe. It was clearly a risk in terms of ordinary, everyday prudence, but I had no hesitation in giving him my blessing. Now I know in a much deeper way why his decision was correct.

It was I who put Joseph Malham in contact with Wilhelm Leisner, younger brother of Blessed Karl Leisner. Today, Herr Leisner is still a very active member of Mother of Sorrows Parish in Berlin Lankwitz, where I have been helping out pastorally for a couple of decades. Not far from there, many Christian martyrs were detained for interrogation at the Gestapo offices on the Albrechtstrasse. And some miles further away stands the Queen of Martyrs Carmelite Convent, founded by sisters from Dachau to commemorate the Christian martyrs, especially those of the nearby Liechtensee.

In the summer of 1996 shortly after Karl Leisner's beatification, I was privileged to be with the Leisner family to concelebrate Mass – the first annual commemoration of Blessed Karl Leisner, Martyr. We are pledged not to forget those who died for their Faith in the Holocaust.

Daniel C. O'Connell, S.J.
Loyola University of Chicago
St.Patrick's Day
March 17, 2000

Chapter I

Mystic in a Train Compartment

Titus Brandsma, O.Carm.

On the evening of January 19, 1942, two men knocked on the door of the Carmelite Friary in Nijmegen, Holland, and asked to see Father Titus Brandsma. The porter did not find the request unusual, as streams of visitors seemed to constantly pour into the parlor of the otherwise silent and peaceful friary on the Dodden-daal. The old and the young, students, journalists, the famous, the anonymous, the troubled and especially the poor all knew they would get a warm smile, spiritual wisdom, practical advice and often a good cigar from the friar known throughout Nijmegen, indeed throughout Holland, as simply "The Professor."

The scholastic nickname was by no means pejorative in origin, nor did it suggest an egghead or lofty academic far removed from the life and struggles of the common person. The title conferred on Father Titus was conferred in love and with respect, the basis of which was his widespread reputation as priest and professor that carried far beyond the dikes and marshes of the Gelderland.

A tireless, prolific author, Father Titus began writing essays and articles as a young Carmelite novice and never stopped. He was an indefatigable champion of education, and through his contributions the first Catholic university on Dutch soil rose in Nijmegen in 1923. He not only became a highly respected professor of philosophy and theology, and in 1932 was named *Rector Magnificus* – a position of great honor held for one year – of that institution as a token of the esteem and affection of the nation's Catholic citizens.

Father Titus had a deep devotion to the spiritual and secular traditions of his homeland, and not only did he promote the language and culture of his native region of Frisia, but helped to revive Marian devotion and pilgrim shrines in a predominately Protestant province. No subject or cause was beyond his eye or interest.

First and foremost, however, Father Titus was a priest, and as such saw his life as a sacrificial journey centered on the divine person of Jesus Christ. The casual acquaintance or passerby could only marvel at his dynamo-like energy and passion. The close observer came close to the source.

The quiet friary in which the two gentlemen waited was both a retreat as well as a re-charge for the friar who was engaged in constant and often nerve-frying activity. As placid and contemplative as were the walls and cloister corridors of Carmel, the friary nevertheless remained a tributary, and not the source of his prayer and peace. He was much too spiritually mature and practically detached to find strength in mere stone.

Father Titus lived his whole life in a total spirit of recollection in the presence of God, whether it was in the cloister, classroom or foreign lecture hall. Forced by the circumstances of place and natural talents into the world of higher education, Father Titus remained silently rooted in a prayerful and constant attention to the Lord. Immersed in the teachings and lives of the great mystics – especially the Lowland Mystics of the Middle Ages – he followed a path of prayer that, while mystical in itself, was characterized more by joy and pragmatism than by supernatural phenomena.

Practicality in prayer should never be confused with ease, as the endeavor to seek God's will and remain in his love was as constant a struggle for Father Titus as it was for his Lowland Mystics as it is for us today. He had no recipe or formula, but fidelity to a basic idea of total abandonment to God's will as seen by the light of one word: love. He made love the driving force and the deepest desire of his life, and he sought God in ordinary circumstances, in every face and situation he encountered in day to day life.

It was the utter simplicity of Father Titus' love for God and humanity, as opposed to a complex theory, that drove so many disparate individuals from all over the country to seek him out.

This unconditional love of God and neighbor, difficult under the most idyllic conditions, had by 1942 become a risky dance of death on the edge of a very sharp blade. Europe at this time was barreling toward the third year of World War II, and the Netherlands were at the moment under Nazi military rule. The forces of Adolf Hitler's Third Reich were blitzkrieging and bulldozing a bloody path across the entire face of the continent, with no signs of halting or even slowing in the near future.

Beginning with the Anschluss with Austria in March, 1938 followed by the annexation of the Czech Sudetenland and culminating in the outright invasion of Poland in 1939, the Führer was intent on making short work of all nations large and small who dared defy the destiny of National Socialism. By 1940, with France on the verge of collapse and England bravely retrenching for a solitary defense, the Northern and Low countries quickly fell one at a time to Hitler's Luftwaffe and Wehrmacht.

With brutal efficiency, the National-Socialistiche Beweging (N.S.B.), the Dutch Nazi Party, slammed a jackboot down on the neck of occupied Holland and began mercilessly cutting every artery of resistance and revolt. Patriots and intellectuals disappeared, churches, papers and youth organizations were silenced or suppressed, and Jewish citizens were rounded up and deported to concentration camps. In Holland they were sent first to Westerbork in the northern part of the country, and later to faraway places in the east with strange and blood-chilling names like Auschwitz, Treblinka and Maidenek.

In the midst of these horrifying and uncertain times, it was quite natural that two young men would seek out Father Titus' help in what could be anything from untangling a spiritual conflict or educational problem to evading a Nazi roundup or interrogation. It was a dangerous time, a time of suspicions and terrors as well as sacrifice and heroism when people were just as likely to risk their life for friends as they were to betray them to the Gestapo.

Many young people, including many of Father Titus' students at the university, were in the underground resistance movement, and all knew of the friar's increasingly vocal opposition to Nazi tyranny.

Despite the difference in years, the young and the stouthearted knew they would find a friend and kindred spirit in the Professor. Yes, Father Titus would be happy to speak with these two gentlemen.

It will never be known whether or not the two men were charmed by their first encounter with the Professor. It would have been singularly odd if they were not, because almost everybody was.

The Friar who stepped into the parlor was a short man, about sixty years old, but possessing a quality of presence and youthfulness of spirit that made actual age irrelevant. His steel gray hair, brushed back to a height that made him seem taller, was the only visible concession to the close of his middle years. Behind the steel rimmed spectacles, without which he was legally blind, were clear, bright eyes that held a warmth and a kindness so memorable that people who last saw them in 1942 remembered them for decades.

Father Titus had a good face, a Dutch face, expressing a straightforward, no-nonsense view of life free from exaggeration or equivocation.

Father Titus wore the long habit of the Carmelite friars – brown tunic, matching scapular and cowl draped wide over the shoulders. In choir or during liturgical functions outside of Mass, he wore a long white wool cape. While teaching, travelling, or engaged in business outside the friary, he would wear a black clerical suit, white Roman collar and a jaunty black fedora.

Like most Dutchmen, Father Titus was often wreathed in the blue smoke of a black cigar, one of the constant luxuries the otherwise poor friar allowed himself. No pious purveyor of showy mortifications, Father Titus lived a life of joyous detachment, yet he enjoyed everything from sightseeing at Niagara Falls and football matches to cigars and a glass of Scotch with his Carmelite confreres in England.

He saw everything as a gift from God that needed to be shared with others. Often, when entering the parlor, Father Titus would be carrying a box of cigars under his arm to share with his guests. "Wherever we are," he would say, "there should be a feast."[1]

---

[1] "The Life and Witness of Father Titus" by Aquinas Houle, edited by Mark Ciganovich, O.Carm. in *Essays on Titus Brandsma: Carmelite, Educator, Journalist,*

He would not have time to make such an offer and receive a reply, as one of the gentlemen immediately identified himself as Steffen of the *Sicherheitdienst* (SD), the security arm of the dreaded Nazi SS. He immediately produced a warrant for the arrest of Professor Doctor Brandsma, who was to be escorted that very night to prison.

While searching Father Titus' room, the security police overturned furniture, emptied wardrobes and desks, and stuffed reams of notes, manuscripts, essays and letters in varying stages of completion, into a valise as evidence. In actuality, the SD had been watching Father Titus for some time, increasingly suspicious of his actions and recent travels throughout Holland. It was the opinion of the Party that sooner or later they would have to arrest Professor Brandsma, a feeling no doubt shared with increasing intensity by the friar himself.

To the SD, Father Titus was not merely the 'Professor', but a living threat to the security of the military government of occupation. Indeed, the Nazis knew a great deal about Father Titus for a long time, a report going so far as to refer to him as a "dangerous little friar."

And now they had him.

Birth and Early Years

To understand an individual in toto, it is essential to understand the soil from which they came. Father Titus was born Anno Sjoerd Brandsma on February 23, 1881, at Oegeklooster, a hamlet in the northern Dutch province of Friesland. His parents, Titus and Tjitsje Brandsma, were devout Catholics in a predominantly Protestant region, and they welcomed this fifth child and first son with genuine joy and a sense of gratitude. Not only did he provide a genealogical continuum to the family, but an extra set of hands on the sprawling and busy farm as well.

Martyr, edited by Redemptus Maria Valabek, O.Carm (Rome: Carmel in the World Paperbacks, 1985), p. 18.

Titus senior, despite the starched, autocratic air conveyed by his photographs, was a warm and loving individual invested in the practical affairs of his family, his faith and his community. No gentleman farmer, Titus senior was a genuine sodbuster who, in between the interminable duties required of him as *paterfamilias* and farmer, still found time to serve the local church, his town and the local schools.

The father was, by all accounts, a solid and respected individual whose Victorian air of respectability and propriety was warmed by a love of family, an appreciation of music and festivals and an unwavering devotion to his Catholic faith.

A photograph of Tjitsje Brandsma, obviously taken in her later years, shows a woman who with her kind, simple face and distinctive lace Frisian cap, could have stepped out of a Frans Hals portrait. Hard working and warm like her husband, Tjitsje possessed a deeply spiritual center that the practicalities of farm and family prevented from straying into sentimentalism or maudlin piety.

It would be wrong, laughable even, to think that life with a future martyr for the Faith was a placid, carefree existence, bathed in warm and ethereal colors. Like all peoples living by the laws of the earth and the constraints of an agrarian economy, the Brandsmas struggled and sacrificed and yet somehow kept body and soul together during good times and bad.

Life on a nineteenth century farm, like today, required a tremendous amount of work and discipline, and the fact that Titus senior found time for the extra-curricular activities in the church and in town politics attests to the family's sense of organization and clarity of purpose.

The Catholic faith into which Anno was born was not only learned at his parent's knees, but observed from the actions of their hands as well. This experiential absorption of faith did more than turn the Brandsma children into good and observant Catholics. It heightened their sense of stimulus and response to God's voice, and five of the six children – two boys and three girls – eventually entered into the religious life.

Giving almost their entire family to the service of the Church, especially in an age and place where farmer children married and rarely lived a few miles from their home, must have caused Titus and Tjitsje a great deal of pain as well as pride. The extent, however, to which the two emotions mingled were forever hidden in the tidy rooms and cozy hearth of Oegeklooster. As they accepted children out of obedience to God, so they gave them back.

That is the family from which Anno came, but what of the soil? With people of the land, it is often difficult to separate the characteristics of one from the characteristics of the other, since they are inextricably linked in an intimate bond few modern urbanites can even begin to grasp.

The rhythms and cycles of the earth, flowing unimpeded through time, hold a metaphysical mirror in front of the people called to work the soil. The coming of darkness and the return of light, the benediction that is rain and the blessing that is the harvest, the death of the land in winter and its eventual rebirth in the spring all represent mystical parallels to human existence not lost on the farmer.

The land, however, like the sea, does not produce starry-eyed dreamers but active contemplatives of the best kind, whose understanding of God and their own humanity comes from a constant, often confrontational, coexistence with the elements. Sandwiched in between the land and the treacherous vastness of the North Sea, Friesland produced a particularly diligent and hardy stock who more than proved this to be true. When seen from the windows of a moving train, the endless expanse of its countryside stretching to the horizon conveys a sense of awe and painterly beauty. Far from monotonous, the marshes, canals and fields, interrupted vertically by occasional windmills and tree clumps, present the viewer with shapes, colors and visual poetry worthy of a Van Ruysdael or Cuyp painting.

There is no equivocation in the land, no obstructions or hidden views, no exaggerations or meanderings. A sense of geometry and certainty, orderliness and determination seems to guide and direct the course of nature in the Frisian countryside. The land is honest, one could say, and it gives exactly what is seen. It is no wonder that during the Reformation certain Frisians held on to the Old Faith with the same fierce tenacity their neighbors showed in embracing the New.

"The Frisian people are an agrarian people, close to the earth," says Father Constant Dölle, a Carmelite author of several books on Titus Brandsma, who remembers Father Titus well from visits to his boyhood home. "They are very constant people, who are militant yet like their silence as well. Titus was his father in his action, his mother in his thinking. A very good combination for Carmel, active and contemplative."[2]

Although the family rejoiced at the arrival of Anno, they soon realized that his delicate health and tiny frame did not bode well for a future career in farming. While not exactly sickly, the young Anno grew slowly and by his tenth year his fragile, bespectacled appearance gave him the look of a hapless victim of the class bully. With his decidedly Frisian nature, however, the reality was far from the perception.

Despite his physical limitations – he never really did grow tall – Anno had a determined, fighting spirit and a budding intellect that impressed his family and teachers from an early age. Unable to wield a scythe or bail hay with the other family members, Anno made do with secondary and tertiary chores around the house and barnyard. In school, however, he excelled and the high marks he constantly received made it clear that his future lay somewhere beyond the fringes of peaceful Oegeklooster.

His world was to be the university perhaps, or the bar, or possibly even the Church. Anno's naturally joyful disposition, his love of family and neighbor, and his growing devotion to the Eucharist, the Blessed Mother and private prayer were counter-balanced with a tenacious and argumentative inquiry into the nature of things that earmarked his Frisian origins.

Whether these were the stirrings of a vocation or simply the adolescent foundations of the adult personality are more or less immaterial. What they do point to is the profundity of Anno's

---

[2] Interview by the author with Rev. Constant Dölle, O.Carm. Nijmegen, The Netherlands, April, 1999.

sense of being; an awareness of people and places that connected him to feelings and emotions far beyond his known world. Anno was beginning to know his own self, and the beauty was not so much that he was attracted to the religious life, but that he was responding to the whole idea of calling and vocation in general, be it marriage, career or the priesthood.

Aware that God was calling him to do something with his life, Anno was nevertheless unwilling to go blindly down roads limited by the circumstances of his birth and health. On the contrary, his questing and questioning foray into faith, science, nature and literature impressed his parents, siblings and the parish priest with their depth and insight.

Anno was not a perfect or a holy child – on the contrary, his parents often found him *too* Frisian for their taste – but he was graced with not only an extraordinary intellect for his age, but a keen sense of listening. Not in the sensory way but in the spiritual way but in the ability to quiet the confusions and frustrations of youth, and recognize the voice of God calling him to a hidden vocation still awaiting revelation.

Anno's first choice for the religious life was the Franciscans. The followers of the *Poverello* from Assisi had attracted young men and women for centuries with their poor and simple service of the Lord, and Anno felt drawn not only to their lifestyle but their ideals as well. With his gentle personality, love of nature and tender way with people, Anno seemed perfectly suited to the Francsican life of prayer and sacrifice. With his parent's cautious blessing, Anno entered the college of Saint Anthony in Megen in 1892. He was eleven years old.

The postulancy of the major religious orders – the first step of young men and women aspiring to the religious life – remained largely unchanged for hundreds of years literally until the middle part of the twentieth century. Spartan, to put it mildly, the living conditions of the postulancy were geared towards quickly weaning the child from home and family, and preparing them for consecrated service in schools, hospitals and missions throughout their country and indeed throughout the world.

Intense rather than harsh, the regimens of the postulancies were intent on focusing the young man or woman on spiritual things rather than those of the world, and the faint-hearted and the luke-warm were soon sent packing. Living in dormitories, the postulants were up early and in bed early, and their days given over to long periods of study, work and prayer punctuated only by meals and communal recreations.

From the start, Anno impressed his superiors with his brains, his spirit and the deepening nature of his interior life. It was obvious, however, that his body was lagging far behind his will to achieve and succeed in his vocation.

If it proved difficult to keep the boy fat and fit on his own farm fed by his own mother, it proved a somewhat more formidable task for the good Franciscans at Megen. Anxious over the thin young postulant, the friars excused Anno from many of the rigorous restrictions placed on the students at Saint Anthony's, and he was fed large quantities of milk, cheese and meat in a futile attempt to fatten up his slight frame.

By the time he returned home for his summer vacation in 1898, Anno realized he would never have the stamina that the life of a missionary or curate required and therefore made up his mind not to return to the Franciscan novitiate at Megen. Still convinced in his depths that the Lord was calling him to a religious vocation, Anno began to search for another, possibly a more contemplative, road down which he could travel in his burgeoning spiritual jour-ney. Perhaps influenced by his cousin Casimir de Boer, a young Carmelite also from Friesland and possibly even by his sister Boukje who was with the Poor Clare nuns in Megen, Anno began to cast his first serious glances at the Order of Carmel.

Carmel

The Carmelites belong to one of the oldest and most respected Orders in the Catholic Church, yet their beginnings are shrouded in the mists and lore of ancient Palestine. The name is taken from Mount Carmel near Haifa, a sacred Jewish site first inhabited by the prophet Elijah and his followers some nine centuries before the birth of Christ.

The prophet is honored by the Carmelites as their founder and patron and by Church tradition as the father of the monastic life, an opinion shared by many of the Church Fathers. The Mount had always been regarded in the Judeo-Christian traditions as holy, and by the Apostolic and sub-Apostolic age Christian hermits were known to be dwelling peacefully on its rugged slopes. By the Middle Ages, travelers and pilgrims to the Holy Land wrote of a flourishing little community of brethren living lives of penance and prayer on Mount Carmel.

Their life was largely cenobitic, or communal, yet with great emphasis placed on private prayer, silence, manual labor and mutual love and assistance. Carmelite devotion to the Blessed Virgin was total and tender, and, seeing Mary as the perfect contemplative who carried God within her while living an ordinary life of recollection and prayer, they sought to do the same.

With the Holy Land ruptured and consumed by the bloody Crusades beginning in 1096, the Carmelites were trapped in the eye of a storm raging between the adherents of the Cross of Christ and the Crescent of Islam. Enduring harassment, privations and ultimately martyrdom, the Carmelites chose to emigrate to the safety of the European continent at the close of the twelfth century, and soon they had flourishing foundations from Cyprus and Sicily in the Mediterranean to Marseilles, France and Kent, England.

With their loose collection of customs and traditions codified as a rule by Saint Albert about the year 1210, the Carmelites quickly adapted to the needs of the bustling, densely populated cities of Europe, and their numbers and reputation for sanctity steadily increased. In the course of time, however, the Rule of Albert was relaxed and modified in regards to fasting and cell retirement to allow for greater movement and ministry among the laity.

Many Carmelites expressed a desire to return to a more rigorous observation of the original rule and contemplative spirit of Carmel, but it was not until the late sixteenth century that a Spanish fireball named Mother Teresa of Jesus – later known as Saint Teresa

of Avila – blazed across the face of Carmelite spirituality and forever changed its course.

Along with several devoted followers, including a diminutive
but dynamic friar named John of the Cross, Teresa began a long
and quite bitter struggle to take the order to its contemplative
roots. After much heated discussion with brother and sister
Carmelites as well as great suffering – especially for John of the
Cross, who ultimately endured imprisonment and torture for his
commitment to the reform – Teresa was granted patents for the
nuns in 1562 and the friars in 1568.

Even though they are now officially split into two branches, the
calced, or shod (O.Carm) and the reformed *discalced* or unshod
(O.C.D.), both are fragrant flowers of the same stem which produced an abundance of saints, writers and holy men and women
deeply in love with God. Aside from Saint Teresa of Avila and Saint
John of the Cross, their number would in time include Saint Maria
Magdalena de Pazzi, Sister Elizabeth of the Trinity and Saint
Thérèse of Lisieux. Saint Thérèse, who would die an unknown
young nun at the close of the nineteenth century, would nevertheless extend great influence over the face of the Universal Church
in the following century.

The goal of all religious life, regardless of the occupations and
charisms of the individual orders, is the perfection of love. In
Carmel, this perfection is achieved through a paradoxical ascent
that takes the contemplative down into the deepest recesses of their
soul. There, in the silent depths of their very self, where deep calls
upon deep, God is encountered and touched through a continual
breaking down and raising up of the soul.

Contemplation is the heart and soul of Carmel, and all work,
apostolic or intellectual, is subordinated to this primary goal. The
tender devotion to the Blessed Mother and Saint Joseph, the majesty
and mystery of the order itself, the spirit of detachment and the
upward ascent of Mount Carmel all represented hooks that Anno
could grasp and use to begin his own climb in life.

The more Anno read and investigated the Carmelite way of life,
the more he was excited at the prospect of joining their ranks. If

the searching seventeen year old did not fully grasp the poetic sub-
limities of the *Song of Songs*, or the poetry of Saint John of the
Cross, he did find the Carmelite way of life very appealing and
felt that as one he could lead a happy, productive and prayerful life.

The Carmelite novitiate at Boxmeer, Holland, had changed little between its founding in 1653 and 1898 when Anno Brandsma
entered its massive stone portals. Nearly four centuries of revolutions,
upheaval and two global wars can do little do destroy the sense of
tranquility that flows through its stone cloisters and peaceful gardens.

It is difficult to say whether it was the excitement of his newly
found vocation, the increasing solidity of his personality or just
maturity that made Anno suddenly begin to grow up. Probably it
was a little of everything. Along with the other novices, he scrubbed
floors, washed windows and dishes, perfected his Latin and recited
the Divine Office in choir with his brothers, all the while drinking in the silence with a thirst that evidenced Saint John of the
Cross' image of the soul thirsting for God.

Clothed with the habit of a novice, Anno took the religious
name of Titus, which reflected his two loves of faith and family.
The biblical Titus, like Carmel in that he is of mysterious origins,
was Saint Paul's Gentile assistant who accompanied the Disciple on
his third missionary journey and was charged with organizing the
church in Crete.

The familial Titus was obviously Anno's father, to whom the
young friar made farewells but honored with the taking of his name
as a lifelong keepsake of home.

With his new life, new name and deepening sense of self and
the presence of God in his life journey, the young friar began to
range spiritually beyond the ordinary novitiate curriculum. Immersing himself in the writings of the great mystics of the Western
Church, Titus developed a lifelong devotion to Saint Teresa of Avila,
the energetic, visionary Carmelite whose practical and love-driven
search for God so matched his own.

After his first year as a novice, Titus translated a book on Saint
Teresa's works into Dutch, and was commended for the polish and
beauty of the finished work. He began to write, first on spiritual

topics for the community, and then on wide ranging topics – spiritual and secular – for the Dutch Catholic periodical *De Katholieke Gids*.

The silence, the focus, the seriousness of his devotion to Carmelite life and spirituality seemed to uncork torrents of thought and ideas in Titus, which poured forth at an incredible speed from his pen on topics ranging from prayer and philosophy to science, art and nature. Some years later, he would write about the grace, artistry and power of one of American boxer Jack Dempsey's prize-winning fights.

Despite the diverse nature of his topics, Titus seemed to unify and anchor them in the depth of God's beauty and love, and His presence in every facet of human existence. Far from narrowing his vision of God, or of squeezing it through the picture book piety of quiet cloister halls, Titus' novitiate years endowed him with the grace to see the divine presence in all things and all peoples.

This passion and growing spiritual insight led him to discover yet another love, one that grew and stayed with him all his life; the great medieval mystics of the Low Countries, or Holland, Flanders and the surrounding areas. The writings of these men and women, including John Ruusbroec, Geert Groote, Hadewijch of Antwerp and Beatrice of Nazareth, illuminated and helped define Titus' own path to God, and he sought his whole life to keep his spiritual 'friends' alive and relevant to his own violent and deeply troubled times.

All Christian mystics through the ages, individuals and collective schools of thought, have tended to be colored and influenced by region and geography to the point where history seems to know them by locale as much as by spirituality. We can, therefore, speak of the English mystics, like Julian of Norwich, Walter Hilton and the author of the Cloud of Unknowing. There are also the Rhineland or German mystics like Eckhart, Tauler, Suso and Hildegard of Bingen, and of course the Spanish mystics so gloriously represented by Teresa of Avila and John of the Cross.

The Lowland or Flemish mystics were one of the greatest and most enduring joys of Titus' life, and he immersed himself in their work and thought with an academic ebullience tempered with a levelheaded pragmatism. Sitting at the feet of fourteenth century mystics did not make him forget he was a friar of the twentieth, with increasing duties and responsibilities outside the convent's rich library.

What Titus sought in the works of the Flemish mystics was something far beyond patriotic identification with spiritual ancestors: it was a common denominator of faith which linked him with people who likewise delved into the mysteries of Revelation, the Incarnation and the Passion.

In his desire to come to a greater knowledge of Christ in the fullness of his Trinitarian life, Titus went deeper into that which transforms the observant life of liturgy and common prayer into the contemplative life, where the inflamed soul experiences a more intense and direct experience of God.

In that respect, the Flemish Mystics transcended nationalistic loyalties and linguistic ties. They taught, along with the Desert and Cappadocian Fathers, the role of the senses in the soul's experience of God, centered on the sense of touch, or embrace, in which contact is made complete.

Blessed John Ruusbroec, the fourteenth century Flemish monk and mystic whose works Titus came to know intimately, understood the concept of the divine touch and infused it into his writings. For Ruusbroec the divine touch of the Beloved, given after the soul has been purified and detached from all earthly attachments, does not constitute an end in itself, but initiates what he calls the "storm of love", in which the soul and God struggle and pine to completely and eternally posses the other.

This touch of the Beloved, known in mystical language as a "wound of love", is not a dull, dead pain with no purpose, but a means through which all human experience, from great joy to great suffering, is transformed into an inflow of the Trinitarian life and love.[3]

---

[3] *John Ruusbroec: The Spiritual Espousals and Other Writings*, translated by James A. Wiseman, O.S.B. (New York: Paulist Press, 1985), p. 115-116.

Not a novel approach to mystical prayer and contemplative life and thought – this spiritually tactile experience of God figures in history from Origen, Augustine and the Spanish mystics to the present – the Flemish mystics spoke to Titus in a familiar spiritual and geographic context that touched his core. He did not digest the material and store it away only to retrieve it as needed for examinations or writing an essay. Titus truly personalized what he read, dove deep into scripture and the mystics, into nature, into solitary and communal prayer, and when he emerged he shared the fruits of his experience with those he encountered in his day to day life.

Titus also learned how to throw himself headlong into numerous projects at one time, often requiring titanic feats of concentration and energy, and quietly bringing them to completion. These talents and disciplines were greatly needed, for after the turn of the century, Titus' life went into high gear academically as well as spiritually.

Ordination and Academic Career

Ordained to the subdiaconate in 1903, the diaconate a year later, Brother Titus was ordained Father Titus on June 17, 1905. "When a man has had a great deal given him," read the Lucan quote on the reverse of his ordination card, "a great deal will be demanded of him." As events in his life would prove, his first sacrifice at the Lord's altar was a wholehearted offering of his entire life.

As it was implicitly understood throughout the province that Father Titus would be a great light shining brightly one day in Rome, the young priest was naturally eager to charge out of the cloister gate into the heady realms of theology and canon law. His superiors sensed an air of precocious presumption, natural in such a brilliant young religious, and chose to hold him back in the Netherlands to be assigned more practical work in and around the Provincialate.

Instead of blazing brilliantly across the academic sky of the Eternal City, Father Titus had to simmer dimly as the friary sacristan. It was a monumental disappointment tempered only by his continual contributions to Dutch periodicals and religious journals.

After such a dazzling ascent of his star, the psychological maturity, and the sharpening of his intellectual skills through sheer determination, Father Titus was once again the weak child at Oegeklooster performing menial tasks around the house while the big people labored in the field.

There was obviously a reason his superiors administered this healthy dose of humility to the young priest and, though it cut deeply, Father Titus looked back on the lesson years later as a necessary and valuable trial that made him realize how much he still had to grow. The coddling and nurturing of his youth was over and now, like the great Carmelite saints he endeavored to know and emulate, Titus realized that Carmel is achieved not so much by a pleasant stroll but by an arduous climb.

In 1906, judged sufficiently reined-in by his superiors, Father Titus was informed that he would finish his doctoral studies at the Universita Gregoriana and reside at the Carmelite's Collegio San Alberto in Rome. Despite the initial thrill of arriving in Rome and achieving the goal he so longed for, Father Titus soon realized that the experience would come at a very high price.

Living for years on a robust diet of Dutch meat, cheese and chocolate to maintain his somewhat mercurial health, Father Titus' system all but shut down in protest against the starchy, spicy Roman fare. The benefits of sleep continued to elude the friar and his academic work load wreaked havoc on his constitution to the point where it became clear to his confreres that Father Titus was a very sick man.

Had he been sent to Rome for rest it would have been difficult enough to keep him together, but given his punishing schedule of classes and perfectionist pursuit of his studies, Father Titus was soon on the road to medical catastrophe. He continued to throw himself into his writing, turning out dozens of articles and essays on numerous topics ranging from theology and mysticism to science and sociology, all sent home to Holland on a regular basis for publication. He also laid the foundations for a Dutch periodical, *Carmel Roses*, and all the while he struggled to offer himself to God and those around him in the celebration of the Eucharist and the exercise of his priestly ministries.

Despite the intervention of his superiors, as well as the tender care and fraternal concern of his confreres, Father Titus' health simply broke down. He was convulsed with crippling abdominal pains, he hemorrhaged, he coughed blood and for days lay curled up in agony on the bed of his tiny cell.[4]

Father Titus tried to see his pains and illnesses as a small share in Christ's passion, and he tried to be cheerful and placid in the face of his intense suffering. Thankful to his brothers for their considerations and charity, he asked that they simply pray for him. His attitude was admirable, even heroic, but it was not the inexpressible storm of love, the wound of love, so beautifully expressed by his Flemish mystics. Not yet. For now, it was sheer, brute pain masked by a childlike sincerity and bravery.

If his superiors had not stepped in and taken charge of the friar's fragmenting life, it is doubtful whether Father Titus would have made it back to the Netherlands alive. As it was, he was put to bed for several months, given a severely restricted diet, an increased sleep allowance and a prohibition of all study and activity except that essential to his doctoral studies.

By the spring of 1909, several months into his radical cure, Father Titus at last seemed to be rebounding. While his health was improving, the medical nightmare of the past several months had done untold damage to the rhythm of his studies, let alone his system, and it surprised no one that he failed to pass his doctoral exams.

Emaciated, weak, and thoroughly depressed by the failure of his Roman sojourn, Father Titus dragged himself back to the Netherlands to rest and wait for a future plan to unfold or be decided for him. Father Hubertus Driessen, a lifelong friend of Father Titus, was himself a brother Carmelite with a brilliant academic background both at home and abroad. Giving the younger man some time to rest and lick his wounds, Father Hubertus organized an aggressive study program and in a few months was ready to send his pupil charging confidently back to the Eternal City.

---

[4] Josse Alzin, *A Dangerous Little Friar: Father Titus Brandsma, O.Carm.* translated by the Earl of Wicklow (Dublin: Clonmore & Reynolds Ltd., 1957), p. 32.

Rested, refocused and energized by his friend with a new sense of purpose as well as a firmer grasp of the doctoral material, Father Titus returned to Rome in the fall of 1909, and when he came back to the Netherlands it was as Doctor Titus Brandsma.

When Father Titus returned from Rome enriched with the dignity of his doctorate, he brought with him a wealth of maturity, an increasing sense of identity and a clearer grasp of his vocation. The unfolding pattern of the past few years, the breaking down and building up, the precocious fragility tempered by intense suffering, the victories snatched from the jaws of defeat, all produced a steadiness and humble tranquility that allowed him to sail forth with a strong rudder and a good compass.

Titus' first appointment was to the faculty of the Carmel at Oss in 1909, and he now divided his increasingly limited time between his classes and the myriad subjects that continued to attract his literary and journalistic attentions. His reputation, always impressive throughout the Carmelite province, began to grow on a more national level. Aside from his preaching, Father Titus spoke at parishes, cultural, civic and social gatherings, and he published works in magazines and newspapers too numerous to count.

Although he continued to translate classic works of spirituality, including those of the Flemish mystics and Saint Teresa of Avila, Father Titus' work was not confined to the rarified realms of mystical theology. Exposed to the recent advances of sociological sciences while studying in Rome, he also began to take a keen interest in the plight of the worker in a new but already very troubled century.

Mystic On The Move

The new century that Father Titus found himself very much a part of, was awash in social, political and scientific conflicts that began in but were left unresolved by the previous one. The Church, finding itself increasingly constricted by the officially secular governments ruling Germany, France and Italy, struggled to reconcile traditional teaching and dogma with the problems brought about by the effects of the Industrial Revolution as well as the writings of Darwin, Marx and Nietzsche.

The poor, common laborer, part of the new sociopolitical juggernaut known as the working class, had discovered a unity in the upheavals and revolts of the past century, and by 1900 was no longer a passive pawn in the hands of monarchs and industrialists. The worker had not only found a purpose and a voice, but power as well, and the Church sought to re-evangelize the poor with the original and authentic freedom and social justice preached in the Gospels.

Beginning with *Rerum Novarum*, Pope Leo XIII's landmark encyclical of 1891 which defended traditional concepts of private property yet called for a visionary recognition of the worker's rights and an end to oppression by the industrialized nations, the Church began to slowly and steadily re-engage workers on their own territory.

Along with countless prelates, priests and laypersons, Father Titus began to ask himself, as he would publicly ask years later as a university rector, what was being done to make Jesus Christ known and real to a brutally marginalized working class trapped in militarized nations arming for Armageddon?

Father Titus knew that before he could hope to change the world by his words, he must first do so by example, and for the first few decades of the century he threw himself into performing the ordinary duties of his priestly, pedagogic and journalistic vocations. He was perspicacious and self confident enough to know that he could not fight at a barricade or move the earth with a literary bombshell like *Das Kapital* or *The Origin of the Species*. His barricade was the classroom, the typewriter and the pulpit, and he used all to maximum effect in the fight to better the plight of the worker and the marginalized poor.

A great distinguishing trait of the Professor, as Father Titus was now known, was his boundless energy coupled with a rapid fire ability to ingest material and then explain it to his readers or students in a highly intelligent yet accessible manner. Never a good speaker in the oratorical sense – his frail body did not allow him to project his thin voice – Father Titus nevertheless enthralled his listeners with the passion of his presentation.

Like a great conductor, Father Titus would use his whole body in his presentation, throwing himself physically behind his words to drive home their force and meaning. He won over listeners with the conviction of his words rather than the volubility with which they were spoken.

Father Titus also had to accept the fact that, despite the breadth and depth of his talents, he was simply not the stuff out of which superiors were made. Even though he would remain a figure of importance in the Carmelite province, his peripatetic lifestyle and preoccupation with countless literary and academic projects made Father Titus content to disappear into the rank and file rather than preside at the head.

This is not to say that Father Titus was either incapable of authoritative positions nor up to the responsibilities they required. On the contrary he was a model of docility and abandonment to the will of God manifested by the decisions of his superiors, who were often younger and less intelligent than he was.

"The superiors know better than Titus Brandsma in what way Titus Brandsma can be useful," he was often quoted as saying.[5]

By the 1920's, with his fame as a preacher, teacher and journalist already reaching national levels, Father Titus was often engaged in a dozen, if not dozens, of projects large and small. He did, however, always remain first and foremost a priest of Carmel, and as such kept himself always in the presence of God. This was not accomplished by rote observations and showy demonstrations of piety, but by a constant return to God in prayer both in his public work and in the innermost solitude of his soul.

The immense concentration of heart and will required for such a whole-hearted consecration to prayer and to people points to how deeply rooted Father Titus was in a constant awareness of God. The duties and obligations of his vocation did not, however, separate him from his fellow human beings. On the contrary it drew him into a deeper love of them and an appreciation of their needs, wants and pains.

Father Titus had a genuine empathy with the poor and the working classes that was not only reflected in his preaching, but in

[5] Ibid.

a Christ-like love manifested in countless ways throughout his day to day life. He was constantly besieged at the Carmel and on the street for material as well as spiritual assistance, and he told his confreres time and again how no one was ever to be turned away for any reason.

He was often seen in the town, begging food, clothing and money for individuals and entire families, and the unemployed usually came to Father Titus for his assistance in finding work in a shop, factory or home.

His ethos was rooted not only in common decency but also in the belief that his vows as a religious needed to be kept real and practical. If the friars did not love the poor and themselves embrace a genuine spirit of poverty and abandonment, he said, then they ran the risk of being materialists hiding behind the Dutch mania for neatness and organization. Without true poverty, Father Titus said, the religious becomes nothing more than a Pharisee in a habit.[6]

A Nijmegen merchant recalled how, pushing his heavy, fruit laden cart in the early morning he would continually run into Father Titus, who was on his way to classes at the university. Throwing his briefcase on top of the cart, the little friar would help the man push his cart up a particularly steep street. What the merchant did not know was that Father Titus was observed many times waiting for the man so that 'happening' to run into him he would be able to assist in the big push up the street.[7]

There was nothing affected, nothing showy about Father Titus, but rather quiet, joyful kindness to God who was present in his brothers and sisters.

More than sincerity and simplicity, Father Titus' constant offering of self reflected a profound sense of unity within himself, and a self knowledge that was cemented in the Spirit with a spirit of love. The tranquility of spirit bred by Father Titus' actions, which

---

[6] See *Essays on Titus Brandsma*: "Life in the Spirit" by Aemilius Breij, O.Carm., p. 92-93.

[7] Interview by the author with Rev. Hein Blommestijn, O.Carm., Nijmegen, The Netherlands, April, 1999.

by their nature cast out all guile and pride, gave him a deep and abiding love for solitude and his cell, but took him, as the same contemplative, back into the world.

"Prayer is life," Father Titus would say of his journey between the cloister and the world, "not an oasis in the desert of life."[8]

In the midst of the hectic pace of his work and ministry, Father Titus turned his attention to the glaring absence of a Catholic University on Dutch soil. Despite their minority role in a nation predominantly affiliated with the Dutch Reformed church, the three million Catholics of the Netherlands were a vibrant and devout people. Following in the far-flung wakes of the explorers and merchant vessels that commanded global trade routes for three hundred years, Dutch Catholics had spread the Faith to the farthest corners of the world.

Burning with a zeal that is particular to religious minorities, Dutch seminaries, convents and friaries founded and maintained flourishing schools, hospitals and religious houses from Europe and the Dutch Indies to Africa and North America.

Despite their apostolic zeal, Dutch Catholics could claim no university of their own on their own soil. From the inception of the project after World War I, Father Titus was an integral mover of this dream, and the early 1920's saw him dedicating countless hours to make the dream a reality.

For the backers of the massive project, a Dutch Catholic university would not merely be an educational milestone in their history, but a living intellectual expression of Dutch Catholics' deep-rooted sense of patriotism as well as their richly textured spiritual heritage.

Bold new ventures call for bold hearts, and, with Father Titus' support and invaluable spiritual and intellectual contributions, the University of Nijmegen opened its doors on October 17, 1923. Doctor Titus Brandsma, forty-two years old, was one of the first of twenty-seven professors hired by the university, and his classes

---

[8] See *Essays on Titus Brandsma*, "Life in the Spirit" by Aemilius Breij, O.Carm., p. 90.

in philosophy and the history of mysticism allowed him to spend increased amounts of time in the company of his old 'friends.'

The lives of the Flemish mystics, like mystical prayer itself, invited Father Titus deeper into the heart of a mysterious love. In these spiritual forbears, particularly John Ruusbroec, Hadewijch of Antwerp, Beatrice of Nazareth and Geert Groote, Father Titus saw not only his spiritual roots but also timeless, practical ways of love and perfection that were not dimmed or obscured by the veil of time.

Because they themselves were so immersed in scripture and constant prayer, the Flemish Mystics were still very much alive for Father Titus, and he worked tirelessly to make them just as real to his students.

With great emphasis placed on the divine touch, joy and optimism, Flemish Mysticism is characterized not so much by the purifying night as the illuminating sun. While suffering is a necessary part of the soul's journey to God, especially in its purifying and cleansing aspects, it is seen as brief in comparison to the glorious light that awaits the faithful and the perseverant.

By His passion and death, Christ raised suffering from brute agony to a share in his sacrificial fruits. Therefore, the person who suffers with a spirit of love and hope does not only suffer like Christ, but Christ suffers with them, and, far from being masochism, the acceptance of suffering is a temporary prelude to inexpressible joys to come.

The Flemish Mystics, like their disciples Geert Groote and Thomas a Kempis, were not passive recluses, but pragmatic, joyful people of prayer and good works. It was at the crossroads of these two virtues that Father Titus met them, emulated them and endeavored to take their message of faith to a new century.

Another project undertaken at this time, almost as massive as the building of a university, was the microfilming of all existing documents written by the Flemish Mystics of the twelfth to the fourteenth centuries.

It was an exhausting labor of love that took Father Titus scurrying to monasteries, convents and universities throughout Europe. The project, which he worked on until before his arrest, carried a prophetic dimension as well, since many of the priceless documents he photographed were later destroyed during World War II bombings.

The one hundred eighty-six volumes, visible over Father Titus' shoulders in a photograph of him in the study of the Nijmegen Carmel, contained photocopies of around sixteen thousand manuscripts gathered during years of loving labor. The complete set of volumes were removed from the friary shortly before it was reduced to rubble during the Allied advance on Nijmegen, and today are lovingly preserved at the Titus Brandsma Institute at the University of Nijmegen.[9]

Titus was immensely proud of his association with the University of Nijmegen, as well as the major role he played in its foundation, and the institution reciprocated with honors that were accepted without the slightest hint of pride or pomposity.

In the 1932-33 academic year, the governing board of the University named Father Titus *Rector Magnificus*, an office of great honor and distinction that touched the friar deeply. A photograph of Father Titus in his black silk gown, heavy chain of office and black velvet biretta also shows the ghost of a smile playing around the corners of his mouth, as though he was taking the honor more seriously than he was.

By now the Holy See was taking a keen interest in the intellectual Renaissance of sorts that was underway in the Netherlands, and Father Titus was asked to travel to Rome and personally present Pope Pius XI with a report on the University of Nijmegen. He also represented the University at the jubilee services for Queen Wilhelmina of the Netherlands and at various academic and cultural events throughout the kingdom.[10]

Yet another one of Father Titus' devotions was to the great Saint Boniface (675-754), the English missionary whose tireless efforts to spread the Faith through pagan Europe were instrumental in converting many Germanic tribes. Martyred with fifty-three companions in Dokkum – a town in the friar's native Friesland – Saint Boni-

[9] Alzin, *A Dangerous Little Friar*, p. 55.
[10] Ibid., p. 50.

face typified Father Titus' ideal holy man of action: building up the kingdom of God with souls as well as with stone.

A spring bubbled up on the spot where the saint was tortured and murdered, and without fail had continued to pour forth sweet water for over a thousand years. The spring, called "near miraculous" by Father Titus, had been a focal point of pilgrims for centuries, and yet it was the Carmelite friar who expanded not only the site, but the deeper significance of the spot into one of national and universal spiritual significance.[11]

He pushed for, and succeeded in, the raising of a shrine to the saint at Dokkum, going so far as to take the ancient stones from ruined abbeys in the area and transform them into living Stations of the Cross that symbolically linked the ancient and present Church in a bond sealed in the Passion and death of Christ.

Father Titus had a great and lifelong devotion to the Frisian people, and he worked tirelessly to help promote their language, customs and culture. He also saw the shrine at Dokkum as a way of universalizing a local custom and making it relevant to the contemporary Church caught in an increasingly irreligious time. The fact that Saint Boniface carried the Gospels to the Germanic peoples and paid for his missionary zeal with his life was not a coincidence lost on Father Titus, who was not blind to the pagan militarism coloring the creed of Germany's growing National Socialist party.

Given Father Titus' deep admiration for and knowledge of the history of mysticism, it is natural to ask whether or not the Carmelite himself was a mystic graced with the supernatural phenomena and manifestations that are so often associated with mystical prayer.

What was the nature of Titus Brandsma's mystical prayer? To answer that would be like the proverbial conundrum of describing the color blue to one who was born without the power of sight. Mystical prayer, by its very nature, refers to ineffable and hidden ways in which God and the individual converse in the silent places

---

[11] Joke Forceville Van Rossum and Kees Waaijman, *Titus Brandsma: A Continuing Source of Inspiration* (Nijmegen: The Foundation: Friends of Titus Brandsma), p. 4.

of the soul. As Saint John of the Cross, Saint Teresa of Avila and indeed all the great mystics of the Church have said, ecstasies, bright lights and sweet odors are the *effects* produced by intense mystical experience, not the goal.

Indeed, as the goal of mystical prayer is total union with God for all eternity, the senses represent a fallible and ultimately transitory part of the soul's journey to the Divine. The senses, being part of the mortal body, carry the seeds of decline and death and are therefore unreliable methods of understanding the soul's progression from the purgative to the illuminative and ultimately to the unitive state. True communion, true prayer takes place is the higher parts of the soul, which, being invisible and unreachable through the senses, remains an unknown mystery in this life.

Being a language of ultimate love, mystical prayer is therefore inexpressible, and the more profound the dialogue a soul has with God, the more inexpressible the substance of what was said and heard. Ultimately, the mystic comes to the point where words, like the senses themselves, fail miserably and the beauty of their experiences can only be expressed in exaltations of the soul; song and poems that attempt to define the indefinable.

What, then, is the criterion, the yardstick, if those words can even be applied, to gauge the progress of the genuine mystic's love of God? "We can be sure," Saint John says, "that we are in God only when the one who claims to be living in him is living the same kind of life as Christ lived." (1Jn 2: 5-6.)

That simple declaration by the Evangelist adequately sums up and defines the nature of Father Titus' mystical life. His accomplishments, his intellect, his reputation throughout his order and through his country are outweighed by the simple fact that he loved Christ and loved like Christ in a way that clearly evidenced a life of total abandonment to the Father's will.

Common courtesies and proper liturgical observations simply make for good manners and good form in a Christian. The depth and reality of Titus' Brandsma's life *in* Christ, however, is shown by his life *like* Christ, in a way so genuine and radical that, like the Lord, it too could end only on Calvary.

Sanctity is arrived at not only by a life of denial, but a life of acceptance as well. Father Titus accepted everything, *everything*, regardless of their extremes, as gifts from the two hands of the same God. From poor health and sickness, exhaustion and agony, to honors and great joys, everything in his life was seen as high and low waves in one 'storm of love' that with every toss brought him closer to the Beloved.

Ultimately, like all mystics, he was able to expand on the themes and rhythms of mystical prayer and the place of mystical prayer in the lives of great saints and holy persons, but he could not quite verbalize his own experiences. There was no secret, Father Titus once said in trying to describe his relationship with God. "I simply skip after Him as best as I can. I put my trust in him and abandon all care."[12]

If he used this unpretentious approach to his own prayer life, he applied it as well to others in a pastoral sense to separate those genuinely in love with God and lost to themselves from those distracted from the reality of God's love by the fantastic and the extraordinary. Such was the case with the follower's of the German stigmatist Therese Neumann.

Aside from carrying on her body the five wounds of Christ, as well as occasionally crying bloody tears, Therese was besieged for decades on end by the faithful, the skeptical and the simply curious, all who vied for the chance to glimpse or speak with the celebrated holy woman.

While not disrespectful of the supernatural phenomena manifested by Theresa, or even doubtful, Father Titus saw beyond the miraculous to the spiritual realities that had nothing to do with bloody tear ducts and unhealed wounds.

Asked what he thought of the celebrated stigmatist, Father Titus replied that he was not so much impressed with Therese's bloody wounds as he was with her ability to live so completely in the presence of God. As proved in these honest and sincere comments

---

[12] See *Essays on Titus Brandsma*: "Challenges in Life" by Redemptus Maria Valabek, O.Carm., p. 46.

about Therese Neumann, where hidden awareness of God was seen as more impressive than bleeding hands, Titus Brandsma was, for lack of a better word, a 'people's' mystic. He was a mystic on the move.[13]

He was, the Dutch writer Godfried Bomans wrote, "the only mystic with an international railroad pass, and he could be holy in a train compartment."[14]

Father Titus was devoted to the study of mysticism, immersed in every facet of it, one could say, and was a pioneer of sorts in his fostering of ecumenical dialogue with the Orthodox churches of the East on the subject of mysticism. Not only did Father Titus feel this dialogue was essential but he also felt that mysticism was a common thread that linked the great faiths of the world on the deepest levels.

True faith, however, was immobilized, if not deadened, Father Titus felt, by confining its expression to liturgical services or seeking its validation in miraculous events.

One afternoon, Father Titus and a confrere were strolling through the garden of the friary, and soon were on the subject of sanctity. When the conversation took a dry, academic turn, Titus stopped in his tracks and asked, "What did your mother mean to you?" "A great deal," the brother responded, "she took care of us." "How did she do it?" asked Father Titus. "Very well," the brother said. "*That*," declared Father Titus, "is holiness."[15]

The older he became and the deeper he was drawn into contemplative prayer, the simpler became Father Titus' ideas on sanctity and how to achieve it. Having written a vast array of essays and devotional works on profound theological and philosophical subjects, Father Titus arrived at a point in his interior life where great truths could only be expressed in simplicity. After a lifetime of struggling to reveal God in boldly written lines, he slowly began to discover Him more and more delicately hidden *between* the lines.

---

[13] Ibid., p. 123.
[14] Forceville and Waaijman, *Titus Brandsma*, p. 10.
[15] Ibid., p. 16.

This was never more apparent than when he undertook a tour of the United States and Canada in 1935, his longest trip abroad, where he gave a series of lectures on Carmelite mysticism to religious as well as lay audiences throughout North America's Eastern Seaboard and Midwest. His speeches, at the University of Washington, colleges in Chicago, Middletown and Niagara Falls, as well as Carmels in New York and Allentown, Pennsylvania, were later gathered together in a wonderful little book called *Carmelite Mysticism, Historical Sketches.*

While staying at the Carmel in Niagara Falls, Father Titus visited and was overwhelmed by the magnificence of the Falls that roared just outside the walls. Like Leonardo da Vinci, he sat transfixed and studiously noted every scientific and aesthetic aspect of the awesome, mystifying, force of water.

"I see not only the beauty of nature, the immeasurable potentialities of the water, but I see God at work in His creation, in His revelation of love. Nevertheless my eyes and ears are also captivated and time after time I return, to see and hear. Many a time this last pleasure even predominates."[16]

Returning to the Falls several times, Father Titus strove to capture the essence of what moved him so deeply by the awesome sight. It was not the sheer tonnage of liquid, hurling down unchecked into the riverbed below. It was not even the force of the water's mass. It was the delicate interplay of light and water that made the sensation of awe possible.

Titus' five senses were invaded and dazzled simultaneously by the force of nature displayed before him, although he admitted sight and sound predominating in the end. He did not, however, simply see the overall composition of elements that created a tourist sensation known as Niagara Falls. His awe was generated not by the spatial, but by the particular.

Father Titus acknowledged every drop of water that comprised the cascading Falls, saw how the sun illuminated every drop like

---

[16] See *Essays on Titus Brandsma*: "Mysticism of the Passion" by Adrianus Staring, O.Carm., p. 122.

trillions of individual crystals. He saw the beginning of the torrent's final descent and how, before returning again to the peaceful expanses of the riverbed, each drop sparkled briefly in the sun. More than just a metaphysical moment in the face of great natural beauty, Father Titus' reflections at Niagara Falls represent a revealing moment in a life already marked by tremendous spiritual insight. His thoughts on Niagara Falls was a revelatory understanding of the sacredness of the present moment in time, which the saints and the great spiritual writers have discovered to be the eternal dwelling place of the unseen God.

By the time he returned to Holland following the North American tour, Father Titus was well over fifty years old and in almost constant pain of some sort. Despite pleas by his confreres to rest and ease up on his punishing workload, Titus pushed himself harder and harder to fulfill the seemingly endless spiritual, literary and academic demands made upon him. The stomach ailments of his youth never went away, and they renewed in frequency and intensity despite several operations that did little to help. He suffered from vertigo, from headaches and from an insomnia that never prevented him from being in his choir stall every morning at five for his pre-Mass meditation.

His vigor, his enthusiasm and sense of adventure in life were his best medicine during this time, and photos taken during this period invariably show him with a bright face and childlike, mischievous smile. Despite his often thin and frail appearance, due to his illnesses and operations, there are no known photos of Father Titus with a dark or gloomy visage.

Father Constant Dölle, a Dutch Carmelite in Nijmegen who remembers Father Titus well, said that it was this contagious and irrepressible joy – not his awesome academic reputation – that made his visits such a welcome event. "He filled the house with a special presence," said Father Constant, "and word of his coming sent an exciting, electric charge through the house among friars young and old."[17]

---

[17] Interview by the author with Rev. Constant Dolle. Nijmegen, The Netherlands, April, 1999.

The 1920s and 1930s were golden periods for the Dutch Carmelites, and aside from taking on new houses in Holland and Germany – projects that were personally supervised by Father Titus – new foundations were being planned in Brazil and the Dutch Indies.

Father Titus, burning with missionary zeal and eagerly searching for new horizons, anticipated being sent to found and guide one of these new foundations. The university work, combined with the endless duties and details he attended to throughout the province, had left him worn out and ready for a change.

While always adept at maintaining a perfect balance of action and contemplation, Father Titus by this time in his life was longing for more solitude and pastoral simplicity. A mission station in the forests of the Amazon or the jungle villages of Java seemed to promise the life of a simple friar among simple people, and Father Titus let it be known he was more than eager to be sent.[18]

His superiors, however, deemed Father Titus much too valuable to the University and the province at home, and all his requests for transfers were denied. Although deeply disappointed, he nevertheless obediently accepted the decisions and quietly returned to his classroom and typewriter.

The impression conveyed by Father Titus during these years, times of contradictions and extremes of success and suffering, is not of a saint gliding through life with ease and certitude but of an honest man trying to keep his vocation real and substantial. It was a challenge that was neither given nor accepted lightly, and his ultimate triumph came at a very high price to his health and his humility.

Like all good religious, Father Titus worked his whole life to overcome himself, to consciously choose paths and make decisions that, while bringing him recognition and plaudits, would ultimately glorify God alone. He was fifty and ill, and at a time in person's life when, despite a high level of sanctity, a person begins to feel old, vulnerable, and closer to the end than the beginning.

---

[18] Alzin, *A Dangerous Little Friar*, p. 60.

Humility is learned through humiliations, and having sacrificed the comforts of married life and the material rewards of a successful life, Father Titus now had to subordinate his own desires and wants to the decisions of superiors who were often quite younger than he. Feeling life closing in on him like the walls of a small room, Father Titus felt that it was time to ask for fresher fields and new horizons in which he could re-charge and regain his inner silence.

It was not to be, however, and the dutiful return back to his ordinary life and duty represented one of the greatest sacrifices asked of him as a religious thus far.

His sense of humility, however, while a grace, needed a predisposed heart and a tremendous force of will to accomplish what God was offering, and to make it real and lasting. The contradictions and pains of his life during this time, which seemed to multiply rather than recede with age, took an incredible amount of courage to accept. Father Titus realized that it was the only way to truly imitate Christ that went beyond surface observations and spiritual lip service.

A wholehearted embrace of Christ means the embrace of the totality of His life, and the culmination of His human life is the cross on Calvary. Not obsessed with pain and death – on the contrary Titus continued to radiate joy to all around him – he seemed to meditate more and more on the nature of suffering.

"Consider life as a Way of the Cross," he said in a 1939 retreat, "but take the cross on your shoulders with joy and courage, for Jesus with his example and grace made it light."[19]

For many people, pain, disappointment, sickness and death are disconnected and isolated catastrophes that can turn life's pilgrimage into a pointless wandering down darkened paths. For Father Titus, these elements were linked together and, viewed in the context of his entire life journey, gave him a linear view of both a starting point and a goal.

---

[19] See Essays on Titus Brandsma: Staring, p. 127.

"Be of good cheer and see grief in a higher light", Father Titus declared joyfully in some notes he made for a retreat, "in which it becomes a free choice and motive for gladness."[20]

Slowly, imperceptibly, Father Titus had begun to transform the very nature of his bodily suffering in a way that merely confirmed the increasing depths of his prayer. He did not simply suffer them or blindly offer them up; both ways would have kept him as the origin and fulcrum of the suffering. On the contrary, he began to subsume his sufferings into the suffering of humanity as a whole, to universalize his pain so as to make it one note in a wider chorus of suffering endured by his brothers and sisters in Christ throughout the world.

His life of prayer and apostolic zeal was slowly becoming wedded to a more *compassionate* view of suffering humanity, which by its etymology means 'to suffer with.'

The ascent of Mount Carmel was never achieved through a theory, but a step by step struggle. As the decade closed out with the grim inevitability of war and horrific suffering on a scale not yet experienced by humanity, Father Titus himself began the most torturous part of his climb. The summit, however, was in view just beyond.

In 1935 Father Titus was appointed spiritual director of the Dutch Catholic Association of Journalists by Archbishop De Jong of Utrecht, a role combining chaplain with that of adviser and confidante. The position was not merely an honorary one, and due to the Carmelite's long association with the journalistic field he played a decisive role in shaping and guiding policy for the organization.

His lifelong passion for journalism, evidenced by the multitude of his works that continued to appear in newspapers and journals throughout the country, was fueled by his recent trip to North America. Studying the advances made in the printed and electronic media fields, including the burgeoning television industry, Father Titus returned to the Netherlands with a new and expanded vision for the journalist.

---

[20] Ibid., p. 127.

The little Carmelite by no means saw himself as a passive the-oretician, and his expanding role in Dutch Catholic journalism became as prominent as his position in the world of philosophy and academia. He was heard preaching over the radio airwaves on various sacred and secular topics, and he regularly contributed stories on practical mysticism to the newspaper *De Gelderlander*.[21]

Hoping to include the Netherlands in the march of journalistic progress, Father Titus threw himself into the study of every aspect of the profession as well as the social standing and economic needs of the individual journalist. He advocated more intense methods of training for the journalist, and explored ways to raise their social profile from craftsperson to respected professional. As with his view of priests and religious, Father Titus saw the journalistic career as a vocation, and he wanted to expand it from mere coverage of the news to a voice that could be heard and could act as an agent for change in the world. This was a noble vision that was needed at the close of the decade more than ever before.

War, Invasion & Resistance

It seems an incomprehensible, mind-boggling case of mass naivete on the part of the leaders of 1938 Europe to think that Hitler would be content with Austria and the Czech Sudetenland. Aside from his ability to fool intelligent statesmen, the trump card that Hitler played to great effect was his oft-stated desire to join together the German peoples scattered and separated by the reapportioning of Europe done at Versailles in 1919.

With England and France failing to stop the Führer in his ter-ritorial aggressions at Munich, the 1930s ended with the German war machine moving unopposed like a juggernaut across the face of Europe. The Nazi and Soviet invasion of Poland in September of 1939 in effect signaled the beginning of World War II, and all the countries not aligned with the Reich braced themselves as best as they could for the blitzkrieg.

---

[21] Forceville and Waaijman, *Titus Brandsma*, p. 10.

With the passing of the Nuremberg Laws in 1935 by the Nazi Party Congress, the Jews of Germany were in effect deprived of their basic human and civic rights by the law of the land. Legal recourse was denied Germans of even partial Jewish descent, inter-marrying between Aryans and Jews were forbidden, and the general atmosphere of hatred and intolerance that was promulgated laid the foundations for the Final Solution that commenced in 1942.

Following in the wake of the initial waves of Nazi infantry and artillery, there poured into the conquered and occupied territories ice-blooded mass murderers whose sole purpose was to identify, isolate and then quickly liquidate all those deemed racially inferior by the Reich. Called, *untermenschen,* or sub-humans, these men, women and children were placed in the brutal hands of various organs of the dread SS, including the SD (Security Service) and *Einsatzgruppen* forces who either murdered them en masse or shipped them like cattle to concentration camps in the east.

Making the work of the SS easier were battalions of local thugs who gladly assisted their German masters in subjugating people whom a short time before had been their fellow citizens.

At the top of the list were Jews, regardless of their national origins, social standing or integration into the culture of their particular homeland. Slavs, gypsies, Communists, the mentally and physically handicapped and the terminally ill followed them. The other head of this beast sought the destruction of any person or group posing a threat to the security of the new order, including teachers, intellectuals, authors, activists and any person who manifested resistance in thought, word or deed.

On May 10, 1940, the forces of the Third Reich invaded the Netherlands along a front running almost the entire length of its four hundred kilometer border with Germany. Lulled into a false sense of security by their close cultural and historic ties with the German people, coupled with a strict national policy of neutrality that Hitler vowed in 1937 as sacrosanct, the Dutch were shocked into a state of numbed disbelief by the invasion. On May 14, a mere four days after the invasion began, the Dutch armed forces under General Winkelman surrendered to Germany.

Strangely enough, an eerie calm descended over the shocked and defeated kingdom, and aside from a frantic scramble by Dutch Jews for boats to England across the North Sea, life in the big cities and countryside for a time returned to normal.[22]

The reason for this was two-fold. First, Hitler saw the Dutch as more or less a kindred people, whose geographic proximity to the Reich was equated with a sociopolitical empathy for all things German. Thinking like Germans, sounding and looking like Germans, Hitler reasoned, the Dutch would be more disposed to the glorious visions of hope and glory promised by National Socialism.

Second, Hitler knew he would be taking on more formidable opponents like England and eventually the Soviet Union once he militarily and politically secured his conquests in northern Europe. Men and materiel needed for these future campaigns would be wasted in policing what he deemed the relatively placid Dutch people. Therefore, for the first year of Dutch occupation, the Führer was content to simply watch and wait rather than crush by force.

This policy, however, was restricted to gentiles and not to the 150,000 Jews thickly enmeshed for hundreds of years in the fiber of the Dutch population.

To oversee Nazi military rule in the Netherlands, Hitler's Reichskommisar, or Reich Commissioner, was Dr. Arthur Seyss-Inquart, a former lawyer and fellow Austrian whose blind devotion to his Führer and the Party was unclouded by the slightest coloring of conscience or remorse until his arrest and trial.

To Seyss-Inquart, who had betrayed his native country by helping the Nazis orchestrate the annexation of Austria, the Netherlands was more of a launch pad into higher party politics than a genocidal proving ground for Nazi racial theories. His rule began with oppressive anti-Semitic laws such as barring Jews from positions of authority and entrance into theaters and cafes that, while harsh, were hardly the draconian measures enforced by his fellows Reichskommisars in the east.

---

[22] Dr. Jacob Presser, *Ashes in the Wind: The Destruction of Dutch Jewry*, translated by Arnold Pomerans (Detroit: Wayne State University Press, 1988), p. 10.

By 1941, however, with the Nazis firmly in control of the Low Countries and beginning to roll victoriously eastward, pressure from Berlin forced Seyss-Inquart to enlist the SS and Gestapo into rounding up Jews and crushing all elements of opposition so close to home.

Seyss-Inquart's efficiency in carrying out Berlin's orders, despite petty jealousies and internal power struggles rocking his Reichskommisariat, was repaid with high flown praise by Hitler, who considered the bespectacled, scholarly looking Austrian one of his most devoted followers. Weak, vain and lusty for power, Seyss-Inquart was more of a cold-blooded administrator than a bloodthirsty dictator who, though he tried to help relieve the suffering of the Dutch as the Reich collapsed, was condemned as a war criminal by the International Military Tribunal and hanged in 1946.

Before his execution in Nuremburg, however, Seyss-Inquart expressed remorse for his crimes and returned to the Sacraments of the Catholic Church. This was a grace that one would, no doubt, like to believe dispensed through the intercessory prayers of Father Titus.

In many ways resistance was perhaps less difficult in the Netherlands than other countries under Nazi rule, and the reason was largely geographic. Unlike Norway, Poland and Greece, where partisans could strike at German soldiers and supply lines and then retreat into the impenetrable depths of snowy forests and mountain caves, the Dutch had no barriers or natural defenses in or behind which they could hide. The flat Dutch landscape was wonderful for painting but woefully inadequate for hiding bands of hard-hitting partisans.

While a fierce and formidable Dutch underground movement was eventually formed, resistance to the Nazis was waged along intellectual lines as well as well as guerilla lines, and suppressing ideas and words proved as formidable a task as seizing rifles, bullets and bombs.

Attempts by the SS to provoke anti-Jewish riots backfired, and the response of the stubborn and outraged Dutch to this attack on their fellow citizens was to organize a strike that brought the occupied nation to a virtual standstill. The irony was that this vociferous, non-cooperative spirit of defiance stoked the ire of the their German overlords, and efforts to crush resistance and its leaders were redoubled by Seyss-Inquart.

Due to the galvanizing sense of pride and a fierce loyalty to both Queen and Pontiff, Dutch Catholics not only enjoyed a tight unity among themselves but also a good relationship with people of other faiths. The Catholic leadership had a particularly good relationship with the Dutch Reformed Church, the predominant denomination in the kingdom, and together many religious leader formed a firm and unshakable front against Nazism with a vigor unmatched by many of their European co-religionists.

As early as 1936, the bishops of Holland saw the face of the beast lurking beneath the official veneer of National Socialism (and it is well to remember that as late as 1937 Adolf Hitler was named *Time* Magazine's Man of the Year) and in that same year refused the Sacraments to members of the Dutch Nazi Party.

While defiance was manifested in heroic and often perilous ways by countless Jews, clergymen, and legions of ordinary Dutch men and women, the Nazis entered Holland with a great deal of information on individuals already known to be enemies of the Reich. One of them was Father Titus Brandsma, whose anti-Nazi writings were well known for years before Nazi tanks rolled across the Dutch frontier.

In 1935, two years after the Nazis came to power in Germany, while the majority of governments were snickering at Hitler as a demagogic street agitator or coolly acknowledging his charismatic power, Titus Brandsma was denouncing Nazi anti-Semitism in the literary and academic circles throughout the Netherlands.

He contributed an essay to a collective work published in 1935 entitled *Dutch Voices on the Treatment of Jews in Germany*, which unequivocally stated that Nazi theories of racial supremacy were fallacious polemics that actually masked deep seated feelings of national inadequacy and inferiority.[23]

---

[23] Leopold George Glueckert, *Titus Brandsma: Friar Against Fascism* (Darien, IL: Carmelite Press, 1985), p. 5-6.

What made Father Titus such a serious threat to the German forces of occupation in Holland was not so much his high profile anti-Nazism as the intelligence of his articulation. He did not simply attack the Nazis as murderous brutes, but attacked the core of Nazi doctrine and its neo-paganistic coloring. Incorporating his beliefs not only into his writings and preaching but his university curriculum as well, Father Titus gave numerous lectures on the evils of National Socialism and its ultimate incompatibility with traditional Judeo-Christian beliefs.

In short, Father Titus stated that according to Nazi philosophy, the good of the individual is subordinated to, or more accurately subjugated by, the good of the superior race, or the *Volk*. Unlike Communist doctrines, according to which the workers themselves theoretically control a workers state and theoretically acknowledge individual rights, National Socialism was predicated on the fanatical worship of a race under the supreme control of a deified Führer. Father Titus believed such a political system precluded a belief in the human family and supplanted the supremacy of God with that of the Führer. Father Titus believed such a system was a threat not only to the peace of Europe but to the entire world.

For these lectures as well as his preaching and published work denouncing Nazism, Father Titus was viciously attacked in the German press. Called a Communist dupe and a defender of what were termed Jewish "bandits", he was a subject for slanderous abuse in Nazi newspapers and journals such as *Fredericus, de Knuppel* and *De Volksche Wacht*.[24]

Father Titus harbored increasing suspicions that he was being watched, and he would tell of the sudden appearance of new 'students' in his lectures, who would take reams of notes and then disappear. If he was frightened or even concerned unduly at this point, he did not let it get to him, and he pressed on in his quiet, steady struggle against tyranny.

Targeting the churches as a key element of resistance in the Netherlands, the Nazis moved swiftly to cripple and crush their

---

[24] Ibid., p. 6.

efforts. Priests, nuns and religious who held supervisory posts in primary and secondary education were ordered to vacate their posts by the summer of 1941, thus severing any links of influence over great segments of children and young adults.

The Catholic press, electronic and printed, was censored, Catholic organizations and youth clubs were suppressed and Jews, who by this time were forced to wear the yellow Star of David on their clothes, were forbidden to attend any Catholic school or institute of higher learning.

Certain members of the Dutch episcopacy, led by Archbishop Johannes De Jong of Utrecht, struck back with a series of pastoral letters and counter-acts of defiance that outraged the Nazis but renewed the determination of the clergy and ordinary citizens to take a stand. A pastoral letter issued in July 1941, signed by the archbishop and the bishops of Breda, s'Hertogenbosch, Roermond and Haarlem, denounced the restrictive measures against the eviction of Catholic superiors from Dutch schools. To insure that the Nazis understood them to be serious, the bishops adamantly held to a policy of withholding the sacraments from all members of the N.S.B.[25]

When the Party demanded lists of all Jewish students, even converts to Catholicism, Father Titus personally drafted a letter to the heads of all Catholic institutes and schools in Holland, exhorting them to hold fast to Catholic policies of non-discrimination in regards to enrollment. Stating that it was Church policy to accept students regardless of religion in their schools, he backed the letter up with personal calls to various ministers of the Department of Education who agreed to do their best to see that these measures would be reversed.

As Seyss-Inquart had promised the Führer that he would annihilate all opposition amongst the Dutch, Father Titus' actions, like so many acts of heroism by clergy and citizens alike, represented a Pyrrhic victory that was followed by even greater recriminations. Bullying and brutalizing the population into submission,

---

[25] Ibid., p. 10-11.

Seyss-Inquart now began a cat-and-mouse game of intellectual chess, in which he hoped to checkmate the last bastions of non-violent resistance in Holland.

The Netherlands had during this time a flourishing press and the Catholic press in particular attracted a large and dedicated readership. This was no secret to the Nazis who, despite growing attempts to corrupt by stealth rather than invigorate through martyrdom, allowed the Catholic press to continue, though with several major caveats.

The first was that the Nazis could not be refused space for articles in all Dutch Catholic newspapers. The second was that the papers had to accept advertising by the Party in every Catholic paper, magazine and journal. These measures were intended to turn the Catholic papers into willing organs of the Nazi party under the façade of journalistic freedom.

For Father Titus, considered the elder statesman of the Catholic press in the Netherlands, these restrictive measures represented an unacceptable compromise not only of freedom of religious expression, but of the very right of human beings to write, think and speak without fear of censorship or suppression. To the Carmelite, the Nazis were not only illegally occupying Holland, but their ideology was now posing a dire threat to the basic dignity of human beings made free in the image of God.

Now Father Titus decided to act. His increasing participation in scattered pockets of intellectual resistance at the university and among the Dutch literati was now re-channeled into a focused crusade to preserve the freedom of the last organs of protest in the occupied Netherlands.

By Christmas of 1941 Father Titus was having clandestine meetings with the archbishop for the purpose of organizing resistance among Catholic editors throughout the country. Many of the editors, flagging or despondent after the closing of several papers, needed encouragement in a way only a dynamic and genuinely spiritual person could offer, and by the end of the year Father Titus was deeply absorbed in his latest and most perilous project.

His attack was a two-pronged offense that was as simple as it was effective. He first drafted a letter to all Catholic editors in Holland:

a fiery broadside that carries as much force today as it did when issued in 1941. Like Emil Zola's "*J'Accuse*" letter to the President of the French Republic during the Dreyfus affair, Father Titus succeeded in unifying a frightened and fragmented group of citizens.

When the restrictive orders came down from the Party, the letter stated, everyone must hold fast to principle despite threats of suppression, harassment or prison. Father Titus called on the editors to prayerfully search their conscience by the light of faith and to stand their ground accordingly.

"The limit has been reached," went the most memorable line from the circular. "The more we are united in refusing, the stronger we shall be."[26]

The letter hit the editors like a thunderbolt, and to prevent the momentum from being lost through wasted time and inertia, Father Titus attacked with the second prong of his offense almost immediately. For the first weeks of 1942 he undertook a clandestine tour throughout the nation, a punishing journey that left him more ill and exhausted than ever. Visiting each editor personally, as well as all the bishops in the Netherlands, Father Titus steeled their resolve with assurances of mutual support and eventual victory.

The sheer force of the little friar's personality as well as the depth of his spiritual convictions proved a potent combination and, in the end, a fairly unified editorial was formed and holding against the Nazis.

By choosing to undertake this mission, which moved him further to the forefront of Dutch anti-Nazi resistance, Father Titus was daily increasing the odds for a head-on confrontation with the Gestapo. This concern, never lost on Father Titus' friends and confreres, was now raised by Archbishop De Jong, who advised the Carmelite to place himself as far out of harm's way as possible in his work. Prudence was advised along with boldness. Before setting out on his last mission to the editors, the archbishop urged caution, reminding the friar that the Nazi authorities would be more disposed to arresting an ordinary priest than the prelate whose orders he was carrying

---

[26] See *Essays on Titus Brandsma*: Winship & Hoekstra, p. 54.

out. Father Titus concurred with the archbishop, and then set off on his mission.[27]

It is important to remember not only Father Titus' psychology in regard to his work during this extremely dangerous time, but also the spiritual sense of abandonment and detachment that allowed him to carry out his mission without the taint of foolhardy heroics or an inordinate desire for martyrdom. It is an important distinction that can easily be blurred in the vagaries of the human psyche.

The difference between a masochist and a martyr is that the masochist rushes headlong into pain and suffering, which he sees as their own reward. The martyr, fully aware of the consequences of his actions, chooses in freedom to do what is right out of love of God, despite those consequences.

Arrest

By the first days of 1942, while few could have foreseen eventual martyrdom it was apparent that Titus Brandsma was a man marked by the Nazis. Writing in defense of the Church, preaching against anti-Semitism since 1935, and now boldly journeying from city to city to organize resistance among the Catholic newspapers of the kingdom against their German oppressors, the question was why had he not been arrested already?

It could be that the Nazis, in their desire to keep from making too many martyrs out of spiritual and secular leaders and persons of authority, simply waited for Father Titus to make the wrong move at the right time. This insured that the arrest could be made under the perverted guise of due process of law. Rather than a question, the situation requires an observation, namely, that Titus was acting in perfect freedom and was not a victim of the circumstances of time and place, tossed helplessly on a sea of fate.

On the contrary, approaching the crossroads of his destiny, Father Titus proceeded out of a choice to do so, out of a freedom to maintain his silence and out of an obligation as a Christian to

---

[27] Force & Waaijman, *Titus Brandsma*, p. 11.

speak out. By marrying the freedom of his will with the actions of his hands, he chose the latter, fully cognizant of every consequence and inherent danger.

Father Redemptus, an elderly Carmelite in residence at the novitiate at Boxmeer, relayed in an interview for this book an incident that illuminates the heart and mind of Titus Brandsma at this time. Despite his years, Father Redemptus is still a vigorous member of the community and, between celebrating Mass and acting as chaplain at a local nursing home, still finds time to tend his beloved chickens.

Speaking through a translator, Father Redemptus recounted his last encounter with Father Titus, which happened there at the novitiate in Boxmeer. Wrapping up his exhausting mission to the editors throughout the country, Father Titus decided to spend the night in his old novitiate before heading back to the friary in Nijmegen.

Father Redemptus was in conversation with Father Titus and another Carmelite, who told the friar that he was meddling in extremely dangerous affairs that ultimately were none of his business. Father Titus, according to Father Redemptus, responded that the whole matter was not one of choice but of obligation: to speak up for right or to sit back and let evil triumph. Besides, Father Titus said, if he did not take the risks it meant that someone else would have to, and he did not know who that person would be if not him.[28]

That was January 18, 1942. The next day Father Titus returned to his friary in Nijmegen where that evening *Sicherheitspolizei* Officer Steffen placed him under arrest. Told to put on an ordinary black suit, Father Titus asked the Prior for a blessing, promised to be back as soon as possible and, stepping into a black police car, roared off into the dark winter night.

Scheveningen

Father Titus was taken first to Arnhem and then to Scheveningen, a seaside town, where he was placed in the police prison with other

---

[28] Author interview with Father Redemptus, Carmelite Novitiate, Boxmeer, The Netherlands. April, 1999.

patriots, resistance members and intellectuals similarly awaiting interrogation and trial. His own interrogation began on January 21, and was no longer conducted by the SD, but by the SS under the personal direction of *Hauptscharfuehrer* Hardegen of Gruppe IV (Church Affairs.)

Swaggering fearlessness was never Father Titus' style, and he did not try to put up brave fronts against the first shock waves of prison life and SS interrogation. No torture was applied, mainly because there was nothing to forcibly extract from the priest. From the start Father Titus acknowledged his work among the Catholic papers of the country, encouraging them to hold firm in the face of Nazi directives in regard to publishing and advertising.

He was, Father Titus said, working out of obedience to Archbishop De Jong and the dictates of his own conscience. While not shifting the blame to either the archbishop or the editors, Father Titus let it be clearly known he was working in concert with a great number of like-minded individuals of influence throughout the kingdom.

Quite cordial and cogent, and definitely not courting disaster and martyrdom, Father Titus expressed his hopes of resolving the issue of his arrest quickly and return as soon as possible to his friary. He made it perfectly clear to Hardegen, however, that he would not compromise his principles or his conscience on these or any other matters. On this point he accepted full and complete responsibility for his actions.

Hardegen obviously knew from the start the stuff of which the little friar was made, and he adjusted his tactics accordingly, though, under the circumstances, did little to correct the criminal perversion of justice he was perpetrating on his prisoner.

Hardegen began engaging Father Titus in protracted interrogatory conversations, in which he hoped to trick the friar into a tongue-tied confession of the Church's avowed hostility towards National Socialism. Father Titus' responses were, however, clear thinking parries to each one of Hardegen's subtle thrusts, and the depth of his moral convictions and intellectual control soon became evident. The limit had been reached, Father Titus stated again, and although reaffirming Catholic doctrine and organizing a unified Christian front was not the primary intention of his mission, he could not deny that it was the ultimate result.

Being so obviously in control of his thoughts and reasoning, Father Titus was prepared for the cat- and-mouse game that Hardegen was playing, and the SS officer redoubled his efforts to match his prisoner point for point. From the transcripts of the interrogation, it appears that the German not only wanted to trap the Professor in a legal context but to beat him at his own game. Father Titus, however, was not so obliging.

Was it, Hardegen asked, the intention of Professor Brandsma to get a clear idea as to the thoughts of every editor in regards to Nazi editorial policies?

Not exactly, replied Father Titus, because not only was he sure that the majority of them would agree with the episcopacy, but that, regardless of what they thought, Church policies of non-cooperative resistance would remain unchanged.

Were the bishops, Hardegen asked, prepared to pressure the editors into falling in line with the Church's position if they refused to follow along?

Aside from the sanctions already outlined by Archbishop De Jong carried by the friar to editors around the nation – to be applied to those papers submitting to the Nazi's restrictions – Father Titus said no pressure was to be applied. Despite threats of financial straits, harassment and possible imprisonment, the editors were emboldened by the Archbishop's declaration that between material loss and moral right, morality must prevail in the end. It was this, Titus said, that swung the editors firmly into the Archbishop's camp.[29]

Hardegen ordered Father Titus to write a document, to be used at his trial, summarizing his beliefs, that would give Party officials an outline of the reasons for his actions. Father Titus closed his statement with a prayer asking God to "bless the Netherlands and

---

[29] See *Essays on Titus Brandsma*: Winship & Hoekstra, p. 55-56.

bless Germany," in the hopes that the two peoples would soon stand again "united in their faith in Him." In writing this, Father Titus not only manifested his paternal affection for Germans as individual persons, but his fervent hope that the inherent Christian good buried deep beneath the Nazi crust would surface again in the future.[30]

Hardegen handed his report to a Nazi judge the next day with an appendix expressing his own thoughts on the matter of Professor Brandsma. In the report, the SS officer stated that Professor Brandsma was an avowed enemy of National Socialism, with a long history of opposition manifested in countless speeches, homilies, essays and articles.

Brandsma, Hardegen said, denied nothing and not only spoke out against Nazi policy in regard to the Jewish Question, but also felt that Christianity needed to be protected from Nazi *Kultur*. Professor Brandsma, Hardegen concluded in a memo to his superiors, was a "dangerous man," but added that he was also a man of true character who was admirably steadfast in his convictions.[31]

While the officials debated what to do with the Carmelite friar, in light of *Hauptscharfuehrer* Hardegen's report, Father Titus settled into the quiet of his cell and the dull routine of prison life.

For Titus, however, the seven week imprisonment at Scheveningen became a time of retreat, of prayer, and, ironically enough, of the first period of rest he had known in years. Writing letters of assurance to his prior and his family, he said that he was in relatively good health, excellent spirits, and was well treated.

While he was not allowed to celebrate or receive the Eucharist, Father Titus was allowed the use of his breviary and a few books. He did, though, set up a small altar in his cell, with a picture of the Sacred Heart of Jesus from his breviary tacked up as the centerpiece. He tacked on the wall a picture of the Blessed Mother, to whom he maintained a deep and tender devotion. "We must go to Mary," he said so often in his life, and in this increasingly uncertain time he held close to her tighter than ever.

[30] Ibid., p. 57.
[31] Glueckert, *Titus Brandsma*, p. 17.

Father Titus, now a prisoner of the Third Reich, had to work for his food and keep at Scheveningen, and he performed menial tasks and cleaning chores around the prison every day for a few hours. To ward off lethargy and boredom, he worked out a daily schedule of work and prayer that, in mirroring his life in Carmel, not only gave a sense of rhythm and structure to the day but allowed him to become immersed in the silence and solitude so long denied him by his professional duties.

He not only devoted several hours of the day to mental prayer and spiritual reading, but also recited the unchanging prayers of the Mass from memory without bread, wine or sacramentary. He walked for about an hour every day, pacing the length of his cell back and forth as long as it took to approximate a brisk stroll through the streets of Nijmegen. Kept busy spiritually, mentally and physically, Father Titus was for the time being relatively left on his own.

His cell, roughly ten feet by six feet, had just a bed, a stool, table and four walls, but it became for Father Titus a monastic cell, a cave on the heights of Carmel, and he became absorbed into a sweet peace that he tried to pour out in words.

Having been granted what looked like an indefinite amount of free time by officials of the Third Reich, Father Titus took the opportunity to work on a project close to his heart for some time. He began an autobiography of Saint Teresa of Avila, without notes or research material but relying solely on his photographic memory of her life and works. In the absence of clean paper, he began writing the book between lines of a book he had there in his cell.

The irony of Father Titus' time in Scheveningen, which from the tone of his letters seemed to amuse rather than terrify him, is that it took arrest and imprisonment to give the friar what he most longed for. Not martyrdom and suffering, but total solitude with God in the silence of his cell.

As a Carmelite extraordinarily receptive to grace, Father Titus had always been able to carry his cell with him regardless of where he was or what he was doing: not a portable, physical structure but a perpetual place of quiet in his heart where he could meet and speak with God when and however God wished. Whether teaching and speaking or writing and travelling, Father Titus was able to maintain that sense of constant prayer, of constant conversation with the Lord.

Now that the teaching and writing and magazines and lectures were finished, the wound of love was opened even wider in Father Titus, and the sweet balm that poured in elevated Father Titus' soul to the point that even poetry proved woefully inadequate in terms of expression.

But try he did, and, despite his being arrested and unjustly imprisoned for doing good, Father Titus sang out his inner joy in verse. Sublimely succeeding in expressing the inexpressible, Father Titus composed a poem entitled *Before a Picture of Jesus in My Cell*, and it expressed the depth of his love and joy in being allowed to share in a small portion of the Passion of Jesus:

> O Jesus, when I look at you
> My love for you becomes more true.
> And yours, I know, will never end:
> You see me as a special friend.
>
> This calls for courage on my part
> But pain's a blessing for my heart,
> For pain makes me become like you
> And leads me to your kingdom, too.
>
> I feel true blessing in my pain;
> Such suffering for me is gain,
> For what your providence will do
> Is make me one, My God, with you.
>
> Just leave me in this cold alone
> Although it chills me to the bone.
> No visitors – no one to see-
> To be alone is good for me.
> For you, Lord Jesus, are right here;
> I never felt you quite so near.

Stay with me, with me, Jesus sweet,
Your presence makes my joy complete.

(Translation by Henrietta Ten Harmsel)[32]

Amersfoort

The solitary and, for the present, relatively harmless atmosphere at
Scheveningen was the last peace and safety Father Titus would
know. After seven weeks he was shipped to Polizeiliches Durch-
gangslager Amersfoort, a small concentration camp midway between
the coast and the German border, where his monastic desert retreat
would turn into a slow and brutal climb to Golgotha.

At Amersfoort, Father Titus found neither solitude nor time to
meditate and write poetry, but on the contrary began to experience
the full dehumanizing fury of Nazi 'justice.' Arriving on a bitterly
cold March 12, 1942, Father Titus and his fellow prisoners were
ordered to undress in the courtyard, and stood naked in the icy rain
for several hours before they were marched inside to have their
heads shaved.

The prisoners were issued itchy wool prison uniforms, each with
a triangle of differing colors to denote their crimes. Father Titus bore
the red triangle of political prisoner and, having had all rights and
identity taken from him as a common criminal, was now Prisoner
No. 58 and nothing else.

Despite the crowded conditions at Amersfoort Prison, as well as
the increase of violence and abuse at the hands of the Nazi guards,
Father Titus immediately began to minister to the spiritual and
human needs of his fellow inmates. Any observed act, particularly
of administering the sacraments, would earmark the offending
priests (called 'Black Vermin' by the SS guards) for severe beatings
and harsh punishments.

The increasing bleakness and uncertainty of Father Titus'
prospects were lightened somewhat by the acquaintances he quickly

---

[32] Forceville & Waaijman, *Titus Brandsma*, p. 13.

made among the other prisoners. Doctors, lawyers, intellectuals, teachers and clergymen of all faiths all heard about the presence of the famed Professor and sought him out immediately.

Forming what was called the Tillburg Circle, in honor of the famed Catholic town in the province of Brabant, the group of intellectuals and clergy made Father Titus their unofficial leader and helped him form a clandestine but highly effective network of prison ministry.

Under the increasingly suspicious eyes of the Nazi guards, Father Titus gave sermons, heard confessions and led talks on key points of Scripture and spirituality relevant to the current Lenten season or on the saint of the day. His health failing but his mind as sharp as ever, Father Titus took the opportunity to introduce his fellow inmates, many of whom were atheists, to the beauties and depths of his beloved Flemish Mystics. Testimonies submitted after the war by dozens of prisoners attest to Father Titus' radiant faith and the effect he had on prisoners of all faiths or no faith at all.

As he was deprived of all of his possessions, including his books, his breviary and even his rosary, the Tillburg Circle managed to smuggle in a copy of Thomas a Kempis' *Imitation of Christ*, a missal and even a rosary – a hand-made affair comprised of bits of wood – that deeply touched the friar. He listened to all, spoke with all, and gave to all regardless of faith or political beliefs. He was soon a revered figure in the prison and came to be known as "Uncle Titus", a Dutch term of great respect and deep affection.

In Amersfoort, Father Titus also tried to perform as many corporal works as possible too, and offered what assistance he could to those in physical pain and discomfort. Confined to the infirmary when his stomach pains began again, he risked a severe beating by sneaking outside to steal rocks, which he heated and placed on the stomachs of his comrades suffering from the same ailments.[33]

None of this escaped the notice of the camp officials who, after Father Titus preached a well-attended Holy Week service, decided

---

[33] See *Essays on Titus Brandsma*: Houle, p. 31-33.

to place the little friar on the 'special treatment' list. It was whispered that he was to be put on the brutal work details that meant almost certain death for the weak and the elderly prisoners. Through the influence of several inmates and a doctor, Father Titus was released from the work detail and assigned to some relatively safe kitchen duties. Before he was able to again run afoul of prison guards or officials, Father Titus was informed that he was being transferred back to Scheveningen on April 28.

It seems that Hardegen and the Nazi authorities had had sufficient time to review the Brandsma case and decide on the next course of action. What that course would actually be was placed squarely on the shoulders of Father Titus himself, thus effectively putting the Nazis in the best possible light and absolving them of any consequences.

If Father Titus Brandsma would promise never again to speak, write or preach another word against the Nazis or the German occupational forces, and would sign an agreement to that effect, Hardegen stated that he would be a free man in a few days. If not, Hardegen said, Father Titus would be sent to Dachau.

At the Nuremburg Trials following the war, minutes from meetings Hitler held with his top advisors in regard to policy for the occupied territories revealed how a systematic elimination of key figures was to be employed to intimidate the populace. Termed 'Night and Fog', the operation saw the arrest of high-profile figures in the fields of politics, academics, literature and even religion, who disappeared without a trace as though they had been swallowed up by a misty darkness.

Hardegen's offer, while not unusual, still represented a departure from the Nazi's normal modus operandi. Whether or not Hardegen wanted to avoid making a martyr out of the high-profile priest or genuinely admired him and wanted to spare him the certain death that Dachau promised such a weak, ill man, the Nazi's offer was seen by Father Titus as an outright bribe.

Having achieved a national reputation for being a staunch and brave anti-Nazi, having endured arrest, prison, interrogation, cold, hunger and beatings for the Faith, Father Titus could have easily agreed at that point to the terms without looking as though he had caved in to their demands. Like Saint Paul, he could have claimed to have suffered stripes for the Faith that went beyond that which was expected of him.

As terrifying as the whole ordeal was becoming for the friar, as sick and frail and utterly spent as he was in his body, he saw what lay inside the prettily wrapped gift offered him by the representatives of the diabolical Nazi Party. Having been unable to break Father Titus through the brutalities and deprivations of prison life, they now tried to simply buy his silence at the price of his conscience.

Father Titus, having now come full circle to where he was on the day of his arrest several months back, once again clearly but unequivocally stated his positions and his beliefs.

The protest which brought the Nazi Party to seek his arrest and imprisonment was non-negotiable for Father Titus. The rights of the Church, manifested in the exercise of authority and free expression in the Catholic press were inextricably linked to the sanctity of basic human rights and freedoms. To stand silent before the abrogation of a single right of a single individual, whether the person be Christian, Jewish or even German, would be tantamount to the abrogation of the rights of all. He could not, Father Titus restated, remain silent and remain a Christian where he saw such wrong, and therefore could never agree to sign such a document.[34]

For Hardegen, the fate of Father Titus was now sealed, for, by refusing to sign the agreement, he instead signed his own death warrant. Granted permission to phone his superiors in Nijmegen, Father Titus called his prior and told him that he was being transferred to the concentration camp of Dachau, probably some time in May. He said that that was all he knew at present but added that all was well and not to worry about him.

On May 16, Father Titus was loaded aboard a cattle car packed with fellow prisoners and they began the long, nightmarish train ride to KZ Dachau, outside the Bavarian city of Munich. Stopping in Kleve, Germany, for a short time, Father Titus was consoled by

---

[34] Alzin, *A Dangerous Little Friar*, p. 99.

receiving the Blessed Sacrament in a Mass said by a German priest. Receiving communion for the first time in several months proved to be a profound consolation for the friar, and it truly strengthened him interiorly and gave him the necessary strength to continue on the darkening path that lay ahead.

Like ink in water, Father Titus' pains began to affect his physical, emotional and, ultimately, his psychological state. His legs and feet were swollen to the point where he could hardly wear his shapeless prison shoes, and his stomach was causing him more agony than ever. He was also suffering from insomnia, dysentery, ringing ears and was experiencing occasional hallucinatory periods.[35]

The German priest who said Mass for Father Titus was horrified by the Friar's pathetic physical condition, and he urged him to write letters of appeal to escape incarceration in Dachau. If he did not, the priest said, it would be the beginning of a quick end.

For the first time since his arrest, Father Titus began to crack under the tremendous strain and suffering he was enduring in every facet of his existence. It was miraculous, to say the least, that he could have gone so long with such a cheerfully optimistic outlook, let alone with enough strength to get his frail body through each increasingly brutal day.

The monumental injustices of his arrest and imprisonment, and the horrors of daily life as a political prisoner of the Nazis understandably pushed Father Titus to his breaking point. The fact that all of this could have been easily avoided had he quietly acquiesced to the Nazi's demands began to tax and torment his soul, and for several weeks despair whispered in his ear like the Tempter did to Christ in the Desert.

Writing a letter stating his situation and asking for another hearing, Father Titus had it circulated among the Nazi authorities with the help of friends back in the Netherlands, many of whom personally tried to intervene with The Hague. While by no means giving in to the Nazis in conscience or principle, Father Titus

[35] See *Essays on Titus Brandsma*: Houle, p. 34.

offered to place himself under house arrest in a Carmelite house somewhere it Germany for the duration of the war, going so far as to suggest Bamberg.

When the Nazis in The Hague were approached with this offer and told that Father Titus was a very sick man, quite possibly on the verge of death, the terse reply came back stating that he should have anticipated such harsh consequences "before rushing into this brawl."[36] All attempts were exercises in futility and, placed once more on the stinking cattle cars, Father Titus left Kleve on June 13 and continuing into Bavaria, arrived at KZ Dachau on June 19, 1942.

Dachau & Death

After ten days in the initiation blocks – barracks where the new prisoners were acclimated to the inhuman, exacting regulations of concentration camp life – Father Titus was assigned to Block 28 as Prisoner No. 30492. The last leg of his climb was now under way.

After almost ten years of mastering the arts of death and systematic brutality on an organized scale previously unknown, the guards of Dachau took a special pleasure in singling out groups or individuals for particularly horrid abuse. Built to house 5,000 prisoners, by the time Father Titus arrived, the bleak, long barracks housed no less than 12,000 human beings, including 3,000 priests, whose day to day existence was based on the whim of their SS overlords.

The frustration and the anger that had temporarily beset Father Titus in Amersfoort and Kleve, the result of weeks of uncertainty and deprivations, began to burn away upon arrival in Dachau and, amazingly enough given the situation and the location, he seemed to regain his spiritual and emotional equilibrium again. A sense of calm renewed itself inside Father Titus and, far from fatalistically accepting the inevitability of his lot, he abandoned himself with an open heart and with open eyes to the Father's will.

If he radiated peace and a deep interior joy at the very moment his life began its excruciating end, it is because through the

---

[36] Alzin, *A Dangerous Little Friar*, p. 103.

conscious choice of his free will he was truly imitating the Lord whom he had followed his entire life. While he naturally felt fear and loneliness, for Father Titus to have regretted his actions or lost all hope would have been more than uncharacteristic; it would have been in effect a denial of the very essence of his life.

The fact is that eyewitness reports, of which fortunately there are quite a few, attest to the exemplary behavior and genuine sanctity manifested by Father Titus in the last painful days of his life in Dachau.

The most detailed account comes from a Dutch Carmelite and fellow inmate at Dachau, Brother Raphael Tijhuis, O.Carm., who related that, from his arrival in the camp, Father Titus knew in his heart he would never leave alive. Calm, patient, but a physical wreck, he nevertheless marched daily to the fields and back again, sometimes after twelve hours of backbreaking work.

His swollen feet covered with festering wounds, Father Titus suffered as well from violent abuse by the Communist guards chosen by the SS for their well-known hatred of the clergy. Fed thin soup and three potatoes a day like his fellow inmates, Father Titus was often clubbed by the block guards for the slightest infraction of the endless camp regulations, ranging from having a dirty spoon to not removing his hat to looking up during work marches.

Brother Raphael personally attended Father Titus, binding the sores on the older man's feet with bits of rags or handkerchiefs. Following the makeshift medical attention, Father Titus would always gingerly get to his feet and cheerily declare, "There, I feel like a man again!"[37]

Brother Raphael also related how awed other inmates were of Father Titus, one group of Polish Carmelites going so far as to say that the friar exuded a deep sense of peace that defined explanation. He continued to hear confessions and speak to small groups whenever and wherever he could, and he became once again a hero, a living standard of sorts, around whom the Dutch inmates rallied.

---

[37] See *Essays on Titus Brandsma*: Tijhuis, p. 65.

The source of peace and joy, so tangible to those who met him, was revealed privately to Brother Raphael with the greatest precaution and care possible. Had it been discovered, the penalties would have been severe indeed. Through an intricate network of priest inmates throughout the camp, the Blessed Sacrament was circulated clandestinely for distribution among the prisoners. It was a great consolation as well as a great hazard, and for many it truly became *viaticum*, food for the final journey.

One night, a consecrated host was passed to an overjoyed Father Titus hidden in an eyeglass fashioned into a makeshift pyx and tabernacle combined. Before he could consume the host, a surprise inspection was called, and Father Titus quickly hid the case in his armpit – like Saint Tarsicius – prepared to protect Christ's body with his own.

For no apparent reason, the guard doing the inspection pummeled Father Titus, flooring him with one blow of his cudgel. While the other inmates stood by helpless, the guard hit again and again every time the friar attempted to rise, leaving him a bloody heap on the barracks floor. Brother Raphael said that instead of going for medical treatment, Father Titus dragged himself to his bunk and collapsed. Awaking in the dead of night, he remained in silent adoration before the Lord concealed in his eyeglass case. "I knew Who I had with me," Father Titus said to Brother Raphael.[38]

The next morning, sore and bruised from the previous night's beating, Father Titus gave the Brother communion and then trudged off to another twelve-hour workday. It was only through these brief encounters with the Eucharistic Presence that Father Titus found the remaining strength to survive and carry on.

After one month of concentration camp work and abuse, Father Titus had withered to a sickly and fragile shell of a human being. The infirmary, in the hands of experimenting SS doctors and brutal Communists, was no better than the barracks and was therefore scrupulously avoided at all costs. However, since Father Titus could

[38] Ibid., p. 85-86.

not simply lie in his bunk and die, he was talked into going to the infirmary and, after receiving at least minimal medical attention, returning as soon as possible. In late July, he was reluctantly taken to the infirmary and almost immediately began a quick decline.

The infirmary at Dachau was, in effect, a charnel house in which SS doctors used inmates as human guinea pigs in a series of horrifying 'scientific' experiments. One set of these experiments, which included everything from freezing and pressure experiments to forced sterilization and electric shocks, was crafted especially for the priests of Dachau. Some of the testing done on the priests at Dachau included being injected with high levels of malaria to gauge how long and how much of the disease could be tolerated by the body's system. Another included healthy priests being injected with a virus that caused ulcers and inflammation of the membranes. Purulent wounds, some as big as a man's hand, covered the entire bodies of countless victims, resulting in excruciating agony, amputations and death.[39]

Since few of the infirmary doctors were brought to justice at the Nuremburg Trials, it is impossible to pinpoint with certainty the dates, victims and precise nature of the experimentations. From eyewitness accounts, however, it is certain that Father Titus was a victim of SS medical experimentation after being taken to the infirmary on July 19.

The woman who killed him surprisingly enough supplies the most reliable witness to Father Titus' extraordinary last days and death. A nurse and an ex-Catholic priest-hater, the woman was a bitter soul and had grown indifferent to the brutal, daily extermination of human life. In a written testimony, the nurse stated that there was something very attractive about Father Titus that she could neither explain nor forget. The nurse caught bits and pieces of conversation, which she listened to with a growing sense of curiosity.

[39] Dr. Johannes Neuhausler, *What was it like in the Concentration Camp at Dachau?* (Munchen: Trustees for the Monument of Atonement in the Concentration Camp at Dachau, 1965) p. 62.

Despite his own pain, the friar began counseling and comforting his fellow inmates, the only thing many of them had in common up to this point was that they were all there to suffer and die. One man was seen speaking, sotto voce, with great intensity to Father Titus, apparently relieving himself of a great burden. She saw another man pouring out his heart to the little friar, tears streaming from his eyes. Despite her own hatred of the Church and the clergy, the nurse allowed Father Titus to ask questions about her life and how she had become so consumed with hatred and apathy. He told her to pray and, taking her hand, gave her his rosary. She laughed. Pray, he told her again, and she would not be lost.

The end finally came for Father Titus on July 26, 1942, six days after he was admitted into the infirmary. The nurse, so filled with hate and rage toward humanity that murder became just another one of her duties, administered a fatal injection to Father Titus. Within a few minutes he was dead. The next day he was incinerated in the camp crematorium.[40]

When the news of his death became official – the cause of death being given as pneumonia – tributes and accolades poured into Nijmegen from around the Kingdom. Archbishop De Jong, writing to Father Titus' Prior at the Nijmegen Carmel, declared that the friar gave his life for the Church in the personal service of his prelate. In 1946, Father Titus' sister received a personal letter of condolence from Queen Wilhelmina of the Netherlands, who had just returned to her country following a war time exile in England. The letters of sympathy that poured into the Carmel after the war were followed by testimonies from fellow inmates of all walks of life and religions, who attested to the heroic sanctity and selfless sacrifice of the friar.[41]

Interest in the life, death and legacy of Father Titus continued to grow in the post-war period, and soon a strong devotion to him began to increase among Dutch Catholics to the point where individuals began offering intercessory prayers to him. As early as 1948,

---

[40] See *Essays on Titus Brandsma*: Staring, p. 154.
[41] Alzin, *A Dangerous Little Friar*, p. 109-110.

two miraculous cures were attributed directly to the intercession of Father Titus. The first was a man suffering from ulcers who, despite several operations, was increasingly plagued with suffering and the debilitating effects of the disorder. After praying to Father Titus, his ulcers disappeared overnight to the puzzlement of his doctors.[42]

The second was a boy who, after being in a car accident, was lying paralyzed and comatose in a hospital bed. The nursing sisters, who had a strong devotion to the Carmelite friar, began praying to Father Titus for the boy's life. In a few days, the boy regained full use of his limbs, again with no medical explanation offered.[43]

In 1955 a commission was formed in the diocese of Ten Bosch in the Netherlands to investigate the life and death of Father Titus Brandsma. Through the evidence given by those who knew him in the friary, University and in Dachau, the commission concluded that Father Titus led a life of heroic sanctity and died a martyr's death for the Faith. After eighty sessions, the commission closed the proceedings and sent the one hundred thirty-six volumes of testimony and evidence to Rome.

Among the prominent testimonies given to the commission, which included statements given by Protestants, Jews, non-Catholic doctors and three bishops, was that of the nurse who administered the fatal injection to Father Titus. Apparently she indeed took Father Titus' advice to pray, as she returned to the Catholic faith after the war. Coming forward voluntarily to give a first hand account of his final days and martyrdom which she had personally brought about, the nurse continually referred to Father Titus as the "Servant of God" and attributed her conversion to his direct intercession.

Beatification & Legacy

Testimony after testimony offered by the survivors of the labor camps – as opposed to the death camps like Auschwitz and Treblinka, where prisoners marked for extermination were killed immediately –

---

[42] See *Essays on Titus Brandsma*: Houle, p. 36.
[43] Ibid., p. 37.

shows how sheer force of will amplified the survival instinct and increased the chances for survival.

On the other hand, Father Titus was not consumed by a burning desire to defend and prolong his existence despite a strong natural sense of joy and passion for life. The one letter that reached his family after his transport to Dachau does not state an unequivocal promise of survival and return, but offers a quiet abandonment to God's will and a prayer invoking the protection of the Virgin Mary and Saint Joseph. He closes with the brief but still characteristically cheerful note of admonishment: "not too much worrying about me."

As the radical abandonment displayed by Father Titus during his imprisonment at Dachau showed neither fatalism nor survivalism – the most obvious extremes one would expect given the situation – the depths of his interior life and prayer at this time are more ineffable and therefore more sublimely beautiful.

Jesus had clearly and lovingly declared the criterion for discipleship to the rich young man of Saint Matthew's Gospel, who ultimately went away sad because he clung so tightly to his life and all the transitory illusions of security it held. All that was required of the true disciple of the Lord was to put God before self, feed the poor and, having laid up spiritual wealth in heaven, "Come, follow me" (MT 19:21.).

In his search for God, Father Titus naturally sought to fulfill the divine will in every undertaking of his life. In so doing, however, he never confused total detachment with total indifference, but sought the sanity between both, which is known as *abandonment*.

Father Titus' brand of spirituality, quite mystical despite also being quite practical, was not geographically oriented; he did not need to be in a cloister or in a choir stall to seek, love and serve God. Able to be "holy in a train compartment", as his friend Godfried Bomans said, Father Titus found his union with God down the constantly widening and narrowing of his spiritual journey. Like a good disciple, Father Titus did not ask how and where he would be called and where it would all end, he simply asked for the grace to love and be faithful until the end.

Pope John Paul II declared Father Titus Brandsma Blessed in Rome on November 3, 1985.

Chapter II
"Let the Little Children Come to Me"

Père Jacques de Jésus, O.C.D.

The city of Linz, Austria, is situated halfway between Salzburg and Vienna on the shores of a wide but not so blue Danube. Like most of the cities in Austria, Linz is a delightful blend of baroque opulence, Hapsburg splendor and *fin de siecle* artistry. Moving outward from the massive Hauptplatz, or city square, with its swirling Bernini-esque column and quaint coffee houses, narrow streets snaking out in every direction teem with raucous adolescents and staid Frauen in gray wool capes and Tyrolean hats.

Again like all Austrian cities, Linz caters to many feelings, many desires, but most of all to the human weakness of the sweet tooth. From the elegant, centuries-old confectioners on the Hauptplatz to the family-run, back street bakeries, Linz offers pastry lovers hundreds of ways to artistically and guiltlessly indulge their passion.

The most distinguishing feature of Linz, however, is the abundance of the churches that stand in baroque magnificence on what appears to be every street corner and down every tiny alley. Everywhere, beginning from the Bahnhof – or railway station – skirting the edges of the city to the top of the gently sloping Postlingberg, onion-domed church steeples soar into the blue Austrian sky like gigantic fingers of yellow, white and oxidized copper. You can hardly go a block in any direction without passing a massive church portal crowned with the ornate coats of arms of some Hapsburg prince or potentate.

Aside from a few churches whose communities have either died out or can no longer maintain the costly upkeep, the sacred spaces of Linz for the most part continue to be just that. Unlike so many

European cities where the churches have been nationalized or turned into multi-purpose cultural centers due to congregational atrophy, the churches of Linz are alive and pulsating daily with spiritual energy.

There are very few signs in Linz proper to recall a more tragic chapter in the history of this magical city of churches and pastry on the Danube, and the kind citizens of the modern city are as far removed from Nazi hatred and intolerance as can be imagined. Indeed, one must go to the history books to see crowds thronging the Hauptplatz, ablaze with spotlights and swastikas, celebrating the *Anschluss* – the joining together – with Nazi Germany in 1938.

The Fuehrer himself had an intimate though unhappy connection with the city, for he failed as a young student in the *Realschulen* of Linz and Steyr; yet its citizens nevertheless joined the rest of the nation in hailing him as a conquering hero come home.

The most ineradicable sign of Austria's other past lies about fifteen miles east of the city, where the wooded Danube valley gives way to gently rolling hills dotted with farmhouses and peaceful hamlets. As one pushes further out into the pastoral expanse of the Muhlviertel, it appears that aside from an occasional tractor and television antenna, life has changed little in the past several hundred years.

The awesome sight of the Tyrolean Alps soaring into the heavens some 75 miles to the south no doubt aids this bucolic sense of idyll. Even on cloudy and overcast days, the mountain range is still slightly visible, floating mistily like stationary clouds of gray and icy blue. It is probably the reality, the sanity and stability of the mountains, even on days when they are hidden, that bring about a deep sense of perpetual exultation, a stirring of the spirit and a turning of the soul towards God.

From the foot of a steep, thickly wooded hill just past the fairy tale hamlet of St. Georg, the climb takes one past neat little houses, ramshackle barns and dark forests that look as though they have fallen straight from the pages of the Brothers Grimm. Sleek, brightly colored tour busses chug heavily up and down the slopes, steering wide of hardy school children of various nationalities, scurrying and shouting all the way up the slope.

Remarkably enough, the variety of languages of the multi-national visitors is transformed into a common and deafening silence when the objective at the top of the hill is achieved.

Konzentrationlager Mauthausen.

Like all the concentration camps preserved throughout Germany and Eastern Europe, Mauthausen is shrouded in a heavy, palpable and ultimately triumphant silence. Despite the size of the crowds entering the heavy stone gate, the entire camp is locked in a silence that seems to be continually regenerated by the life force of the 86,000 human beings murdered here by the agents of Adolf Hitler's Reich.

The silence of Mauthausen is a presence that often feels more real than the visitor walking its stone pavements and neatly organized barracks, gas chambers and crematoria.

At first glance, with its squat towers and long stone ramparts, Mauthausen could appear to be a crusader castle, transplanted from the deserts of Palestine and plunked anachronistically atop an Alpine hill. What hangs from the grim walls of Mauthausen, however, are not the shields and swords of Teutonic Knights, but endless rows of somber plaques and markers silently honoring the tens of thousands of men and women who met horrific deaths here at the hands of the SS.

There is one plaque, initially harder to find in the veritable sea of bronze and marble, which hangs among the national monuments located on the sweeping slope that begins just outside the prison walls. The more artistically impressive monuments built by nations including Israel, the Netherlands, Hungary, Poland and the former Soviet Union, crowd the scene. There is a Menorah rendered in an abstract style, soaring granite columns, a heroic sculpture group and a stylized, neoclassical *tempietto*. Despite the varying styles and sizes of the monuments, they seem to interweave and flow effortlessly together along the lush, peaceful slopes.

Following the footpath through the cemetery, the monument to the French dead of Mauthausen rises out of the grass with a placid, quiet dignity. It stretches like a long stone fishhook, the curve which, when rounded, reveals a wall of marble plaques, pictures and an occasional flower arrangement or a vigil candle.

In the center of this heart-moving mass of marble and stone, one plaque seems to stand out from the rest. Perhaps because it is at dead center on the wall, perhaps because it seems to draw the memory of the man honored into the collective memory of his comrades:

+

A LA MÉMOIRE DU
R.P. JACQUES DE JÉSUS
LUCIEN BUNEL
DE L'ORDRE DES CARMES DECHAUSSÉS
DEPORTÉ AUX CAMPES COMPIÈGNE,
SARREBRUCKEN, GUSEN ET MAUTHAUSEN
MORT A LINZ LE 2 JUIN, 1945
VICTIME DE SA CHARITÉ
POUR LES PERSECUTÉS.
PER CRUCEM AD LUCEM

+

TO THE MEMORY OF
REV.FR. JACQUES OF JESUS
LUCIEN BUNEL
OF THE ORDER OF DISCALCED CARMELITES
DEPORTED TO THE CAMPS OF COMPIÈGNE,
SARREBRÜCK, GUSEN AND MAUTHAUSEN
DIED AT LINZ ON JUNE 2, 1945
VICTIM OF HIS CHARITY
FOR THE PERSECUTED.
BY THE CROSS INTO THE LIGHT

+

Or perhaps it is the realization that, like the plaque, the life of Père Jacques of Jésus, OCD, begins and ends with the Cross.

Birth and Early Years

When asked to write an autobiographical sketch, Abraham Lincoln quoted a line from Gray's *Elegy* to indicate that the story of his life was to be found in "the short and simple annals of the poor." It is an apt summation of the life that ended in Linz but began on January 29, 1900, when Lucien Bunel was born to Pauline and Alfred Bunel in the town of Barentin, France.

Barentin is situated in the heart of the province of Normandy, a misty, lush land with rugged coastal beauty, a long, often tumultuous history stretching back to Celtic times, and a rich Catholic soul that seems to mingle organically with the salty air and sandy soil.

William, Duke of Normandy, launched his invasion of England in 1066 from these shores, and the resulting conquest led to the establishment of his progeny as its kings and queens for hundreds of years. Joan the Maid, a peasant girl who rallied the beleaguered forces of France against the invading English, was captured, tried and burned as a witch in 1431 in the Norman capitol of Rouen.

And centuries later Thérèse Martin, another extraordinary young woman who would be known one day around the world as Saint Thérèse of Lisieux, came to exert a tremendous influence over Western spirituality from behind the walls of an obscure Carmel in the Norman hamlet of Lisieux.

As Normandy is a land deafened by the roar of the North Atlantic, so it has resonated with the cacophony of war, from the clanging of swords in the twelfth century to the crash of artillery in the Allied invasion in June, 1944. It is a land softened by picturesque abbeys and venerable churches, by rolling verdant meadows populated by a hardy stock that clings to values and traditions long jettisoned by urban cousins deeper inland.

By 1900, however, Barentin, like Normandy, like France, and indeed like the whole of Western Europe, had become a hotbed of discontent and unrest arising from a working class pushed to the wall. Uprooted from their agrarian and artisan roots by the Industrial Revolution half a century before, the common laborers of Barentin, like their comrades throughout Europe, lived out their lives in factories and sweatshops producing goods for the world.

Alfred Bunel, one of millions of laborers caught in the cycle of drudgery and backbreaking work, was a spinner in a textile mill near Barentin. Working twelve hours a day, six days a week, in oppressive, hazardous conditions was not out of the ordinary for the common laborer of the day, and Bunel père dutifully sweated without complaint to feed and house his growing family.

Abstaining from tobacco and alcohol to save money (a rarity if not a heresy among the wine loving French) Alfred was a hard working, simple man of integrity and convictions that were manifested in the unpretentious unfolding of his day to day life.

Pauline Bunel (nee Pontif), a few years her husband's senior, was a formidable, irrepressible woman, who refused to let the socioeconomic constrictions of her birth prevent her from ruling in her small sphere of influence, namely, her home and her family.

Even in old age, Pauline Bunel looked like a Grande Dame of the *ancien révgime*: fine, sculpted features, piercing eyes and a bearing that was noble even when she was seated. Affectionate, protective, yet intolerant of opposition or contradiction of any sort from her brood, Pauline ran her family and her house with discipline and orderliness worthy of one of Napoleon's marshals.

Despite the few francs her husband's pay brought to the pot, Pauline somehow managed to keep an immaculate house, keep her children well groomed, and stretch a few potatoes, bread, and an occasional cut of beef into substantial meals three times a day. The Bunel children recalled also how the mother instilled a respect for adults in them, insisting that elders be addressed as "*Sir*" and "*Madame.*"

The Bunels may have been poor, but in their integrity and sense of self they were anything but peasants.

Pauline loved all her children, but she doted particularly upon her lively, wide-eyed third child Lucien. Closer ties generally bind parents to children who are sickly or experience traumatic and life-threatening illnesses when young – precisely that befell baby Lucien when he was just a year old.

Struck down with an illness, from which the doctors held out little hope of recovery, little Lucien was all but given up for dead by everyone, except his devoted and determined parents. It was a brutal law of averages, common to every peasant family, that now seemed to dictate whether or not baby Lucien would survive this illness. Up to the early part of the twentieth century even the most minor childhood illnesses cut a wide swath through the families of rich and poor alike. Among the poor in particular the loss of one or more children to the most common illnesses was, tragically enough, all too common.

True to form, Pauline would have none of this and, left with nothing but her desperate, unwavering trust in God's mercy began a novena to St. Germain, a traditional favorite among the poor folk of the region. On the ninth and final day of the novena Pauline gathered baby Lucien and her husband and trundled off on foot in a cold rain to the shrine of St. Germain, seven long miles from Barentin.

Lashed by the icy rain, shivering from the cold wind blowing over the empty Norman countryside and terrified at the prospect of losing her child, Pauline poured out her heart to God at the base of the statue of St. Germain.

The mother pleaded for the baby's life in exchange for totally surrendering him to God at the age of twenty.

As soon as she finished her prayer, Lucien, who had been on the verge of death, a situation certainly not helped by the seven-mile trudge in the cold rain, suddenly cried and kicked out the first signs of health he had shown in weeks. Later, gurgling milk at the cottage of a farmer couple near by, Lucien laughingly confirmed the parent's unshakable convictions that God had granted their child an instantaneous and miraculous cure.[1]

The lightning-like transformation of her baby from deadly illness to bouncing health seared Pauline to her depths, and, seeing God as living up to his side of the bargain, she never forgot her obligation to do the same. Although it broke her heart to do so, she indeed gave her son to God almost twenty years later. Almost twenty years after that her broken heart was crushed to learn of the death of her child in the faraway city of Linz, Austria.

Yet Pauline always remained faithful to her bargain, and though she suffered every pain reserved for a mother's heart alone, she

---

[1] Carrouges, *Père Jacques*, translated by Salvator Attanasio (New York: Macmillan, 1961), p. 15-16.

always remembered the day the hand of God personally touched her poor family on a cold, windswept field in Normandy.

Youth & Vocation

Lucien fully recovered from the illness, and he grew strong and healthy in the expanding Bunel household which eventually grew to seven children – six boys and one girl. His whole being, however, was deeply and indelibly stamped with the seal of his miraculous recovery and his mother's prophetic consecration of his life to the Lord.

Outwardly young Lucien's life differed in no way from the multitude of children who grew up in the shadow of the textile mills of Barentin. He played make-believe games in the street and lost himself in the deep woods and spacious fields around the town. He stood in awe of his older brother Alfred, a devout factory worker from the age of twelve, who attended daily Mass, and he himself became a conscientious protector of his younger siblings.

As he grew into childhood and adolescence Lucien gave every indication that mentally, emotionally and spiritually he was a typical youngster of the working class. He did, however, exhibit several traits, good and not so good, that separated him a little apart from the others.

In school he did quite well, and his consistently excellent grades and voracious appetite for books gave clear indications of a future that did not include the sweatshops of Barentin. Lucien also possessed an extremely kind and generous nature and, though like all children he loved animals and responded to the wonders of nature, he was unique in that even at an early age he demonstrated an amazing level of love and common consideration for family, friends and total strangers.

Despite this innate sense of kindness and concern, Lucien was by no stretch of the imagination a saintly child, blessed with a cherubic temperament and given to miraculous encounters with heavenly beings. He was a normal and lovable – which means often difficult – child, and the full grain of his personality included not a few rough edges that required much attention.

His kindness and warmth were curiously mingled with a stubbornness and intransigence that, fermenting into a fierce pride during adolescence, put him on a collision course with every elder and authority figure who crossed his path. He grew as a creature of conflicting extremes of self-giving and self-assertion, a sign not only how human he was but of how hard he would have to work in later life to master his dominant faults.

He could bristle easily when challenged, fought defiantly when he could not get his point across and had a lifelong passion for humor and practical jokes. This last character trait, which would become so warm in his later years was, in his youth, often caustic and exercised at the expense of others. With time, however, he mellowed and he left a great deal of this puerility behind with his childhood toys and books. What was left was the fiery animating spirit behind his actions, and an exuberant personality that was attractive to everyone he met.

It was no surprise to anyone, then, that from about the age of five Lucien declared his intention to be a priest. In those days this was not an unusual desire, as one would have been hard pressed indeed not to find a boy or girl of the region who did not consider, or at least dream of, the priestly or religious life.

With Lucien it was not simply a case of dress up or playing Mass; he actually seemed to grasp the essentials of the priestly vocation in the totality of his actions. He 'baptized' his sister's dolls and 'preached' sermons to his playmates, but he also served daily Mass every morning at 6:30 and helped organize after school activities and religious processions for the village children. His brothers and sister also recalled his daily scripture reading and the hours he spent in the parish church, absorbed deeply in solitary prayer.[2]

When M. Bunel approached the good and kindly parish priest, Abbé Ternon, with his son's desire to enter the seminary, the Abbé concurred immediately, as he felt for some time that Lucien was being called to the priestly life. A holy and solid shepherd, the good

---

[2] Ibid., p. 20-21.

Abbé was sure this was not the case of a dreamy youth seeking an escape from the depressingly limited horizons of Barentin.

Lucien was a hard-working, dedicated young man being drawn deeper into God's presence in the Sacraments and in his neighbor, and the Abbé was committed to doing everything in his power to help him respond to the Master's call.

The major, if not the only, problem was money. Scholarships were rare and the Bunel family was very poor, so that, financially, sending Lucien to the Pétit-Séminaire – the minor seminary – was as likely as sending him around the world on a Grand Tour. Abbé Ternon suggested to M. Bunel that he ask his wealthy employers for the money, but, finding begging of any form repellent, the father demurred in the hopes of finding another way.

Lucien, however, had no such inhibitions and he set out on his own to beg money from the wife of the factory owner, a haughty women who condescendingly welcomed the boy into her parlor. After listening politely as Lucien poured out his priestly desires and bemoaned the financial straits preventing them from becoming a reality, Madame quietly dropped a few centimes – literally a few cents – into his hand and showed him the door.

Lucien, who never felt anything but pride in being a member of the working class, was mortified and, sickened with shame and humiliation, went home in a daze and wept in his mother's arms. For the rest of his life Lucien remembered that cruel day with profound sadness.

This inauspicious approach to his seminary career defeated neither the boy nor his parents, and at the beginning of the term in October, 1912, Lucien boarded a train for Rouen and the Pètit-Sèminaire. The money question they left in the hands of God.

Seminary & Military Service

Once ensconced in the seminary, Lucien adjusted quickly and became a standout among the mixed group of young men linked, for the most part, only by a common spiritual goal of priestly service. Raised in a poor but warm and loving religious family, Lucien had no problem with cold baths and dormitory living, and he saw the lean fare and rigid discipline as means to toughen up his body and spirit.

Although something of a rebel, who thought nothing of challenging professors or directives he did not respect or acknowledge, it was apparent that Lucien had made the right decision and was where he was supposed to be.

The years spent in minor seminary, like the novitiate of a major religious order, were a time for laying the foundations of the priestly life and character, a time for silence, meditation and immersion. It was a time when the young seminarian was nurtured, protected and guided spiritually and emotionally by other priests, young and old, who had once started out on the same road.

Lucien, with his infectious, mischievous humor and love of pranks, threw himself wholeheartedly into the social dimensions of seminary life. He thoroughly enjoyed recreation and the spiritual camaraderie, and he formed friendships that were destined to last a lifetime.

On a deeper level, the solid academic air and disciplined regimen of the Pètit Sèminaire began to take some of the edge off his rather sharp temperament, and he began re-channeling his mental and spiritual energies towards his studies and interior life. His prayer life began to deepen and unfold, and he continued his boyhood practice of spending long hours in front of the Blessed Sacrament in silent prayer and meditation. His childhood experience of solitary walks through the Norman woods melded with his maturing spirituality, and Lucien began to crave greater solitude in which he could remain silently in God's presence.

This desire for greater solitude, however, was a luxury which the young seminarian would one day have to relinquish. The placid, nurturing atmosphere of the Pètit-Sèminaire was in effect a respite and haven in which the seminarians could rest before the hectic realities of parish life set it. As a curè in a parish Lucien would be busy from before till after dusk with the spiritual, emotional and physical needs of his flock. Mass, confessions, sick calls, social ministries, youth ministries and the endless practical demands of running a parish would all consume Lucien's time, and he would have to learn to simply weave his contemplation into the fabric of his priestly life.

His superiors, often as critical of Lucien as he was of himself – and them –, had come to see Lucien as an excellent student and a promising priest, and they let it be known that they expected him to proceed to the Grand Sèminaire.

Money, fortunately, had ceased to be a critical factor in deciding Lucien's fate, and he could concentrate wholeheartedly on his studies without distraction. Sister Marthe, a nun from a convent outside Rouen, had become a close friend of Lucien and, in the absence of Madame Bunel, had clucked over him like a protective mother hen. She had gone to M. Bunel's new employer, whom she knew quite well, and this time the results of the mission were quite different.

The Badins were wealthy, but they were also devout and generous, and they gladly welcomed the chance to 'adopt' the dynamic, personable young seminarian. The whole family treated Lucien like a son and a brother and when he was ordained it was the Badins who bought the vestments for his first Mass.

There were, however, greater crises threatening Lucien along with his fellow seminarians and citizens throughout France, with immense implications for the course of history and the lives of millions. The peace of Europe, held together by a complex system of treaties as well as by common blood ties between many of its kings and queens with the great matriarch Queen Victoria, was shattered a mere fourteen years into the new century with the assassination of Austrian Archduke Franz Ferdinand in the Balkan backwater of Sarajevo.[3]

On the morning of the day when the gun salvos announced Europe's first world war, a war which would engulf Europe and spread abroad, England's Foreign Minister Sir Edwin Gray spoke for an entire generation whose established order was about to disappear forever. "The lights are going out all over Europe," he said gloomily

[3] Ibid., p. 26-27.

as he watched the gaslights of London dim, "and I don't know if they shall be lit again in our lifetime."[4]

The German, British and Russian Empires, the monarchs of which were cousins, fell into opposing Allied and Axis camps and, together with France, Austria-Hungary, Belgium and dozens of minor kingdoms, principalities and republics, were by the summer of 1914 engulfed in total war. The global conflagration known as World War I affected Lucien deeply: it aroused a strong sense of patriotism but was to be personally devastating for him and his family.

The men of the Bunel family, loyal sons of France, answered the call, and in rapid succession, M. Bunel, Alfred junior and André were soon in uniform. The Pètit-Sèminaire at Rouen, less than a hundred miles from the front, was transformed into a military hospital, and the seminarians were transferred to temporary quarters nearby. With a collective pall hanging over the nation now at war, Lucien anxiously waited out his own uncertain future.

With three members of the Bunel family serving in the armed forces, the resolution of the poverty crisis threatening Madame Bunel and her remaining children rested squarely on the shoulders of her seminarian son Lucien. If one or more of the others did not return from war and soon, Lucien would have to give up his hopes for the priesthood and become father, brother and provider for his younger brothers and sister. Given his age and his family situation, M. Bunel was soon mustered out of the service and allowed to return home. André was taken prisoner by the Germans but eventually released. Alfred, the beloved eldest son and brother, the daily communicant who walked silently through the woods of Barentin, was killed in action on the Western Front in 1917.

Lucien faced yet another obstacle to his studies: his approaching eighteenth birthday in 1918 brought the distinct possibility of his own participation in the war. At eighteen Lucien was obliged to complete two years of compulsory military service, a prospect that

---

[4] Susanne Everett & Brigadier Peter Young, *The Two World Wars* (London: Bison Books Ltd., 1982), p. 21.

would wreak havoc with his planned departure to the Grand-Sem-
inaire that same year.

The anxieties of his life at this time, a tangle of personal tragedy
and the uncertainties of his future, was mellowed with his eagerly
anticipated departure for the Grand Sèminaire in the Fall of 1919.
Six months later, however, he was called up for military service, and
soon after that Lucien was in the uniform of the 82nd Artillery
Regiment outside Paris.

Not surprisingly, Lucien adjusted relatively well to army life,
having always lived a communal life of discipline and simplicity,
and he eventually rose to the non-commissioned rank of mess
sergeant. Coming from the sanctified atmosphere of the Pètit and
Grand Sèminaires, Lucien was, however, horrified by the atheism
and immorality rampant through the ranks of the military, and he
quietly set about an apostolate of example among his comrades.

Knowing that heavy-handed proselytizing would have a drastic
counter effect on the cynical soldiers of his unit, Lucien won them
over first and foremost by friendliness, cheerfulness and respect.
As mess sergeant he was entitled to kickbacks and petty graft from
the food supplies and purchasing agents, but instead he saw to it
that all monies went to supplies for the men. He never let his military duties interrupt his Mass and prayer schedule, and soon he
was taking groups of the men with him.

Within a short period of time, Lucien had won the respect and
affection of his comrades, none of whom bore unbounded oceans
of love for the clergy, and by all accounts his military service was
a great success personally and professionally. He was by no means,
however, sheltered from the realities and temptations of barrack
life and once, while walking through the Montmartre section of
Paris, was approached by a lady-of-the-night plying her trade. More
saddened than scandalized, Lucien spent the evening praying for
the unfortunate young woman.[5]

---

[5] Francis J. Murphy, *Père Jacques: Resplendent in Victory* (Washington, D.C.:
ICS Publications, 1998), p. 23.

Though raised in poverty and having constantly fought the battle of the poor in myriad ways, Lucien was nevertheless sheltered from full contact with the cynical atheism, hatred and destruction that would come to uniquely characterize the twentieth century. First in the sheltering warmth of his family's bosom and then in the rarefied realms of the seminaries, Lucien had seen and experienced life through a lens of faith, piety, security and the rewards of perseverance in prayer and hard work.

"The short and simple annals of the poor."

Thrown into military life with hardened men further jaded and spiritually emptied by the ravages of World War I, Lucien attracted and won over his fellow soldiers not through pious practices but through the peace and strength emanating from the depth of his convictions.

It was a maturing and profoundly affecting experience on many levels, but most of all on a spiritual one. Like Jesus and his disciples, Lucien left the warmth and security of his known milieu and went out among men and women, the cynical and the unbelieving and the oppressed worker. For the first time he was not among his own, and he risked their rejection and their abuse and their attempts to make him believe less like he did and more like they did. He held fast to his faith and his bedrock beliefs, and in the end despite an atmosphere polluted by atheism, the strangers he met became his brothers and sisters in Christ.

The apostolic zeal burning within him, this love of souls whom he wanted to bring to God, mingled with his constantly intensifying desire for solitude and his growing attraction to the contemplative life. That is why, though he was still in the uniform of a French soldier, Lucien decided to become a Trappist monk.

The Call Of The Cloister

Like his decision to study for the priesthood, Lucien's attraction to the Trappists was not an impulsive whim but was based on prayer and reflection begun when he was sixteen years old. To Lucien, the Trappists with their poverty, austere asceticism and long hours devoted to communal and solitary worship of God, seemed to exemplify the best means by which he could lead a hidden life of love and prayer.[6]

Indeed, next to the Carthusians – monks who live out their monastic lives in almost total solitude and silence – Lucien could not have chosen a more ascetical and demanding way of life than the Trappists.

It was a decision that, surprisingly enough, was supported by many people who had become intimately associated with Lucien on his spiritual journey. His spiritual director advised prudence but did not wholly rule out the idea of his joining a monastic community. Another source of support was the Leroy family, relatives of the priest in whose parish Lucien's military camp fell.

The Leroys became, like the Badins, as close as family to the young seminarian and he became a regular fixture in their home. As he did for Abbé Ternon in Barentin, Lucien organized field trips and hikes for the children of the parish for the priest, and he became a beloved figure among the young and old of the area.

Madame Chalot, the Leroy family grandmother, became a particularly dear friend and confidante of Lucien's, and her warm and genuine piety became a source of great strength for him. Madame Chalot stood in place of the missing Pauline Bunel, and she accompanied Lucien on pilgrimages to shrines and religious sites throughout France. She took a mother's interest in the soldier-seminarian's health and spiritual well being, and she listened as he poured out to her his joys, aspirations and deepest desires.

First among these, was the sanctity he knew he could achieve in the monastic life.

France, despite the horrors and spiritual vacuum brought about by World War I, had begun to experience springtime flowering of Catholic spirituality touching not only the religious, but the social and cultural dimensions of the nation as well. More then just a reactionary swing of a metaphysical pendulum, this flowering stemmed

---

[6] Carrouges, *Père Jacques*, p. 35-37.

from a genuine sense of renewal based not on lofty theological doctrines but on a simple spirituality of love.

France, along with the rest of the world, had less than a decade before the outbreak of the Great War, discovered the *Story of A Soul* (1898), the deceptively simple and childlike autobiography of Sister Thérèse of the Child Jesus. Though she died at the close of the nineteenth century, Sister Thérèse, who would be canonized in 1925 and known as Saint Thérèse of Lisieux, proclaimed a simple way of love and total surrender to God in everyday and unheroic ways, hence, her "little way", that in its radical originality prophesied many teachings of the Second Vatican Council (1961-1965.)[7]

Charles Pèguy (1873-1914) was a great poet of France who, though he was not a member of the institutional Church, was a fervent Catholic in his heart. His verse was a fiery meld of deep spirituality and an undying patriotism that in his mind was exemplified by St. Joan of Arc. Peguy, like Lucien's brother Alfred, was killed on the Western Front in World War I.

Another great source of inspiration to French Catholics of the post World War I era was Charles de Foucauld, the desert mystic and inspirer of a later foundation of the Little Brothers of Jesus. A rakish, debauched atheist in his youth, Charles entered the military and had a radical conversion experience while on leave in Paris. Charles retired to the silence of a Trappist monastery to dwell in expiatory silence with God. From there Charles moved on to a Poor Clare convent in Nazareth, where he acted as sort of hermit-handy man, and then to the vast silence of the African Sahara where he was murdered by bandits in 1916.

"I must want to suffer cold, heat, or anything else," Charles would write in 1903 in his spiritual journal, "liking it, enjoying it, so as to have a bigger sacrifice to offer to God and to be more closely united with Jesus." The words of the solitary hermit of the Sahara

---

[7] Patrick Ahern, *Maurice & Thérèse: The Story of a Love* (New York: Doubleday, 1998), p. 7.

could have come from the mouth of the restless young seminarian/soldier.[8]

Lucien realized that this wave of renewed spiritual zeal was not a knee-jerk reaction to the rational materialism of the new century but a quiet revolution of faith and love accomplished by the faithful endurance of individual men and women. The atheism and Mass-destruction of the still-young twentieth century was being combated in France by the greatest outpouring of missionary and apostolic fire since the Counter-Reformation. It was a time of spiritual giants, of poets and martyrs, of desert mystics and simple souls accomplishing great things for God.

Lucien wanted to join them in their great and saintly deeds while still young, he wanted to conquer souls for Christ and felt the optimum way to accomplish his task was through the sacrifice and solitude of the monastic life.

While utterly sincere in his spiritual convictions, Lucien was only twenty-one and his rhetoric was still outdistancing his judgment. Eventually, the one who put the firmest foot down in the matter was she who had endured the greatest suffering in his life journey.

When Madame Bunel was told about Lucien's plans to abandon the diocesan priesthood for the austere anonymity of the Trappist cloister, she flew into what, by all accounts, was a tremendous rage. Confronting her son in the cottage of Madame Chalot, Pauline threatened to disown her son if he set a foot in the monastery.

With one son dead and another married and concerned with a family of his own, a third disappearing forever into Trappist life was unacceptable and not to be tolerated while she was alive. The bargain Madame Bunel had made with God was to give her son to the priesthood, with its visible ministry to people in their day-to-day lives. The thought of stone walls and hidden cloisters had never crossed her mind.

With Lucien still in uniform, it was agreed that for the time being the question was academic and could not be resolved until

---

[8] *Charles de Foucauld*, Writings Selected by Robert Ellsberg (Maryknoll, N.Y.: Orbis Books, 1999), p. 74.

he was released from active duty. Calming his mother's fears, Lucien agreed to put his plans aside until mustered out of the service but first declared his intention to make a retreat at the Trappist abbey of Soligny.

Despite the icy conditions of the unheated monastery, Lucien immersed himself in the silent depths of his first real taste of monastic life. Whether praying communally in choir with the other monks or alone in his cell, Lucien felt very much at home in the monastic setting and sought a revelation in regards to his future. Even though he thoroughly enjoyed his monastic retreat, he later confessed somewhat humorously that he barely got through the first day without succumbing to the bitter cold of the unheated cell.[9]

Finishing the retreat with a more realistic grasp of the monastic life, Lucien agreed to return the Grand-Sèminaire and his studies for the diocesan priesthood. He did, however, take with him a commitment to live a monastic life wherever he went, and carry with him an internal cell where, even in the midst of his hectic schedule of study and work, he could retire to silent conversation with the Lord.

Institution Saint Joseph

Released from military service in the spring of 1922 Lucien returned to the Grand-Sèminaire, where he refocused his energies entirely on his studies and spiritual life. During the 1924-25 school year, the last before his ordination to the priesthood, he was ordained sub-deacon and then assigned as proctor, or dormitory supervisor, for several months at the Institution Saint Joseph, a large boarding school for boys in Le Havre. There Lucien found the pace of his life beginning to increase frenetically and felt a corresponding need to intensify his dedication to solitude and silent prayer.

A bustling, industrialized port city choked with steamers and liners from around the world, Le Havre afforded Lucien contact with students of all faiths and nationalities. Like the seminaries

---

[9] Murphy, *Père Jacques*, p. 25.

Pètit and Grande as well as the military, the Institution Saint Joseph required proactive and energetic engagement, and Lucien, never known for his timidity, established himself in the school's bustling life.

At first, the students of the Institution Saint Joseph, like their superiors, did not know what to make of the tall, dynamic proctor. Well into adulthood, Lucien presented a figure that was to some curious but to all memorable. His close-cropped hair, topping off a body lean from years of self-denial, gave him a decidedly monastic look. Dark, piercing eyes that also held a perpetually mischievous glint were kept from looking hawk-like by the large steel-rimmed glasses he constantly wore.

Perched atop a prominent but noble Gallic nose, the spectacles managed to give Lucien the curious look of an ascetical university professor. It was an interesting physiognomic combination, to say the least, and played its part in making Lucien a figure that commanded great respect as well as great affection from his charges and colleagues.

While not yet a teacher, as proctor Lucien was a walking watchtower who missed nothing and tolerated little disobedience from the often rowdy and rebellious young men in his charge. Lucien quickly discovered the emotional and physical stamina required of a teacher, especially a disciplinary guide of young men trying to discover themselves and their path in life. The Institution therefore proved an invaluable proving ground for the spiritual and leadership qualities that would bloom so gloriously later in his life.

He learned every twist and turn of the mind and personality of the child and the young adult, their possibilities and their limitations, their fears, struggles and their hopes. Being thrown headfirst into the energetic world of school children not only gave Lucien the chance to refine his communication skills with the young adult, but allowed him to begin formulating radical pedagogic ideas he would implement in a few short years.

The students at the Institution Saint Joseph, like all students everywhere, were particularly fascinated with the staff's private lives, and Lucien was no exception. Spying on him from around corners, through windows and atop school roofs, the boys took to observing their proctor to see what he did during the rare hours he had to himself.

Having sequestered himself in the rear part of the building, far from the tumult of classroom and dormitory, Lucien de-constructed his already tiny room into his very own monastic cell. Stripped of all surplus furniture, his cell contained a bed, a table and chair, a crucifix, a few books and a handful of devotional images. To the astonished wonder of the hidden eyes, Lucien was often observed entering his cell, falling to his knees and praying for an extended period of time with his arms extended cruciform.[10]

It was also during this time that Lucien continued his rigorous ascetic practices – geared towards quieting his passions and mastering not only the desires of the flesh but of his impetuous personality as well.

As for his human passions, Lucien was a vigorous, healthy man who, as he approached ordination, understood more completely the depth of the sacrifice of the celibate life to which the priest is invited. With his heart full of love for the Lord and the gift about to be his, Lucien had no regrets about his vocation but, as he confided later in life, the joys of the married life, especially having children, were offered up with great difficulty.

As he had in the cold Trappist cloister, Lucien encountered not only God in the cramped and barren cell, but his very self as well, and in the deepening of his ascetical struggle he acquired far greater gifts of insight into himself.

He ate little, he drank water only – and that in small quantities – and was never known to sleep more than four or five hours a night. This last was a punishing deprivation, especially given the stamina required to constantly supervise dozens of energetic schoolboys. And, as he had done during the better part of his life, Lucien continued to spend long hours in silent prayer before the Blessed Sacrament in the chapel.

---

[10] Carrouges, *Père Jacques*, p. 56.

As much as possible, Lucien also tried to get into the countryside and woods for relaxation and meditation. Having immersed himself in nature as a child, he saw nature as a wonderful catalyst for deep dialogue with God, and, as he recommended later in his life, he often made his post-Communion thanksgiving while walking in the woods.

While some of Lucien's mortifications often took on a thin veneer of affectation, his asceticism did reflect a sincerity and genuineness evidenced by his unconditional love and deep respect for all people he encountered in his widening circle of friends, students and acquaintances.

As he rapidly became a favorite of the students, with whom he formed deep and mutually respectful bonds, so did Lucien impress his superiors at the Institution. His zeal, his dedication, his generous and kindly disposition and his seemingly bottomless capacity for work were noted with great admiration. Like Lucien's superiors at the seminaries, the priests at Saint Joseph saw a few rough edges and room for improvement, but on the whole predicted good things for the deacon and they gave him high marks.

One of the greatest of those predictions, promised by his mother in the rain over his sick little body, was fulfilled on July 11, 1925, when Lucien was ordained a priest in Rouen Cathedral.

Abbé Bunel

Now a priest, Abbé Bunel celebrated his first Mass in the less ornate but more intimate church in Maromme, the town to which his family had moved when he was still a young seminarian. The day was one of profound and inexpressible joy for Lucien, his parents, his siblings and the countless people who had helped and prayed him along the way to this moment in his life.

Having achieved this plateau in his life after great perseverance, struggle and many setbacks, Lucien quickly realized that his ordination marked only a milestone on the way, not a culmination, and he began seeking toeholds for climbing to the next level.

A pilgrimage to Rome and Florence soon after his ordination gave him a respite of sorts, and he drank in the spiritual as well as the cultural magnificence of the Eternal City and the Cradle of the Renaissance. There is a particular resonance to the churches, shrines and holy sites of Rome when seen for the first time by a newly ordained priest, and Abbé Bunel was profoundly touched as well as honored to be able to celebrate Mass and administer the sacraments within them.

After the brief Roman sojourn, which turned out to be the first of several trips to Italy over the next several years, Abbé Bunel returned to the archdiocese of Rouen to await his first assignment. To no one's surprise, he was assigned right back to the Institution Saint Joseph, this time as teacher rather than proctor. His natural talents for leadership, his sense of easy fellowship and camaraderie and a conveyance of genuine spiritual depths were not lost on the Archbishop of Rouen, and his re-assignment was seen as beneficial to all concerned.

Given the teaching posts in English and religion for the lower school, Abbé Bunel threw himself once again headlong into his work with a vigor that was still mingled with an unflagging desire for the monastic life that never quite went away.

As he had done as a major seminarian, now, before the school term began, Abbé Bunel returned to the prayerful simplicity of the Trappist cloister at the abbey of Notre Dame du Port-du-Salut. Increasingly comfortable with the rhythm of monastic life and the praying of the Divine Office, the young priest became a welcome guest who impressed the abbot as a zealous soul with genuine signs of a contemplative vocation.

Abbé Bunel, despite his passionate leaning towards the cloister, was fiercely loyal to the archbishop of Rouen who made his education and ordination possible, and he felt that abandoning his diocesan career before it truly began would be dishonest and dishonorable. With the same renewed vigor he mustered years before when he felt called to the monastic life, Abbé Bunel renewed his commitment to the diocesan priesthood, which even now had begun to demand all his time, energies and devotion.

From the evidence of Lucien's life thus far, and the testimonies of those who knew him personally and professionally, the impetus for his tremendous concentration of will and disciplined commitment did not arise simply from blind filial obedience to his Bishop and superiors.

On the contrary, though indeed obedient, hardworking and extremely dedicated, Lucien was already living his life in a spirit of sacrifice, of self-offering and immolation in the moment-to-moment unfolding of his life. It was a sense of sacrifice born of prayer and a constant return to the writings of past spiritual masters who by now were intimate friends of the young priest.

As a Frenchman and a devotee of the great works of spirituality, Lucien clearly absorbed the basic premise of loving and serving God as put forward by the Jesuit author Father Jean-Pierre de Caussade (1675-1751) in his classic *Self-Abandonment to Divine Providence*.

In what is undoubtedly a masterpiece of spiritual wisdom and common sense, Father de Caussade's book – actually collected letters to a convent of Visitation Nuns – declares that that love of God and the fulfilling of the Divine Will is not achieved by waiting for the optimum moment in a particular situation or vocation. On the contrary, Father de Caussade wrote, God is found in the present moment, the sacred now that begins unfolding at our birth and ends in the consummation of our earthly journey.

All one must do to love and serve God with the fire and passion of the Saints, says Father de Caussade, is seek to do the Divine Will in the ongoing present wherever one may be.[11]

Through his zealous, forward-looking plunge into the active apostolate of the secular priesthood while curtailing his backward glances at Trappist abbeys, this salient point of abandonment slowly came home to Lucien. The result was that a certain calm and peace descended on him that was in direct proportion to the fruitless struggles he was abandoning.

The courage and tenacity shown by Abbé Bunel in his recommitment to the diocesan priesthood, in light of his passion for the

---

[11] Fr. Jean-Pierre de Caussade, SJ, *Self-Abandonment to Divine Providence*, translated by Algar Thorold (Rockford, IL: Tan Books, 1987), p. 6-7.

monastic life, did not merely reflect a personal sense of virtue and integrity, but mirrored broader sociopolitical tensions running deep in the very fiber of French life.

By the time Lucien was born and well into young adulthood, France was in the throes of the most strident anti-clericalism it had experienced since the Revolution of 1789 some hundred years before. This tension, abating somewhat during the reign of Napoleon I with the signing of the Concordat with the Vatican, after decades of historical ups and downs, had by 1905 come to an ugly political head.

That fateful year saw the passing of the *Loi de Separation des Églises et de L'État*, or, the Law of Separation of the Churches and the State. Promulgated on the basic premise that the Republic of France was an officially non-religious state, the law entailed drastic reductions of Church power and property that succeeded in dividing French Catholics and raising the ire of the Vatican.

While the Law included endless and tangled prohibitions on everything from priests' salaries, public liturgy and the wearing of clerical dress in public, the most serious article was that which dealt with Church property throughout the Republic.

The Law of 1905 in effect nationalized all Church property, including residences and seminaries, and placed them in the hands of lay administrators. The administrators, known as *associations cultuelles*, were comprised of laypersons who became the official governors of all Church property in France. Responsible for the liturgical use, upkeep and even sale of churches, convents, parochial schools, seminaries and rectories, the associations also had the power to simply close the buildings if taxes could not be raised for their maintenance.[12]

While the Vatican responded with official pronouncements of outrage, most notably Pope Pius X's 1906 encyclical *Gravissimo officii*, the government successfully restricted the authority of the Catholic Church in France, using the legal machinery of a democratic state.

---

[12] *The Catholic Encyclopedia*, edited by Charles G. Herbermann, Vol. VI (New York: Robert Appleton Company, 1909), p. 185-186.

"We have extinguished in the firmament lights which shall not be rekindled," triumphantly thundered Minister of Labor M. Viviani to the Chamber of Deputies in 1906, "and we have shown the toilers that heaven contains only chimeras."[13]

The workers, the laboring mass who represented the traditional core of French Catholicism through the ages, had by 1920 become more and more enamored of the tenets of Socialism and the international labor movement. Encouraged by the establishment of the worker's state in Russia in 1917 and the voice of Labor now being heard in Parliaments throughout Europe, the French laborer of the post-World War I period was more likely to be found in a mass meeting than at Mass.

Lucien had encountered this growing anti-clericalism himself even in his hometown of Barentin, and later during his early days as a soldier. When he had left Barentin as a twelve-year old for the Petit-Seminaire, the village laborers sneered at him as a soft-skinned malingerer, using service to the Church as a way of shirking his common worker heritage. In the barracks, the soldiers reveled in lewd remarks and indecent behavior in his presence as a way of mocking him as well as his Church.

Despite the early twentieth century revival of French piety, the flowering of spiritual literature and the example of countless holy men and women, the Church during these tumultuous years was seen by many workers as siding with old power structures and therefore part of a problem rather than a solution. Priests, nuns and religious, struggling for their very existence in a new and legally anti-clerical age, lived precarious existences in a fishbowl scrutinized by a cynical and suspicious populace.

Lucien, like his brother priests before him, did not immediately receive the respect, admiration and affection of the people with the oil of ordination. On the contrary, the respect of the people had to be earned and held daily not simply by his piety, but by the example of every facet of his life.

[13] Ibid., p. 189.

Restlessness & Recommitment

It was in the hectic, often draining pace of his daily activities that Abbé Bunel made a discovery of something precious that would have been denied him in the monastic life, namely, the joys and rewards of the apostolic life. With his buoyant zeal and sparkling personality Lucien was a magnet for souls, and he quickly became a favorite at the school and indeed throughout the city of Le Havre. Not only students, but also professional persons, dock workers and men and women of all faiths and backgrounds became his friends. Many became his spiritual children and recipients of his already profound wisdom and counsels.

In short, by giving up the struggle to attain the cloister, Abbé Bunel discovered that in fact he was naturally a tireless shepherd of souls and a very good teacher.

He was a firm believer in the classroom-without-walls concept, and he used the surrounding world as a means to help students integrate school-acquired knowledge into the practical aspects of their lives. He organized field trips to the seashore, forests, and the docks of Le Havre to understand better the beauty of God's creation and the unpleasant realities of human life.

However, while he was a genuinely pious priest, an extremely gifted teacher and a fun loving, ebullient individual, Abbé Bunel constantly appeared to his colleagues as being on a road all his own: a solitary, distant road they neither saw nor understood. While never mean-spirited and never known to have uttered an offensive remark about anyone, Lucien still retained enough Norman fire to put him at odds with anyone who challenged his teaching style or methods. Although beloved by many, he was still something of a hothead, and his superior, Monsignor Blanchet, was led to sigh, "One Abbé Bunel at Saint Joseph is fine."[14]

The children, though, had an immense affection and growing respect for the Abbé that not only deepened but also transcended language and nationalities.

---

[14] Carrouges, *Père Jacques*, p. 53.

In 1928, while acting as chaplain to a troop of Boy Scouts formed especially for the poor children of Le Havre dock workers, Abbé Bunel took them on a long-awaited jamboree to the English coastal town of Plymouth. Having already mastered the English language as a teacher, Abbé Bunel led the boys in a lively, congenial exchange of songs, games, food and traditions with their English hosts. Engaged in an intimate discussion with his Protestant counterpart, Abbé Bunel spoke of the joys of his life as a Catholic priest. Describing with what must have been great beauty and poetry the Mass, the dogmatic mysteries of the faith and the ever deepening life of sacrifice and love to which all Christians are called, the French priest impressed the English scoutmaster with his sincere, spontaneous revelations.

Reluctantly ending the evening and friendly discussion, Abbé Bunel led the French boys in evening prayer and then gave them each the traditional blessing. Deeply moved at the sight, the English scoutmaster approached Abbé Bunel the next day and, prodded by his troop, asked if the priest would bless the Protestant boys in the same way before the night's end. Abbé Bunel was as delighted and touched as the English troop and that night, as they saw their French counterparts do, each Protestant boy knelt down in front of the priest to receive his blessing before retiring to his tent.[15]

The inexpressible feeling of love the souls for the English children flowed out of Abbé Bunel like tears of joy, and he treasured the memory his entire life. The next few days, he noticed several of the English scoutmasters watching his Mass from a respectful distance, as though they were trying to glimpse something of that mystery of love of which he spoke so eloquently by the dying embers of the campfire.

Carmel

It was not long before Abbé Bunel's reputation spread from the confines of the Institution Saint Joseph to the bigger world outside.

---

[15] Ibid., p. 64-65.

When he was not performing his duties as a teacher, Abbé Bunel could be seen hop-scotching across Le Havre to say Mass, hear confessions and give spiritual direction to the laity and religious in parishes and religious communities throughout the diocese.

Though an exemplary priest whose reputation was now beginning to cross denominational boundaries, Abbé Bunel was still unsatisfied and unfulfilled in the depths of his professional life. The lack of directional clarity that had troubled Lucien for several years, came to a sudden halt on the bright summer morning of July 12, 1927.

Having continued to crisscross the archdiocese as a popular priest, confessor and homilist, Abbé Bunel by chance wrote and asked the superior of the Carmel of Le Havre if he could come and celebrate Mass for the nuns. When a favorable reply was received from Mère Marie-Joseph de Jésus, Lucien arrived at the convent unaware that his life's course was about to be drastically altered.

Abbé Bunel certainly knew about the existence of Carmelite nuns in France, and his life had already crossed paths with Carmel on several occasions that had made lasting impressions on him. In regards to their particular charism and spirituality he had yet to be illumined from the inside.

Like so many French Catholics, Abbé Bunel had a great affection for St. Thérèse of Lisieux, and not only did he immerse himself in her autobiographical *Story of A Soul*, but also rejoiced in her canonization in 1925. He also read and reread the autobiography of Sister Marie-Angelique, in whose book he made the startling discovery that there were Carmelite friars in France as well!

It was, however, in conversation after Mass with Mère Marie-Joseph that Abbé Bunel began to feel the fullness of Carmel enter an increasingly empty space in his life. Opening up his frustrated heart to this kind and wise woman, who would become from that day an intimate friend and confidante, Lucien listened enraptured to the superior's detailed description of Carmelite life and day-to-day spirituality.

The call of Carmel, Mère Marie-Joseph said, was dual in nature. The Carmelite friar is called to a life of constant prayer, solitude

and intimate conversation with God in the silence of the cell, only
to return to the world as a teacher, preacher and pastor to share his
contemplative fruits with the people of God.

For Lucien, who had been caught in an exhausting, vacillating
struggle between the contemplative and the apostolic lives, it
seemed as though the Carmelites offered what he had been searching for his entire adult life. He felt as though he had discovered like
a hidden vein of gold the balance of the two great passions of his
life: the silence of the cloister and the clamor of thirsty souls. This
revelation filled him with an intoxicating joy.

"The Carmelite Order is my ideal of the religious life," Abbé
Bunel excitedly wrote to Mère Marie-Joseph soon after their visit.
"To live in solitude with God, in intimate contact with Him, and
then to leave the cloister to bring Him to souls, to let Him be
known and loved, then return to plunge back into the retreat to
renew oneself with prayer. This is what draws me!"[16]

Abbé Bunel's journey to Carmel, however, proved to be more of
an ascent than a plunge, and the myriad obstacles that soon loomed
before him merely fueled his ardor for the climb.

No sooner had he discovered the hidden, joyful spring of Carmel
than the school term once again began. The school year, demanding and draining as ever, was followed by various twists and turns
that proved just how far Lucien still was from resolving his career
anxieties.

He had not entirely abandoned the Trappist idea, although an
entirely cloistered life was becoming less likely. Under the influence
of Père Labigne, director of Rouen's archdiocesan missionary program, Abbé Bunel was also giving thought to the missionary life.
If this was not already enough, he was also giving consideration to
the Franciscans, the Dominicans and the Eudists.

Loosened for a while after his discovery of Carmel, the tangled
knot of Lucien's vocational dilemma once again seemed to tighten,
and it was probably his prayerful perseverance along with his sound
spiritual direction that prevented him from choking altogether.

16 Ibid., p. p. 87.

Abbé Arson, pastor of the dock worker's parish in Le Havre, was considered one of the holiest priests in the Archdiocese. A devotee of Saint John Vianney, Abbé Arson made bi-annual pilgrimages on foot from the port of Jaffa to Jerusalem and the sites of the Holy Land. It was natural, therefore, for Abbé Bunel to seek the assistance of this holy priest to help him through the dense fog of his vocational crisis. It would take a wise priest and placid soul to help discern the will of God in the variables that seemed to be swallowing him whole, and by all accounts Abbé Arson was precisely the man for the job.

Abbé Arson urged a steady course and saw no reason for the young priest to diverge from the path that clearly pointed in the direction of Carmel – a direction that was slowly being accepted by Lucien as well.

While he was respectful of the diocesan priesthood and of other religious orders, none of these callings seemed to demand the levels of spiritual commitment and excellence from Lucien that the Order of Carmel did. While Lucien did not presume to know the will of God, he did possess a level of self-knowledge that allowed him to see the imperative need for a community to stabilize his temperamental spirit. Only under a monastic rule with the fraternal support to be found in communal life could Lucien hope to curb the "immense pride" and "frightening spirit of independence" that he knew to be deep-rooted in his soul.[17]

With this tremendous amount of internal turmoil and mental drain, Lucien made himself a prime candidate for mental and physical calamity. Having already been felled by what he termed a "nice little bout with typhus" the year before, Abbé Bunel was once again in the infirmary in the winter of 1928. Exhausted, feverish and still unsure of his future, Lucien received the illness as a graced period of mortification and suffering, as well as a time to seriously concretize his next steps in life.

The following summer Abbé Bunel made his annual retreat, no longer at the Trappist abbeys of Soligny and Port Salut, but at the Carmelite Friary at Avon, near Fontainebleau. It was a newer

---

[17] Murphy, *Père Jacques*, p. 47.

foundation, but the handful of friars in residence were elderly and in dire financial straits. The building itself was a shambles, and the friars, let back in the country only a few years before after an uneasy peace was made between the Vatican and the French Republic, lived in conditions that were primitive at best.

To Abbé Bunel, however, living in the ramshackle, dilapidated buildings with the Carmelite friars was as sweet as if he were dwelling in a cave on the slopes of Carmel itself. The zeal of the few old friars at Avon, their spiritual vigor and their determination to renew the spirit of Carmel in France was like a living force, and it quickly inflamed Lucien's soul.

Up to this point, the deep desire for union with God in silence and the barrage of priestly obligations in the world seemed to swirl around Lucien in two diametrically opposed orbits. While his discovery of Carmel eased his sense of anxiety in regards to the future, he still needed to bridge the gap, to link in his mind the two opposing orbits and, by uniting struggle of the world with the spiritual struggle, to see them as one in the journey to God.

That link was Saint John of the Cross (1542-1591), whose works were recommended to Lucien by Père Jean de Jésus-Hostie, the Carmelite novice master at Avon with whom the young engaged in lengthy spiritual conversations.

In his growing relationship with the friars, Lucien was becoming increasingly familiar with the great Carmelite mystic, reformer companion of Saint Teresa of Avila and Doctor of the Church, whose spiritual writings and poetry rank among the most sublime works in Western literature. Born Juan de Yepes in Castile to weavers of probable Jewish descent, John entered the Carmelite Order and made a name for himself as a promising young priest and scholar. When he supported the Reform of the Carmelite Order as put forth by the dynamic Saint Teresa of Avila who, though many years older, looked upon the wise young friar with great admiration, John was spirited away by brother friars content with the status quo.

Imprisoned for nine months in a darkened room the size of a large closet, John maintained his faith and probably his sanity by composing poetry in his mind. The poems, which were later written down once he escaped, speak of the journey to God down darkened paths, or nights, in which the soul is stripped of every comfort and security and must rely on pure faith alone.

This stripping, a purification of the soul that scours away all worldly attachments and human conceptions of God, leads the soul through the three stages known as the purgative, illuminative and ultimately the unitive. The spirituality of Saint John of the Cross, which has often misunderstood as a complexity of mystical esoteria, is actually a model of simplicity and common sense. For John the journey to God is accomplished simply by loving God, and all acts inherent in that journey flow from the paramount virtue of love.

Desperate as Lucien was for answers and for direction, he did not simply read Saint John of the Cross and meditate on the texts. Delving headfirst into the Saint's *The Spiritual Canticle*, Lucien literally broke the words open, ingesting and relating them back to his own often confused search for direction and clarity.

Reading Saint John of the Cross gave Lucien further insight into his own struggle to find God's will, and like a man on a mountain, he was able to see a great distance with sparkling clarity before clouds and mist once again moved in. As Saint John of the Cross states in his *Ascent of Mount Carmel*, the journey to God up the slopes of the holy mountain entails a surrender of all and a reduction to nothing in order to receive everything. Out of this came his famed concept of 'Todo y Nada', 'All and Nothing.'

The paradoxical beauty of John's approach resides in the fact that in the desire for God one must even give up the desire itself – rooted as it is in limited human intelligence and fallible sense perceptions – and enter the divine presence in nakedness and night.[18]

Slowly, like the steady rise of the sun on the eastern horizon, the meaning, clarity and purpose that eluded Lucien for so long slowly began to dawn upon him. Having just put his foot on the slopes

---

[18] *The Collected Works of Saint John of the Cross*, Rev. Ed. Translated by Kieran Kavanaugh, O.C.D. & Otilio Rodriguez, O.C.D. (Washington, D.C.: ICS Publications, 1991), p. 121-123.

of Carmel, Lucien already grasped the answer to the question which had eluded him for several years: how could he best serve God in his vocation? Abbé Bunel felt he arrived at the answer at the end of his retreat. He had decided to enter the Order of Carmel.

Going directly to Archbishop de la Villerabel's chancery office in Rouen, Abbé Bunel was undeterred when he found the Archbishop away. Requesting by letter to be allowed to enter the Carmelites, the young priest was told in no uncertain terms by the Archbishop that, with the school year about to start, it was an impossible request that could not even be considered.

Even though his path was clear and his determination unflagging, there were to be several turnings of the seasons before his dream would be realized. Even a few years before, Abbé Bunel would have been devastated and completely undone by the interminable delays, but now, confident in his future, he simply waited patiently.

He began intensive correspondence with his Carmelite friends, whom he already considered to be confreres, and he began signing his letters as a Carmelite would. He also sent another letter to Archbishop de la Villerabel, asking to be released from pastoral service in Rouen and to be allowed to enter Carmel. Citing the necessity of his services at the school, the archbishop again denied Lucien's request.

As much as these setbacks irritated Abbé Bunel, they did not deter him from his path. He sensed the nearness of his goal, he felt a proximity to "The song of the sweet nightingale/the grove and its living beauty/in the serene night/with a flaming love that is consuming and painless." *(The Spiritual Canticle.)*[19]

Lucien now understood a little more the meaning of Saint John of the Cross' painless, consuming flame. A soul is united with God only after a purifying journey leading through several stages. The purification of the soul, like that of the finest gold, is ultimately accomplished through fire.

In 1929, a year after his first request, Abbé Bunel again approached the archbishop for permission to enter the Carmelites.

---

[19] Ibid., p. 50.

This time the archbishop was more disposed to the idea but, still reluctant to give an immediate release, replied with an answer that was yes as well as no.

He asked Abbé Bunel to wait two years before entering, a trial period predicated on the maxim that time makes love pass, love makes time pass. If at the end of those two years the young priest still desired the Carmelite way of life, the archbishop would release him. Obedience and patience, Archbishop de la Villerabel said, would not go unrewarded. Though he freely admitted his bitter disappointment, Lucien agreed to the two-year trial period. True to his word Archbishop de la Villerabel finally granted Abbé Bunel the necessary dispensation from service to the archdiocese, thus effectively removing the last obstacle from his road to Carmel. It was 1931, exactly two years after his last meeting with the archbishop.

It was with conflicting emotions that Lucien packed his bags and made his farewells to students, teachers and numerous friends at the Institution Saint Joseph in August. Many people, including his superiors, thought his entrance into the cloister a dreadful, even selfish, mistake that would deprive children of a superlative teacher and spiritual guide – needed all the more now during a period of such apathy and agnosticism in higher education and the professional world.

Not surprisingly, the parents of Jewish and Protestant students who, along with their Catholic counterparts were pained to see their sons lose such a good friend and a sterling moral example, expressed some of the greatest sorrow. Though he would carry them all in his heart and his memory always, Abbé Bunel was now looking forward in a new direction, and he rushed to Carmel like an exiled pilgrim returning home from a long journey.

Carmelite Novice

In 1931, like today, Lille was a noisy industrial city situated near Flanders in Northwest France. It was into the Lille Carmel that Lucien came to begin the novitiate he desired for so many years. With Lille being an industrial city as well as an urban center, the

Carmel was something of a contemplative misfit, but despite the smoke, the bustle and the interminable rumble of motorcars past its front doors, a sense of peace and quietude was successfully maintained. Although at thirty he was ten years older than the average novice, Lucien was absorbed into Carmelite life like water in a fertile furrow. After completing the novitiate retreat, he was clothed in the habit of a Carmelite novice, trading in his black priest's cassock for a brown tunic, scapular and hooded white mantle. It was a ceremony that touched Lucien very deeply, and, despite the uncertainty of what lay ahead, his sense of anxiety regarding his future had evaporated in the prayerful silence of his new home. As a symbol of his rebirth to a new life, he was given a new name as well. From the day of his clothing, Abbé Lucien Bunel would now be known as Frère Jacques de Jésus.

As a diocesan priest, Frère Jacques had lived a life of relative independence that, aside from his teaching duties at the Institution, allowed him to come and go and generally do as he pleased. As a novice Frère Jacques had to surrender the direction of his life into the hands of his novice master, an act of abandonment and trust to which all aspirants of the religious life are called.

While it is a nurturing, warm feeling for the novice to know that everything in their life is taken care of, for a man of Frère Jacques's fiery temperament and admitted pride it was often taxing, and the novitiate was for him an intense process of breaking down and building up. The counterbalance to the initial culture shock of the cloister, which he expressed in continued letters to friends and family, was the unbounded time given Frère Jacques for silent prayer and solitude in his beloved cell. His purpose as a religious now was constant prayer, and the joy he felt at finally receiving this gift poured out of him in exuberant letters.

"My life is entirely cloaked in silence," he wrote after his formal acceptance into the Carmelite novitiate, "and is passed almost completely in the choir in an affectionate encounter with God, or in my cell where I again meet God as everywhere else for that matter."[20]

---

[20] Carrouges, *Père Jacques*, p. 99.

He no longer had to create monastery cells in school dormitories or flee to Trappist Abbeys for a few days of silence. Now it was real and permanent, and, far from burning out, Frère Jacques's intensity of prayer and zeal for God and souls continued to grow and deepen behind Carmel's walls.

He was not, however, a fugitive from life and the responsibilities that recently had weighed so heavily upon him. On the contrary, his rapid assimilation into religious life and the spiritual maturity he manifested showed his superiors he was indeed on the right vocational road. His entrance into the cloister did not turn him inwards and away from others in a sort of self-centered ecstasy; he continually returned to his brothers and all he came into contact with. Like Frère Laurent de la Résurrection, a 17th century Carmelite of great sanctity and wisdom, he not only found God in the silence of the chapel but among the "pots and pans" of his day to day chores.

Though few in number, the Carmelite friars at the Lille novitiate were an impressive array of talents by whom no would-be contemplative *poseur* could safely pass. Among Frère Jacques's superiors were a future archbishop, an admiral in General De Gaulle's navy; his fellow novice, Frère Philippe de la Trinité, would later become provincial superior and in 1947 write the first biography of Jacques de Jésus, as well as a deeply moving poem eulogizing his martyred confrere.[21]

Outwardly Frère Jacques changed little from the Lucien Bunel known to the outside world. His radiant joyfulness and natural ebullience made him a welcome and beloved member of the small Carmelite community. His passion for pranks did not end with his entrance into the cloister, and the bending of rules or house customs he found pointless or annoying brought the occasional reprimand from above.

On the whole his superiors and his brother friars sensed an extraordinary presence in Frère Jacques, and his gentleness, his

---

[21] Philippe de la Trinité, *Le Père Jacques: Martyr de la Charité* (Paris: Desclée de Brouwer, 1947), p. 495-501.

kindness and his unforgettable smile made an extremely deep impression on everyone he met. His talents, his organizational skills and most of all his extensive experience in the field of education were not lost on his superiors as well, and soon they were planning ways to put the active dimension of his Carmelite spirituality to good use.

Headmaster of the Petit-College

For some time the Carmelite Province of Paris had considered opening a secondary school for boys attached to one of their friaries. Called a *juvenat*, this particular type of school was more than a college prep or private religious academy. The *juvenat* was geared towards the attracting and fostering of possible vocations to the priesthood and religious life, especially the Carmelites.

Having been devastated by France's anti-clerical suppressions and exiles, the struggling community of Carmelite friars saw a *juvenat* as a practical means of increasing vocations to their life. The school, to be located on the grounds of the Carmelite friary at Avon, near Fontainebleau, required a dynamic, energetic headmaster, and the province knew they had exactly the right man. Frère Jacques was still in simple vows when the province appointed him headmaster of the school at Avon. He made his first profession of vows on September 15, 1932 – a year and a day after his reception into Carmel – and having celebrated his first Mass as a Carmelite was now known as Père Jacques de Jesus.

It was somewhat unusual for a newly professed friar to be saddled with such a monumental project, but Père Jacques's superiors had full confidence in his commitment to Carmel as well as his abilities to bring the *juvenat* project to fruition. On March 15, 1934 Père Jacques de Jesus was formally named Headmaster of the Carmelite's school at Avon, which was placed under the patronage of Saint Thérèse of Lisieux.

The school opened in October, 1934 and, like its headmaster, soon proved to be a dynamic and unique exception to the prevailing norm. Contrary to what the provincial councilors envisioned, the school was molded and shaped from the start by the bold and often unorthodox vision of Père Jacques.

He was adamant that the school did not become a glum, claustrophobic factory for stamping out Carmelite novices. Père Jacques hand-crafted the school using the same techniques and tools he had employed while at the Institution Saint Joseph in Le Havre. The school was to be an open, stimulating environment where young men could grow in character and spirit regardless of their vocational choices.

In another display of his educational foresight, Père Jacques was cognizant of the positive effect bright surroundings had on students and their mental outlook. He forbade grim classrooms, drab colors and Spartan refectories serving indigestible food. Bright colors, hand picked by Père Jacques, covered the classroom walls, and students and professors ate together as a family at tables covered with tablecloths and good cutlery. Insistent that their minds be opened to the beauty of the world and not just crammed with facts and figures, Père Jacques took groups of students on nature hikes and to exhibitions of works by Picasso and Matisse. He also continued to imbue them with a love of poetry and great literature.

Many of the students, born after the anti-clerical exiles, had never seen a friar or a religious in a habit, and Père Jacques did not want to make them think the school – or the Catholic Church, for that matter – was the enemy of joy, beauty and fun. Père Jacques, said a former student, wanted "everything to laugh and sing."

There was a motive underlying all of Père Jacques's actions as Headmaster that went far beyond a desire to give students a liberal education and exposure to the world. He wanted to give them a sense of turning and re-turning to the sense of the divine, the presence of God in every person, place or thing they encountered.

"He showed me God", said a former student of Père Jacques years after his school days, "through Bach and Beethoven."[22]

---

[22] Carrouges, *Père Jacques*, p. 116.

As Headmaster, Père Jacques literally had free and unchallenged power over the school, but he never was a grim, authoritarian figure. This was evidenced by his seemingly limitless capacity to execute pranks and practical jokes. His love of teasing was endless and it ranged from the innocent habit of tripping up students during nature walks and handing out false demerits to elaborate hoaxes employing sound effects and several accomplices.

He had a youthful passion for team sports and competition, and he regularly joined the boys in soccer games, playground antics and organized snowball fights. He would beam with pride if he was on the winning side and the countless times he fought for the losing side he was know to mope around about for the rest of the day.

While perennially and charmingly child-like, Père Jacques still knew how to distinguish being child-like from being childish and he never once sought acceptance as one of the boys. He knew his place as well as he knew the students' limits, and, as he learned at the Institution, discipline was imperative to keep friendliness from straying into familiarity. Influence-peddling by wealthy parents on behalf of their sons was wasted on Père Jacques, and the occasional expulsion of a student was not unusual.

If he asked the highest levels of excellence from his students, he did so first by example. The few years of peace and restful solitude enjoyed in Lille soon came to a halt for Père Jacques as Headmaster at Avon. Once responsibility for the students' education and spiritual welfare was placed on his shoulders, Père Jacques began pushing the levels of his endurance tirelessly, and he never stopped.

He continued his habit of sleeping no more than four or five hours a night, along with his ascetical practices in regard to food, the cold and his senses. After a full day in the school, regardless of how exhausted he was, Père Jacques would visit every student in the infirmary. One student, quarantined in the infirmary for over a month, received a visit and gifts from Père Jacques every night, and his parents received daily notes updating them on their son's condition.

If Père Jacques's health was strained by his feverish pace, his relation with his Carmelite community suffered as well. In another unprecedented move, Père Jacques had transferred his living quarters out of the Carmelite friary at Avon and moved into a corner cubicle of the student's dormitory. Though still deeply connected to his brother friars in everything but physical presence, Père Jacques rejoined the community only for major feast days and school holidays. For a religious community, especially one with such a strong contemplative dimension like the Carmelites, Père Jacques sudden independence caused some friction among his confreres.

Also, given the fact that Père Jacques's journey to Carmel had been fueled by his burning desire for solitude and silence, his sudden and complete return to the noisy apostolate of a school for adolescent boys could be seen as a kind of equivocation.

In fact, Père Jacques's life at this time does reflect something of a contradiction, especially if seen by the light of the contemplative desires that had burned in him for so many years. If there were any contradictions, however, they arose from a sense of duty and proved to be transcended by the grace of God. As a Carmelite, Père Jacques was under obedience to his superior and having been assigned the Headmaster of a growing, high maintenance school he did not want to run it with one foot in the cloister and one in the classroom. The school required all of Père Jacques's time and energies, and the only way he could be a complete success in his profession was to be totally present to the moment wherever he was and whatever task he was undertaking.

Saint John of the Cross helped Père Jacques move deeper into both the mystery of God and of his own journey into the darkness of pure faith. The twists and turns and supposed dead ends of his life had begun to spill out into a deeper reality like streams into a vast ocean. The essence of the Mystical Doctor's words had crystallized in Père Jacques's spiritual life to the point that he no longer needed particular places or times in which he could have God to himself in perfect silence.

No one was more aware than Père Jacques of a sense of divine irony in his life, especially when, after distancing himself from the tumult of the classroom, he was led back into that same world through the doors of Carmel. For Père Jacques, it was no longer a

question of silence or noise, apostolic activity or contemplative solitude, but the complete and total fulfillment of God's will.

His journey was now on a path that originated from the deepest
recesses of his very self and was not spatially dictated or geographically conditioned. He still snatched a precious moment of silence in
early mornings or late at night, and solitary walks through the vast
forest surrounding Avon as always invigorated his soul. Now, the
hallways, classrooms and playing fields of the school were his cell
as easily as any room in the silent depths of the friary could be, and
so it was his ever deepening commitment to God's plan that
allowed him to remain continually in His presence.

In becoming outwardly less monastic, Père Jacques was becoming inwardly more Christ-centered. From the seemingly endless testimonies of his students, it seems apparent that his life was becoming a sacrifice of love, given with an open hand and open heart for
his students, his brother friars and all he came into contact.

Père Jacques professed his solemn vows in September, 1935. His
superiors continued to be impressed with his commitment and his
spiritual maturity as a priest, religious and headmaster. Though
some of his fellow friars may have been resentful of his freedom and
unorthodox administrative methods, Père Jacques ultimately was
judged by results. With the school attendance swelling, new buildings planned and Père Jacques's reputation as an educator spreading throughout France, the provincial superiors knew better than to
tamper with such success.

Sergeant Bunel

As the decade drew to a close and the war machine of Adolf Hitler's
Third Reich cast the dark shadows of war over Europe, it became
clear that France would need Père Jacques as much as the students
of the school. Having annexed Austria in the *Anschluss* of 1938, the
Führer then turned his wiles towards the seizure of the Czech Sudetenland. Letting loose an irrational polemic that fooled intelligent
statesmen throughout Europe, Hitler demanded the return of the
expanse of Czechoslovakia cutting into Germany that held a large

number of German-speaking Austrians. The Sudetenland was, the Führer thundered, a 'dagger' thrust into the back of innocent Germany.

British Prime Minister Neville Chamberlain returned from emergency meetings with Hitler in Munich, waving a worthless accord that he claimed would guarantee "peace in our time", while German forces marched into the Sudetenland. England and France, realizing that in betraying their ally Czechoslovakia they had unmasked Hitler's megalomania and continental blood lust, began preparations for a general mobilization.

Once again, Père Jacques answered France's call and, having been recalled to active duty in 1939, was assigned as Mess Sergeant with the 21st Artillery Battery near Bazailles. As he did twenty years before when first called up for active duty, Père Jacques became a friend as well as a spiritual father to his men. Fiercely loyal to France and the ideals of democracy, Père Jacques was intent on doing his part to defeat the Nazis and their spreading doctrines of hatred and racial superiority.

His keen mind and practical perspicacity, refined from years of teaching and outsmarting adolescent boys, made him realize that boredom, demoralization and inertia were just as deadly an enemy as the Wehrmacht waiting across the Rhine. As Mess Sergeant Père Jacques continued to combat petty thievery and corruption among the officers and non-commissioned officers who were lining their pockets with commissariat graft. He printed a camp newsletter, formed groups to discuss topics ranging from spirituality to politics and in general reached out to all his men in a fashion that made deep and lasting impressions on many.[23]

Not surprisingly, Père Jacques constantly sought out the underdog, the outsider in the barracks, and soon his closest companions and admirers were not just practicing Catholics, but Communists and socialists among the ranks as well.

Billeted in a civilian farmhouse, as was the French military practice when barracks filled to overflow, Père Jacques had the good

---

[23] Murphy, Pere Jacques, p. 73.

fortune to be the welcome guest of Madame Comon and her young son François. Given a small, cold room with a cot and a few sticks of furniture, Père Jacques transformed the glorified store-room into his own monastic cell where he could lose himself in prayer, spiritual reading and the sacrifice of the Mass.

When not about his military duties, Père Jacques tutored young François and assisted Madame Comon in her chores about the farm. He also took long walks in the countryside, absorbing the quiet, pastoral magnificence of the forests and meadows. This was a time of special graces for Père Jacques, and everything, from early Mass, to the flowers and trees, to the spiritual direction he gave to the countless soldiers who sought him out, infused his soul with an exuberant sense of joy and peace.

He called his hermitage Duruelo, in honor of the lonely farm-house near Salamanca in Spain where in 1568 Saint John of the Cross began living Saint Teresa of Avila's reform of the Carmelite Rule. It was less than ten years later that the friar was kidnapped by his fellow Carmelites, locked in an unlit room in Toledo, and began composing in his mind poetry expressing the soul's journey to God through the dark night of purification and inner poverty.

The joy, the peace and the simplicity of Duruelo was followed in the Saint's life by the imprisonment, suffering and utter loneli-ness of Toledo. In emulating the Saint's sweet Duruelo, surely the realization that his own Toledo may not be far away was not lost on Père Jacques.

In the winter of 1940, some half a year after World War II began with Hitler's invasion of Poland, Père Jacques was informed that he was to be re-assigned as the divisional chaplain. The other soldiers, grown very close to the Carmelite priest, protested this move with a petition bearing the signatures of one hundred soldiers who did not want Sergeant Bunel to leave them. In fact, before any action could be taken on the petition, Père Jacques and his entire division were suddenly moved into the war zone to prepare for a German attack.[24]

---

[24] Ibid.,p. 79.

Captured during the French retreat in June of 1940, Père Jacques was imprisoned with his entire unit in a German prisoner-of-war camp at Luneville. In the six months he spent as a prisoner of war Père Jacques continued to exercise his functions as priest and soldier in a way that befitted his dignity in both vocations. Despite German censorship his sermons at Sunday Mass contained exhortations to his comrades to keep up the fight against both Nazi might and ideology. He once again organized get-togethers and discussion groups on wide-ranging topics, and his bravery and personal sanctity won him the respect of his beloved comrades in arms.

When the Nazis decided to remove the prisoners deeper into Germany, Père Jacques's status as a chaplain allowed him to be released and sent back to France. This was the last act of reciprocity and military courtesies Père Jacques would received from the hands of the Nazis. By 1940, with France fallen and split politically between Free French resistance and Marshal Pétain's pro-Nazi Vichy Government, it became clear that the Armageddon known as World War II was about to begin in earnest.

One of the first orders of business on the agenda of France's Nazi overlords was the rounding up and deportation to destinations back east of all those deemed *untermenschen* or racial inferiors. First on the list naturally were the Jews. Rounding them up en masse or plucking them out one at a time proved to be an ordeal, a bloody business certainly not to the liking of many French citizens, even among many officials of the Vichy Government. Thoroughly integrated into French culture, society, industry, politics and the arts, the Jews of France, according to historian Pinchas Lapide, were among the most fully enfranchised in Europe.[25]

Undaunted, the Führer dispatched the infamous SS butcher Adolf Eichmann – later hanged as a war criminal in Israel – to France in hopes of expediting the deportation process. As a compromise, Eichmann agreed temporarily to leave the native French Jews alone,

[25] Pinchas E. Lapide, *Three Popes and the Jews* (New York: Hawthorn Books, Inc., 1967), p. 188.

and instead concentrated on the deportation of some 20,000 displaced Jews.

Outraged French citizens of every faith, political stamp and walk of life were cemented together in a unified front, and soon Jews throughout the Republic were being sheltered and aided by Catholics, Protestants and operatives of the formidable French Resistance.

Despite increased censorship, violence and the lingering effects of the ultra-rightist *Action Francaise party*, opposition to Nazi atrocities against French Jews thundered from many pulpits and the deportations were combated by elaborate underground networks and shelters. In 1942 Cardinals Suhard, Gerlier and Lienart issued joint protests against the dreaded *Service du Travail Obligataire* or *STO* (Obligatory Work Service) that sent young Frenchmen back into Germany as slave laborers. For their opposition to oppressive Nazi laws throughout the Republic the bishops were called senile, dissolute lackeys of Jewish industrialists and Bolshevik agitators.[26]

In regards to the increasingly explosive situation concerning Jews in the Republic, the Catholic and Protestant hierarchy of France were, in spite of some regrettable exceptions among the clergy, courageous in their outspoken denunciations of the Nazi policies. Aside from their opposition to the *STO.* Cardinals Gerlier and Suhard joined the bishops of Montauban, Marseilles, Albi and Nice in aiding the Jews of France with their hearts and hands as well as their voices. In 1942 three bishops and two cardinals signed a joint letter protesting the persecution of the Jews and submitted it to Marshal Pétain of the Vichy government. In the previous year Cardinal Gerlier, Primate of France, composed an open letter of support to the Grand Rabbi of France and issued a pastoral letter exhorting French Catholics to fight against anti-Jewish atrocities, shelter Jewish children and offer Jews every possible assistance.[27]

---

[26] Carrouges, *Père Jacques*, p. 141-142.

[27] Philip Friedman, *Their Brothers Keepers* (New York: Crown Publishers, 1957), p. 49-51.

Archbishop – later Cardinal – Jules Gerard Saliege of Toulouse, spry and indefatigable at seventy-five, issued one of the most impassioned pleas of his or any other age in defense of his Jewish brothers and sisters. Personally composing a denunciation of Nazi anti-Semitic policies in France, Archbishop Saliege ordered it read from every pulpit in his Archdiocese.

"There exists a human morality which imposes duties and recognizes certain rights," declared the Archbishop, "that can be violated, but they must never be suppressed. Lord, take pity on us! Our Lady of God, pray for France! Jews are men. Jews are women. They are our brothers. A Christian cannot forget that."[28]

Despite Nazi attempts to suppress Archbishop Saliege's protests, including a foiled plan to arrest him at his residence, his broadside washed over occupied Europe like a tidal wave. Not only was it heard in hundreds of churches, but was smuggled out of France and came to be recited in prison camps and army barracks, read in the pages of the Vatican newspaper "L'Osservatore Romano" and even heard over the airwaves of the BBC.[29]

In Rome, Pope Pius XI, the wiry, no-nonsense pontiff who did little to conceal not only his opposition but sense of revulsion towards Hitler and Nazi ideology, had already outraged the masters of the Third Reich with his 1937 encyclical *Mit Brennender Sorge* ("With Burning Anxiety"). Writing in German rather than the traditional Latin, Pius concentrated mainly on the abrogation of Church rights, i.e., suppression of youth movements, attacks on the clergy, opposition to confessional schools, but he did stab at the heart of Nazism as a pagan political system as well.

Citing numerous violations of the 1933 Concordat signed between Germany and the Vatican, Pius declared that in attempting to supplant Christianity with worship of the state and the deification of the Führer, Nazism rendered itself incompatible with both faith and reason. "Anyone who, in a sacrilegious misunderstanding

[28] Lapide, *Three Popes and the Jews*, p. 189-190.
[29] Ibid., p. 190.

of the essential differences between God and creatures," the Pope
stated, "between the Man-God and the children of men, dares to
raise up a mortal, even were he the greatest of all time, alongside
Christ, or even over or against Him, would deserve to be told that
he is a prophet of nothingness, to whom would apply the dreadful
words of the Scripture: He who resides in heaven cares nothing for
them."[30]

The plight of the Jews in Germany caused tremendous grief to
the Pope – whom Mussolini called a stubborn old man – and he
spoke out in their behalf both publicly as well as privately. During
an audience with Belgian Catholics shortly before the World War
he would not live to see, Pius, with tears in his eyes, made the magnificent declaration that "spiritually, we are all Semites." For his
courageous stand, the pontiff was viciously attacked in the Nazi press,
where he was denounced as a "half-Jew" and a secret Freemason.[31]

It was into this dangerous, explosive atmosphere that Père Jacques
returned as Headmaster of the school at Avon in November of 1940.
With his patriotic convictions strengthened and tested in the fire of
war and the privations of prison, Père Jacques was every inch ready
for whatever challenges, darkness and sufferings might lie ahead.

The School to which Père Jacques returned was markedly different from the school he had left. Like the students, like the French
people, like Père Jacques himself, the school had been changed and
transformed by the experience of war. Having been seized by the
occupying Germans, the School was used as a barracks before being
returned to the Carmelites. Both the student body and the faculty
had been diminished by the various vicissitudes of war, while food
and other supplies were less available because of rationing and
scarcity of stock.

With his indomitable vigor and optimistic energy, Père Jacques
soon had the School operating at full steam despite the lack of man-

---

[30] Pope Pius XI, *The Church in Germany* (Washington, D.C.: National Catholic
Welfare Conference, 1938), p.11.

[31] Anthony Rhodes, *The Vatican in the Age of the Dictators: 1922-1945* (New
York: Holt, Rinehart and Winston, 1973), p. 192.

power and the barest of essentials. Classes resumed, and activities geared towards the students' physical health and cultural enrichment mingled with a constant attention to the boys' spiritual growth as well.

Since he had been in the crucible of war and had experienced first hand Nazi injustice, hatred and oppression, Père Jacques's conscience would not allow him to bury his head in the sands of Avon, at least not while so much horror and brutality still raged around him and throughout France.

Unremitting resistance was for Père Jacques a spiritual as well as a moral obligation, and once ensconced again as Headmaster he immediately began to make contact with the local Underground. Soon he was an active operative of the French Resistance, working in concert with the Mayor of Avon, his superior Père Philippe and even the Mother Superior of a local convent of nuns.

Gifted with a cool mind, a keen insight and a redoubtable fighting spirit, Père Jacques was also the custodian of the lives and welfare of several dozen students. While he expressed little concern for his own safety, he knew that if he were arrested the boys might suffer out of guilt by association. After consulting with Père Philippe, Père Jacques agreed that he would continue his activities in the underground, sheltering Jews, refugees and fugitives from the forced labor force, while his superior would assume all responsibilities for his actions. That settled, Père Jacques got to work.

By 1943, the School at Avon had become a key link in the local Resistance network. Young men seeking to escape induction into the Obligatory Work Service (*STO*) were sheltered at the school or were farmed out to families in the area until false documents and safe passage to neutral Spain could be secured.

The heart of Père Jacques at this time went out especially to his Jewish brothers and sisters, and the sheltering and protecting of Jewish families became his top priority. With the assistance of the Mayor and the local nuns who were already sheltering Jewish families, Père Jacques threw himself into this bold new cause that held as dire consequences for him as it did for those he was aiding.

Living in wartime conditions and being an active participant in anti-Nazi activities, Père Jacques began to meditate more and more on the subject of death. Not in an unhealthy, fatalistic way, but in a deeply Christian way that made him long to see the face of Christ even if it meant passing through the gate of his own Calvary. Like a friend offering his hand in the dark, Saint John of the Cross once again reached out to Père Jacques from the depths of his poetry and showed him more clearly the path to the summit of Carmel.

"To come to the knowledge you have not," the Saint wrote in his diagram of the Ascent of Mount Carmel, "you must go by a way you know not. To come to enjoy what you have not, you must go by a way in which you enjoy not."[32]

These no longer were simply words meditated on or prayed over. The darkness and the light, the "*Todo y Nada*" of the Mystical Doctor were unfolding for Père Jacques in reality, in time and space and in flesh and blood at a quickening rate. While it did not take a prophet to realize that he was involved in a dangerous business that held dire consequences, Père Jacques nevertheless sensed that his days were numbered. Writing to his brother René, Père Jacques conveyed his sense that he could be arrested any day and possibly shot, and he began to settle school accounts and teachers' advance salaries.

Suffer The Children

By the opening of the 1942-43 school year Père Jacques was personally responsible for the sheltering of numerous Jews and refugees at the School. Included among these was Lucien Weill, a teacher from the Lycée Carnot in Fontainebleau who, forced from his teaching post due to his Jewish origins, was asked by his friend Père Jacques to join the faculty at the School. Sheltered in the adjacent friary were several seminarians evading the labor draft.

At the beginning of the school year Père Jacques enrolled three boys he introduced as Jean Bonnet, Maurice Sabatier and Jacques Dupre. Enrolled in the school, they were quickly assimilated into

---

[32] *The Collected Works of Saint John of the Cross*, p. 111.

the welcoming student body. What the other students did not know at first and was revealed later only to the upper classmen, was that their real names were Hans-Helmut Michel, Maurice Schlosser and Jacques-France Halpern. The boys were Jews, complete with false Christian names and identity cards, whom Père Jacques had agreed to shelter from the Nazis at the School.[33]

While he constantly weighed in his mind the consequences that could befall his students, Père Jacques was determined to put his life on the line to save the lives of these Jewish boys. He was not now nor did he ever actively seek his or any other person's martyrdom. He was choosing the only path open to anyone professing the love of Christ. Besides, Père Jacques said, should he be captured and shot he would be setting the best possible example for his students to follow.

With so many dangerous operations being coordinated literally under the noses of the German forces in and around Avon, it was simply a matter of time before one or the other would be exposed.

On January 15, 1944, while Père Jacques was conducting morning classes, a squad of SS soldiers led by a particularly brutal Gestapo officer named Korff barged into the schoolyard. From the tortured confession of a captured member of the Resistance Korff learned all about the underground, the shelters, the false identities and the Jewish children being sheltered in the school. While Père Jacques was held at gunpoint, the three boys were seized, ordered to pack and under a hail of kicks and blows from the soldiers were led out of the school. All three would die in Auschwitz.

Korff, having found a cache of documents linking Père Jacques to the Avon Resistance network, told the Headmaster to pack and prepare for an immediate departure. At first Père Jacques was pale and noticeably shaking, and his fellow friars had to assist him in packing his battered valise. As he was led past the boys, shivering at attention in the schoolyard under the machine guns of the guards, Père Jacques regained his strength and his composure. Giving the

---

[33] Murphy, *Père Jacques*, p. 90.

students a loving farewell glance, he shouted out "Au revoir, les enfants!" "Goodbye, children!"[34]

The boys shouted back "Au revoir, Père Jacques!" Despite Korff's bellowing for silence and the threats of the armed guards, the students began a spontaneous, thunderous applause that continued until Père Jacques disappeared forever through the courtyard gate.

Arrest and Imprisonment

Père Jacques was imprisoned first in Fontainebleau, where he could be interrogated while the Gestapo decided his fate. It was more of a house arrest than prison, and for the time being he could have books, send mail and even receive food from nuns at the nearby Carmelite convent. A welcome relief from the cramped uncertainty of jail life was the arrival of a local electrician named Guémard, arrested for his Communist affiliations. Greeted warmly by Père Jacques, M. Guémard, who had never met the Carmelite before or even spent any length of time with a Catholic priest, felt that they met as strangers but soon were "like brothers."

In between endless games of checkers with his new friends Père Jacques managed to establish a regular schedule of prayer, spiritual reading and exercise that was neither ostentatious or intrusive. He even managed to secure, to his great delight and relief, a small table that he used as an altar for celebrating Mass.

With the complicity of an Austrian jailer named Willi, Père Jacques was given many freedoms as well as conduits to friends and family outside. Indeed, the first Mass Père Jacques offered in the dank depths of the cell was for Willi's son, killed in action while serving in the German army.

Even Korff, the cold-blooded Gestapo officer who was known to kill religious without any compunction, expressed a twisted sort of admiration for Père Jacques. To Père Philippe, the provincial superior who tried repeatedly without success to secure Père Jacques's

---

[34] Carrouges, *Père Jacques*, p. 144.

release, Korff expressed not only the improbability of Père Jacques's release but also his regret that such a man was not a Nazi.[35]

While Korff did not subject Père Jacques to any torture during interrogation, neither did he have the slightest intention of letting him go. With ties to the Resistance and Underground firmly established, Père Jacques was too great a security threat to simply set free.

On March 6 Père Jacques and several dozen prisoners were led, manacled and under machine gun guard, into a truck heading somewhere to the north of Fontainebleau. Their destination was Compiègne, a name famous throughout French history as a rendezvous for famous personages. The railroad car in which the victorious French accepted the surrender of Germany in 1918, enshrined in Compiègne as a testament to the 'criminal pride' of Imperial Germany, was symbolically used by Hitler in 1940 as the place where he accepted the surrender of defeated France.

The camp at Compiègne, though officially a Nazi prison camp, was relatively lax and lenient compared to what awaited the majority of the prisoners farther into Germany and Eastern Europe. Red Cross parcels could still be received and letters could, with difficulty, be exchanged with loved ones. Aside from reading and exercise, Père Jacques immediately began an extensive camp ministry to any and all in need materially, medically and spiritually.

As he had in Fontainebleau, Père Jacques bypassed the comfort and security of the priests's barracks and the Catholic cliques in the camp and began seeking out the minorities and the outcasts. Still wearing his rough brown habit, Père Jacques was seen by his comrades continually rushing from one end of the camp to the other. Distributing his Red Cross parcels to the poorest and most dejected inmates, doing what he could to assist the sick and the dying and boldly carrying out his priestly functions, Père Jacques acted as if he were still Headmaster at the School.

Père Jacques's Masses were apparently quite a profound experience for those who attended them and it was observed that Mass

---

[35] Murphy, *Père Jacques*, P. 96.

attendance, fairly small and lethargic before the Carmelite's arrival, swelled to a regular attendance of several hundred prisoners.

What moved so many inmates, many being former or non-Catholics, was the way in which Père Jacques became completely absorbed in the Mass, especially during the consecration of the bread and wine into the body and blood of Christ. It was as though in the fear and privations of his imprisonment the friar was actually tasting the bitter desolation of Jesus in Gethsemani with Calvary still to come.

Père Jacques also organized his ubiquitous discussion groups, now confined, however, to spiritual topics like charity, perseverance, constant prayer, chastity and purity. Far from finding topics like chastity in prison amusing, the inmates found them relevant and profound subjects for introspection and meditation. Being exposed to unprecedented levels of cruelty, injustice and perversity and, in many cases, having been separated from wives and families for the first time, Père Jacques's listeners clung to his words like a drowning person to a buoy.

Some of the highest praise of Père Jacques came from Communist prisoners, to whom he reached out not in attempts to proselytize but to befriend. Père Jacques had known several Communists through his work with the Resistance and found them to be patriotic, honorable and fiercely dedicated men and women. At first a curious, almost comic anomaly with his brown habit and gaunt visage, Père Jacques soon had the confidence of the Communist prisoners, who in turn put the word out that the priest was to be trusted.

"Père Jacques," said the Communist Émile Valley who was interned with the Carmelite, was "a Christian as Christ wanted one to be."[36]

The Carmelite's apostolic zeal, noted by all, was more closely observed by the SS prison officials. Severely reprimanded by the camp Kommandant personally, Père Jacques's found his name on

---

[36] Carrouges, *Père Jacques*, p. 160.

a list of prison agitators requiring more specialized treatment. On March 27, having been forbidden to preach, hear confessions and celebrate Mass, Père Jacques was placed in a convoy heading for yet another unknown destination. The morning of his departure, groups of prisoners clustered about the priest, some wishing him the best, some asking or promising prayers, some simply reaching out to shake his hand.

Père Jacques's road now began to darken considerably, both figuratively as well as literally, and the boring, relatively lenient atmosphere of the French jails and prisons were replaced by increasingly hellish environments as he moved into the Third Reich. The prisoners, including Père Jacques, were en route to the prison camp of Neue-Breme in the German town of Saarbrücken.

Neue-Breme

The jailers at Neue-Breme were no longer the young soldiers and old Prussians of the Wehrmacht, but the cold-blooded troops of the *SD* or Sicherheitsdienst (Security Services) whose raison d'etre was the systematic extermination of all *untermenschen* and political opponents. Built up as the intelligence wing of the *SS* by its Reichs Leader Heinrich Himmler, the *SD* was comprised of brutal, cold-blooded butchers whose ranks included Reinhard Heydrich and Adolf Eichmann.

With the unequivocal approbation of the kommandant, the guards systematically subjected the prisoners to gruesome tortures and executions without even a shadow of concern for military law or the Geneva Code. Men were beaten to death, shot, hung or torn to pieces for sport by ferocious guard dogs. Diverse racial, political and religious groups were thrown together to foment divisiveness and prevent solidarity among the prisoners. Another favorite game of the guards was to throw younger men into barracks dominated by groups of sexually perverted prisoners.

Neue-Breme was built upon a foundation of insanity and barbarism, and its inmates referred to the place itself as a "death camp". Extraordinary levels of mental and physical fortitude were needed just to get through the daily horrors, and it was with great difficulty that decent, honest men kept from being ruled simply by instincts of survival and self-preservation.

Père Jacques was by no means protected from these vile outrages against human dignity, and, having been identified as a priest he was subjected to numerous beatings and public humiliations. One of these, according to a fellow priest-prisoner at the camp, entailed Père Jacques being stripped naked and forced to carry an eighteen foot beam around the prison's fetid pools in a horrid parody of Christ's road to Calvary.[37]

Once they were thrown into Neue-Breme, it became increasingly difficult for the good men among the prisoners to keep up morale, hope and decency, let alone lead an apostolic life of sanctity and charity. Père Jacques tried to do both, despite the beatings, the daily horrors and starvation as well as the flare up of his old intestinal condition, enteritis. By rule of the Kommandant there were to be no Masses, no lectures, no preaching. In fact, silence was enforced at all times except for a short time in the barracks at night.

Père Jacques did, however, continue to inspire by his presence alone, and the overwhelming charity that he showed to all by a look, a smile or a simple act of courtesy had the same effect that his lectures did. Forbidden the use of words, Père Jacques was now forced to conduct a 'silent ministry' whose power was revealed by the response it drew from those he was serving. Prisoners would whisper God's praises as they passed him in the prison yard or during work details, and often a voice exclaimed a salutation to the Blessed Virgin out of the dark in his barracks.

Far from embittering Père Jacques or filling him with remorse or anger over his worsening situation, his imprisonment and all the attending sufferings seemed to fill him with an ineffable sense of peace and clarity that continued to radiate from deep places.

Overjoyed and humbled to have been able to share, naked and bruised, in just a portion of Christ's Passion, Père Jacques was felt honored to have suffered stripes for God's precious little ones. In

---

[37] Ibid., p. 170.

letters and private conversations he expressed deep gratitude at being able to protect and care for children of the same race as Jesus.

Père Jacques was indeed drawing closer to the "Living Flame of Love" spoken of so magnificently by Saint John of the Cross, and his face, according to one inmate, was "radiantly transformed" as if he were moving towards the light's source there in the hell of Neue-Breme.

The depth of Père Jacques's interior life did not distract him from the horrendous suffering endured by his comrades on a daily basis. The infirmary was a particularly foul corner of the camp, and far from being a place of healing and rest for the sick and the dying, it was more of a butcher shop where nature finished off the work begun by the SD guards.

Assigned to the infirmary by the *SD* Kommandant, Père Jacques immediately began to transform the barracks from a filthy, vermin-ridden hole into a clean, efficiently run clinic. Woefully inadequate by medical standards, Père Jacques's reformed ward was nevertheless infinitely better than what it was before.

With the help of a Communist prisoner who offered his services to Père Jacques, the new infirmarian scrubbed the barracks top to bottom, bathed the men and bandaged their wounds with pilfered bits of cloth or even scraps of paper. Denied medicines, Père Jacques did what he could for the desperately ill and helped those without hope of living die with dignity and in peace. Weakened himself to the point of exhaustion, Père Jacques often went entire days without food, offering his potato mush meal to another prisoner more desperate for nourishment than he.

What pierced Père Jacques most deeply was that through this nightmarish ordeal he was denied the strength and joys that the Eucharist would have given him. Indeed, when asked again for permission, the Kommandant again refused to allow the priest to celebrate Mass, preach or administer any of the sacraments.

While Père Jacques could not receive the Christ Eucharistically, that is, under the species of bread and wine, he did radically welcome Jesus in the very way the disciples were told they could encounter the Lord. He fed Christ by feeding the hungry, he comforted

Christ by comforting the sick, he assisted Christ by assisting the dying. It would be some time, however, before he himself would receive the call to enter into the Father's house.

In April of 1944, the Kommandant informed Père Jacques that he was being transferred to another camp. Defying all precedents and, indeed to some, all logic, Père Jacques dared to speak back to the camp commander, saying that he preferred to stay behind and continue his work in the infirmary. Taken aback that anyone would chose to stay in such a vile, disease-ridden place like the camp infirmary, the Kommandant refused the request.

In late April, Père Jacques again boarded another stinking boxcar that carried him into eastern Germany, crossed the Austrian border and finally stopped in the Baroque city of Linz on the Danube.

Mauthausen

Officially, the concentration camp of Mauthausen was categorized as a labor camp and not a death camp, as were Auschwitz and Treblinka. Those camps, further to the East, existed for the primary purpose of systematically exterminating millions of Jews, Slavs, Gypsies and all those classified by the Nazis as *untermenschen.*

Mauthausen was legally classified as a Category III Labor Camp, where criminals and 'anti-social' elements were committed to useful labors in the nearby stone quarries. Opened in 1938 and under the command of *SS-Standartenführer* Franz Zieries from 1939 till the end of the war, Mauthausen soon devolved into a hellish killing factory with one of the highest mortality rates of any concentration camp in the Reich.

As Nazi forces swept across the face of Europe, prisoners of war and undesirable persons of all races were sent to Mauthausen from the occupied countries, swelling the stone fortress swelling from 1,100 men and women in 1938 to a staggering 114,500 in 1944. To carry the overflow, some thirty satellite camps were built in the surrounding area, where the prisoners were tortured, executed, starved and worked to death in quarries and munitions factories. Like slaves of the Roman emperors or Egyptian pharaohs, the majority of Mauthausen's inmates were laborers in the stone quarries, forced to carry rocks twelve hours a day up some 150 steps at the quick march and down again for another load. Falling rocks, injuries and exhaustion killed hundreds while some were released from service to the Reich by throwing themselves to death on the rocks below.[38]

Despite the appalling rate of deaths from various methods of murder – the final death count in Mauthausen and its satellite camps was put around 120,000 – the numbers were apparently not high enough to satisfy the statisticians of the SS. In 1941 gas chambers using the new lethal gas Zyklon B were installed, mainly as a way of expediting the murder of the increasing numbers of Jews, Poles and Russians arriving from the east as well as soldiers and resistance members from Holland, France, England, Greece, the United States and elsewhere.

After 1941 the smoke and stench of Mauthausen's crematoria working around the clock continually blackened the blue sky and fouled the pure alpine air.

When Père Jacques arrived at this efficiently run self-contained city of death, he was no longer the conspicuous Carmelite in the brown habit, taking charge and engaging in endless forms of spiritual and medical ministrations. With his shaved head and gaunt face, wasted frame and dirty uniform, he was now simply one of thousands of slave laborers whose fates was in the hands of cold-blooded thugs.

Though he now looked like his fellow inmates, somehow even now Père Jacques managed to stand out and radiate a remarkable sense of decency, charity and love. Having survived the initial quarantine, a brutal testing period that determined who was fit for labor and who was doomed to extinction in the gas chambers, Père Jacques was assigned to the satellite camp of Gusen I.

In Gusen, as in Mauthausen and all other Nazi labor and extermination camps, there was a sort of philosophy of survivalism, a creed that unofficially determined who would live and who would

[38] ???

die. While the whim of the SS had a great deal to do with the selection process, the inmates themselves likewise had a great – possibly a greater – part in determining their fate.

In Gusen, as in the other concentration camps, death was a constant competitor that could win in an instant with the help of disease, starvation, a bullet, a noose or the blow of a rubber truncheon. If a prisoner could survive by sheer force of will, so could they succumb to a apathetic disregard for life known throughout the camps as "going under." Once the will to live was surrendered, it was a mathematical certainty that the prisoner would soon die or 'go under.' For Père Jacques, the contemplative who sought solitude with God the better part of his life, the dark night in Gusen, deepening into blackness, was to be alleviated by the love and support and the presence of other people as brutalized and lonely as he was.

Having lived his life giving unconditional love to so many people, Père Jacques was now to receive love in return when it was needed most and in the most un-loving of places on earth.

Secret Ministry in Gusen

Having previously been in camps of predominantly French-speaking inmates, the riot of nationalities in Gusen, ranging from Finnish and Greek to Spanish and Hungarian, made Père Jacques feel for the first time truly isolated, lost and dejected. In his utter and complete loneliness, compounded by the daily horrors and threat of execution, Père Jacques's dark night had become an agony in the garden.

Placing himself under the patronage of fellow Norman Saint Thérèse of Lisieux, Père Jacques asked not only that he be given the strength to persevere in fulfilling whatever God's plan held for him, but also that he receive some sign of her favor. His prayer was almost immediately answered: that night a Frenchman introduced himself and brought Père Jacques into a circle of French speaking prisoners interned in Gusen.[39]

---

[39] Murphy, *Père Jacques*, p. 108.

Through the camp intelligence network word gotten around among the French inmates of the arrival of a kindly, good-hearted and holy friar. Aside from Henri Boussel, the young man who introduced himself to Père Jacques, there were the French poet Jean Cayrol and dozens of others who came to protect and look out for Père Jacques much the same way he had cared for the Jewish children at Avon. Soon the immediate circle around the Carmelite friar grew to a community of sorts encompassing many nationalities, faiths and political affiliations.

Renewed by this life-link with French comrades, Père Jacques soon began a surreptitious ministry among Catholics and non-Catholics in any kind of need. Through the machinations of his comrades the priest soon acquired a breviary, devotional books and, amazingly enough, bread and wine so that he could celebrate secret Masses on major feast days. At first assigned to fourteen-hour days of work on construction of a reservoir, he was later able to secure relatively light work as a weapon's inspector in Gusen's munitions factory. This was a blessing compared to the brutal, deadly work in the quarries three miles away at Mauthausen to which so many wretched souls were still condemned.

Crammed into the three-tiered bunk beds of the Gusen barracks, which reeked of human waste and were crawling with vermin, Père Jacques managed to cling desperately to Saint Thérèse of Lisieux – his 'Little Flower' – even in such madness and filth. Though after a few months Père Jacques's health began to break down – typhus, dysentery and tuberculosis were taking a frightful toll among the inmates – he continued to work tirelessly on behalf of his brothers, who, he said, were suffering more than he.

Aside from his faithful band of French comrades, Père Jacques also became a friend of the Polish prisoners quartered in his barracks. As in many other concentration camps, Poles were the predominant ethnic group at Mauthausen and, by the time the French Carmelite arrived, many had become numbed into a catatonia of lethargy and hopelessness. Père Jacques learned enough Polish to hear confessions and speak basic phrases to them and make himself available to them as a friend as well as a spiritual guide. These poor inmates who, like the Jews, had borne the brunt of Nazi hatred and oppression, responded in kind, and countless Poles came to dearly love and respect the French Carmelite in return.

Even if no one had known he was a priest, Père Jacques would have inspired and endeared himself to his comrades simply by his joyful example. The sick and the dying were, as always, a great concern for him, and he regularly upset some of his fellow prisoners by foregoing his own meals to ensure that the ill received more food than he. Soon, however, some of his French comrades were making the same sacrifices.

It is here that Père Jacques's deep spirituality and continual imitation of Christ became most clearly manifested. Not only was he living a life of heroic sanctity in the hopeless hell of a concentration camp, but was inspiring others by example to do the same. Still, despite the relative improvement in his working conditions, Père Jacques was subjected to eleven-hour workdays that aggravated a pulmonary infection and diminished his physical strength to dangerously low levels of endurance. While the inmates were able to snatch bits and pieces of news concerning the collapsing German war effort, inside Mauthausen and its satellite camps the sadistic SS guards maintained a brutal grip that did not slacken even slightly.

Liberation and Death

The starvation, the diseases, the work, the demoralizing effects of concentration camp brutality all took their toll on Père Jacques, and by early 1945 he was worn out physically and racked by a persistent, hacking cough. As winter gave way to spring, it was apparent that Nazi Germany was in the throes of military death. The Allies, having staged the greatest amphibious invasion in history, were pushing inward from the Normandy beachheads they secured after their June 1944 landings.

The Soviets, having thrown back the cream of Hitler's Luftwaffe and Panzers at Stalingrad, were now on the offensive and driving deep into the heart of the Third Reich from the east. With the victorious Allies closing in on Berlin from all sides, by April of 1945 it was a mathematical certainty that the war would soon be over.

In the concentration camps throughout Germany and its provinces, including Mauthausen and its satellite camp Gusen I, there was little joy but a tremendous amount of anxiety and fear. The rumors abounded that the Americans would soon liberate them, but as of yet the prisoners were still under the iron-fisted control of the *SS*. Adding to the horror was the persistent rumor that under orders from *SS* top command a scorched earth policy was to be enacted at all concentration camps. In other words, the *SS* were to destroy documents, raze the camps and exterminate all inmates so as to leave no proof of Nazi atrocities.

Regardless of the rumors of the collapsing German fronts, the situation in the concentration camps remained grim and gruesome. In Gusen, as in Mauthausen and all the other camps, the constant hunger of the inmates had devolved into an epidemic of starvation that was adding an element of mad desperation to the omnipresent aura of horror. Supplies of all sorts were simply non-existent and the search for food of any sorts was the driving force of the skeletal inmates, still bullied and brutalized in the quarries and munitions factory. In Mauthausen, instances of cannibalism were reported after the war.

For Père Jacques, suffering horribly from the cold, hunger and the effects of his failing lungs, every day and every pain was an invitation to immerse himself more deeply in the mystery of Christ's passion that few could understand. Like St. Thérèse – under whose protection he had placed himself – Père Jacques made daily offerings of his life and his heart to the Sacred Heart of Jesus, asking that his love be purified and made worthy in the immola-tion consuming his body. It was the same prayer offered by Thérèse as she lay dying, gasping for air on her tubercular deathbed some fifty years before in Lisieux. The genuineness and power of this total self-offering made such an impression on his friends that soon others were joining Père Jacques in this daily prayer.

The mystery of Père Jacques's love as his life drew to a close lies in the fact that, while he was prepared to offer his own life in expiatory oblation to God, he fought like a lion to insure that others had what they needed to live and survive. Despite the wrath it incurred in his friends, Père Jacques passed on almost everything he had or acquired to those more in need than he. By this time the resourceful and redoubtable friar had developed something of a scrounger's reputation in the camp, and he mysteriously seemed to acquire food, clothing and cigarettes out of nowhere.

His heart went out especially to the young and the frail, and any warm clothes, sweaters, socks or underwear he could secure would be passed on to some shivering young Pole or dying Russian Jew. The meager starvation rations, hardly able to keep one man alive, were routinely divided up by Père Jacques and given to younger men on the verge of 'going under.' Giving away his food was a dangerous habit that irritated his friend Henri Boussel to no end, but when Boussel reproached Père Jacques for doing it, he received the reply that, being a priest, he was obliged to set a good example.[40]

Anticipating liberation rather than extermination, an international committee was formed in the growing chaos, for the purpose of assuming control of the camp after the inevitable collapse of Nazi military power. Père Jacques was deeply honored to be selected as the representative of all French prisoners in Gusen I and, despite his worsening physical condition, he busied himself with his new duties.

The first signs of hope arrived in late April, when officials of the Red Cross arrived in Gusen and began removing prisoners from France and the Low Countries. The contingent of haggard prisoners, with Pere Jacques at their head, made the terrible trek up the road to Mauthausen with several dying en route. On May 4 with rumors that American tanks were seen in the hills around Mauthausen, an air of anxiety and uncertainty added to the nightmarish pall that already hung over the camp. The next morning at 11:30, as several tanks of the 11th Armored Division of the American Third Army rolled through the main gate of Konzentratrionslager Mauthausen, the SS and SD officers abandoned their posts and surrendered to the Allied soldiers.

[40] Carrouges, *Père Jacques*, p. 241.

Despite the fact that he was emaciated and weakened from tuberculosis, Père Jacques moved into action with the camp committee to assist the small American force in liberating the camp, aiding the desperately ill and the dying, and rounding up their former *SS* and *SD* jailers.

By the second week of May, however, it was apparent that Père Jacques was a dying man. Too weak to stand, let alone carry out his duties as priest or committee member, the Carmelite had shriveled down to a mere seventy-five pounds.

Despite his protests he was airlifted to Linz after the formal liberation of the camp by the main body of the American force. After several weeks' of treatment in the French military hospital, Père Jacques was moved to St. Elizabeth's Hospital, where the doctors could do little but make him comfortable.

Ravaged by the effects of tuberculosis and pneumonia, Père Jacques was reduced to communicating by nods of the head or monosyllabic words. Often he simply said the name "Jesus" over and over again. Visits from friends also liberated from Mauthausen as well as letters from Carmelite brothers in Avon brought grateful smiles to the sunken face of the friar or were rewarded with a whispered "merci."

On June 2 Père Jacques slipped into a coma and, attended to the end by a French priest himself just liberated from a Nazi prison, died shortly before midnight clutching a crucifix and his rosary. Père Jacques de Jésus experienced his final liberation.

Dressed in a Carmelite habit borrowed from the Carmelite friars in Linz, the remains of Père Jacques were interred temporarily in the crypt of the Carmelite church. Several weeks later they were transferred back home to the friary at Avon, where he was buried again in the friar's cemetery behind his beloved school.

It did not take long for the story of Père Jacques to spread beyond the once again peaceful grounds of Avon or the stone walls of Mauthausen. Père Philippe de la Trinité wrote the first biography of his friend and confrere in 1947 and several others appeared over the next few decades. In 1985 Yad Vashem, the international memorial to Holocaust victims in Israel, honored Père Jacques with the title "Righteous Among the Gentiles" for his work in sheltering Jewish children during the Second World War.

In 1987 celebrated French film maker Louis Malle, himself a student of Père Jacques during the war at the School, made an autobiographical account of his friendship with one of the Jewish boys hidden by the priest at the school. The film, entitled *Au Revoir les Enfants* after Père Jacques's final farewell to the students, was an acclaimed triumph that won numerous awards.

In 1997 the United States Holocaust Memorial Museum in Washington honored the memory of Père Jacques with a temporary display, proclaiming his noble work as a Rescuer.

In 1990 the Bishop of Meaux officially opened the cause for the beatification of Père Jacques de Jésus, the first step towards eventual canonization – officially proclaimed sainthood – in the Roman Catholic Church.

Chapter III
"Vinctus Christi"

Karl Leisner

"On Wednesday, March 22, 1933, the first concentration camp will be opened in the vicinity of Dachau. It can accommodate 5,000 people." Heinrich Himmler, Police Commissioner of Munich, signed this news item which appeared in the *Münchner Neuesten Nachrichten* on the day before. With a stroke of his pen, Police Commissioner Himmler had signed into existence the first of the camps in which the Nazis would come to destroy millions of innocent men, women and children, including six million Jews.[1]

The camp was built on the site of a World War I ammunition factory, which itself had been built on a vast, marshy swampland hostile to human habitation since the Middle Ages. Being a mere ten miles north of Munich, Dachau was well in sight of the Alps which provided a splendid if ironically beautiful site for the prisoners trapped in this Bavarian hell.

The first inmates of Dachau were political prisoners; communists, socialists and the ragged remnants of the street fighting parties that opposed the now victorious National Socialist,or Nazi, Party. The suspicious burning of the Reichstag in Berlin the previous month had given the new Chancellor Adolf Hitler the excuse he needed to declare a state of emergency throughout Germany. By suspending the constitution carefully framed by the well meaning but ultimately impotent Weimar Republic, Hitler created a police

---

[1] Doctor Johannes Neusler, *What Was it Like in the Concentration Camp at Dachau?* (München: Trustees for the Monument of Atonement in the Concentration Camp at Dachau, 1965), p. 7.

state in which the basic rights and laws provided for the protection
of German citizens were suddenly and indefinitely revoked.

Commissioner Himmler himself would propel himself in a few
short years to the forefront of Nazi criminality where, as *Reichsfüehrer*
of the dreaded SS and the feared head of all German police forces,
he would help orchestrate the greatest mass-genocide program in
modern history. Hitler's devoted bloodhound, Himmler was given
a long leash indeed and the camp built to house 5,000 would soon
comprise a complex of several satellite camps that together would
eventually house over 200,000 inmates. Out of these, almost
70,000 would perish from the combined effects of torture, disease,
starvation, exhaustion, execution and medical experimentation.[2]

Although Jews were first and foremost on Hitler's list of *untermenschen* – those tagged by the Nazis as sub-human species without
title to basic human rights – they were joined in Dachau and dozens
of similar camps throughout the Reich by Poles, Russians, Gypsies
and people of every nation, religion and political persuasion on
the face of Europe.

There was another population in Dachau, however, that separated it from the other labor camps scattered throughout Germany
and the occupied territories. Dachau was, by the outbreak of the
Second World War, home to no fewer than 2,000 priests – predominantly Polish – representing 144 dioceses from 25 nations.
Called "black vermin" by their SS captors, these priests, monks and
religious brothers were imprisoned along with Jewish, Protestant,
Orthodox and Muslim clergy as well. Arrested for any number of
reasons, these men were in Dachau primarily because by thought,
word or deed they posed a threat to the Führer's tyrannical rule.

Out of these 2,000 priests imprisoned by the Nazis, over half
would die by various means before the war's end.

In Advent of 1944, eleven years after the opening of Dachau and
five years into World War II, another document was written that
was to have a profound effect on hundreds of inmates, but upon

---

[2] Ibid., p. 22.

one in particular. This document was diametrically opposed to the proclamation of hatred and intolerance issued by Himmler in 1933. The name of the inmate concerned was Karl Leisner, and the document would not only change his life but also would mark a first in the whole bloody history of the Nazi concentration camps.

At thirty Karl was still awash in youthful energy and buoyancy, though the ravaging effects of tuberculosis were daily encroaching on his once-robust constitution. With his blonde hair routinely shaved to a stubble by the camp barber and increasingly drawn face, Karl had the gaunt, hollow look that would be forever associated with post-liberation photographs from Nazi concentration camps. Despite his tubercular lungs and consumptive appearance, his blue eyes twinkled from behind steel-rimmed glasses with a placid, joyful expression that conveyed a curious mixture of open warmth and ineffable contentment.

However, on this Third Sunday in Advent known as Gaudete Sunday – words from the Introit of the Mass which tells the faithful to *Gaudete in Domino semper*, Rejoice in the Lord always – a thin veil of anxiety glazed over the sparkle of Karl's youthful joy. The document issued for the young man could have been his death warrant, and, since what was about to take place was strictly against camp regulations, could very well have been paid for with his life.

Secrecy, absolute and total secrecy, was the watchword for the day but, with the document duly approved and signed, the historic event was now set to proceed. It was not easy and it was not safe for any of the parties involved and the preparations that brought Karl to this day involved the secret participation of numerous men and women on both sides of the barbed wire. They included a cardinal, two bishops, a Protestant and Jewish prisoner, and an underground network of civilians, clergy and inmates whose courage, daring and resourcefulness would have made the finest Allied intelligence services proud.

Karl Leisner was a deacon and, having been sent to various prisons and concentration camps since his arrest by the Gestapo in 1939, an inmate of Dachau for four years. Now it was December 17, 1944 and, despite what the inmates were told about having no rights, dignity nor even a human identity, Karl Leisner was about to be ordained a priest at an altar in one of the most horrific places on the face of the earth.

Birth and Childhood

The world into which Karl Friedrich Wilhelm Maria Leisner was born on February 28, 1915 in Rees, Germany was a world that had already chosen a path of devastation and self-destruction on a scale it had previously not known. Karl's native land was engulfed in the second dreadful year of the First World War, named so because almost every nation on the face of the earth was somehow affected by the horrendous conflagration. Despite the early victories of German and Austro-Hungarian forces, by Karl's third birthday the stalemate on the Western Front coupled with the American entrance into the war had shattered the Axis power's dreams of victory.

In 1918, with German troops in retreat or open revolt like their former enemies throughout Russia, Kaiser Wilhelm II fled Berlin into Holland and the nation quickly devolved into violent civil war. Despite the post war upheaval and the crippling inflation that shattered the German economy, Karl's parents managed to maintain a stable and deeply spiritual home environment for their growing family.

Karl's father was a respectable, hard-working paymaster on the civic payroll whose professional duties took him from Rees – where Karl was born – to Immenstadt and in 1921 to the town of Kleve in the Rhineland. It was in this picturesque town on the Rhine, with its quaint streets and medieval spires, that Karl grew to from a bouncing toddler to an energetic adolescent.

Karl had a great devotion towards and affinity for his native Rhineland that was physical, emotional and spiritual in nature. Physically, he took immediately to this splendid land of canals, vineyards and deeply cleft gorges that towered over the most navigated river in the world. Castles nestled high above the river drew out the romantic in young Karl, and his childhood imagination was populated with Crusader knights and evil lords hallooing down toll demands from crenellated keeps.

Emotionally, Karl manifested the tenacious constancy of the Rhenish character that often bordered on obstinacy and defiance. As the buffer between Germany and France, Belgium and the Netherlands, the Rhinelanders have always been fiercely patriotic folk who have clung to their customs and language despite topographic re-shuffling, border tensions and the tumult of war.

Even as a child Karl evidenced a strong independent streak that had to be constantly harnessed and re-channeled by his parents into school and household chores. Though not excessively zealous about school young Karl possessed a keen sense of curiosity about everything and anything, and, from an early age, was constantly asking questions about the workings of the world.

Another particularly Rhenish aspect that Karl exhibited at a tender age was his deep and exuberant sense of God's omnipresence in the world. Though not a precociously pious child, Karl displayed a natural inclination towards things spiritual that was rooted not only in his family life but also in the rich black soil of the Rhineland itself.

The lush, fertile land through which the Rhine snakes not only has Christian roots stretching back into the second century after Christ, but was also home to some of the greatest mystics in the Western Church. From the same soil, the same towns, fields and valleys through which the young Karl romped had come men and women of God whose lives and literary works greatly enriched the Medieval Church.

Following in the wake of Saint Bernard of Clairvaux, the Cistercian writer, crusader and reformer who represented one of the great lights of Medieval spirituality, the Rhineland Mystics endeavored to move the Faith from Neo-Platonic philosophical systems to a simple love of and search for the God-Man Jesus Christ in the ordinary flow of daily life.

Influenced by the life and message of saints like Bernard and Francis of Assisi, authors such as Hildegard of Bingen, St. Gertrude the Great, Mechtild of Magdeburg and, of course, Meister Eckhart, placed less emphasis on scholastic speculation and looked more towards the inward, often ineffable, journey of the soul towards God.

Basing most of their work on actual mystical revelations, many of the Rhineland Mystics were nevertheless pragmatic visionaries who promulgated the lay vocation to sanctity and contemplation. Writing and preaching during a day and age when the spiritual life, let alone mystical prayer and contemplation, was relegated to vowed religious, the Rhineland Mystics championed the active/contemplative apostolate for men and women in the midst of everyday life.

Although the Rhineland Mystics flourished in the 13th Century their rich spiritual legacy was felt throughout the Rhine River Valley, which was considered one of the most staunchly Catholic regions in northern Europe.

The overarching devotion of Karl's life was a tender devotion to the Mother of God that not only reflected another Rhineland tradition, but also expressed a key element of the very fiber of Karl's being. From his childhood through his adult years, up to his arrest and, ultimately his death, Karl nurtured a genuine love of the Blessed Mother that carried him through dark times of illness and persecution.

He began making yearly pilgrimages to the Marian shrine at Kevelaer, near Kleve, which remained a tradition he continued as long as he was able. He had a strong devotion to the medal of the Thrice-Miraculous Madonna and even on his deathbed, in great pain and unable to speak, he struggled to look towards an image of Mary on his night stand.

Had Karl's life unfolded differently, and had he been spared the horrors and tribulations that finally consumed him, he probably would have maintained a pleasant, cheerfully pious reverence for the Blessed Mother typical of Rhineland Catholics. However, the fires through which he passed, tempered and strengthened this boyhood devotion into so tender a filial love that his gratitude was manifested by a total offering of his whole being. "The Mother of God needs but to move her little finger," Karl once wrote during a particularly dark time, "and everything will be set right again."[3]

---

[3] Otto Pies, S.J., *The Victory of Father Karl* (New York: Farrar, Straus & Cudahy, 1957), p. 8.

Growing Spirituality

Karl's deep spiritual center did not turn him into a miniature monk, a recluse contemplating the divine from behind the mullioned windows of Medieval Kleve. On the contrary, any attempt to understand Karl Leisner must be made through an appreciation of his vigorous and robust love of laughter, friendship and the awesome splendor of nature.

Hiking, camping and mountaineering are as endemic to the character of German youth as baseball, pizza and dances are to American youth. Beginning in his boyhood and steadily increasing in his teens and young adult years, Karl became a passionate outdoorsman, and, along with his friends, was almost constantly on a bike, a forest trail or an Alpine mountain slope.

Karl was blessed with excellent health from childhood, and by the time he was a teenager he was planning extended outings with his friends throughout the beautiful Rhineland countryside. As he and his friends grew older, they received permission to push further into Germany and then across the border by foot or on bike into Switzerland, France and the Netherlands.

While Karl began each trip with a prayer to the Blessed Mother and the group never missed Sunday Mass regardless of their distance from a church, this was simply a time of carefree fun and exciting adventure for the boy and his friends. Often joined now by Karl's younger brother Willi,, the group of friends became a tight-knit band of merry men who seemed to sense the fleeting nature of youth and wanted to drain every ounce of life from it before the time passed.

They hiked across the verdant countryside or trudged up Alpine trails, they swam and whooped like Indians in the forest and told ghost stories around crackling campfires. While this energetic bond with the outdoors is common to almost all German youth, it was for Karl a time of profound growth and maturity on many different interior and exterior levels.

Emotionally, these lively forays into the woods and mountains nurtured a growing dimension of leadership and responsibility. It is one thing, however, to say that Karl was a natural born leader, a completely different thing to add that he seemed to know where he was leading.

It was Karl, barely into his teens, who organized the first boy's club in Kleve, which was to be so instrumental in shaping the character of the man. No ordinary club with secret codes and hidden headquarters, Karl's boys club was professionally organized along the lines of established Boy Scout troops and church youth groups.

Aside from planning excursions and camping tours during school vacations, Karl's club had officers, kept minutes of all meetings and put on plays and Christmas pageants during the holidays. Any money raised was inevitably given to charity or put back into the club coffers. On occasion punishment – usually in the form of a river dunking or whack with a canoe paddle – would be meted out to unruly or mischievous members of the organization.

More than just a testimonial to Karl's keen Germanic sense of order and discipline, his organization of the Kleve group shows a striving for purpose and a commitment to an ideal greater than the natural world he continually set off to explore.

On a spiritual level – hidden and therefore deeper than even Karl knew – this time represented a fallow period of waiting and listening during which the Lord was planting the first seeds of vocation in his questing and energetic soul. While he was making no obvious movements towards the priesthood, Karl was nevertheless manifesting a profound leaning towards something beyond the normal proscriptions and expectations of adolescents in Kleve.

This growing passion to explore the natural world and his own intensifying search for God led Karl to begin a diary at the age of thirteen in 1928. It was a remarkable commitment from which he never swerved or wavered, and the resulting sixteen volumes written in his neat script bespeak an insight and depth of feeling that truly manifest a gifted and perspicacious young man.

While they recorded forever the pranks, pitfalls and wonders encountered during his travels throughout central Europe, Karl's diaries also began recording his growing and often tumultuous aspirations and passions. More than a keepsake, the diaries became for Karl a friend, a parent and a confessor rolled into one and he opened himself – often with startling frankness – across the pages of the swelling volumes.

The subjects broached in the diaries were limited only by the range of his thought and, aside from emotions, confusions and secret longings, Karl expressed his feelings about his spirituality, his family and the increasingly ugly face of German politics. His adolescent honesty and youthful vigor would serve him well in his spiritual growth but would eventually come to do him great political damage in years to come. After Karl's arrest the sixteen volumes of his diary were seized by the Gestapo and used as evidence of his clandestine work with the Catholic Youth Movement and his opposition to Nazism. The diaries were miraculously found after the war, waterlogged but intact, in the ruins of the bombed-out Gestapo headquarters in Münster.[4]

Karl fearlessly dealt with any subject, and he frankly discussed the frustrations and passions typical of a healthy adolescent. First and foremost at this time was girls; not only their charms and attractions but how difficult it was to remain mentally and physically chaste until it pleased God to call him to marriage and fatherhood. The personable young man was becoming more attracted to girls and they to him, and, far from being prudish and icy, his philosophy shows a healthy psychology towards women and a genuine respect for them as equal partners in the call to reflect God in the sacrament of marriage.

Out of this commitment, this open and hearty interaction with girls, there evolved an ethos in Karl's life that allowed him to freely mingle with young ladies and enjoy their company and friendship, yet maintain a code of gentlemanly and decent behavior.

As his diaries evidence at this time, Karl was beginning an intense, introspective search into not only the workings of nature and the observations of his faith, but the meaning of his existence. Karl knew he was young, and that youth would soon pass and be replaced with the responsibilities and choices of adulthood. While

---

[4] Ibid., p. 10.

fully capable of whiling away the days of youth in the mountains and forests of the Rhineland, Karl was also intent on being prepared for the day when the Lord would call him to the next plateau.

The mortar of this foundation upon which he hoped to build was a deepening interior life centered on basic liturgical devotions. He simply did not go to Mass as a passive participant, but placed himself in the presence of a great mystery of suffering, love and redemption. He began seriously reading scripture in his early teen years, and he committed himself to a daily reading of several Gospel verses. Ruminating, pondering and digesting the words of Christ and the key events of His life and death, Karl discovered almost by accident the ancient art of *lectio divina*, or sacred reading, in which the Gospels are not so much read as slowly ingested and savored like nutritional and life-giving food.

He began filling his diaries with thoughts and reflections on his scripture reading, which he began more and more to see through the lens of his own life experience. The words of scripture began to crackle and sparkle with an increasing fire, mainly because he constantly re-directed them back to himself. He must, he said, make the choice to be "...either a saint or a scoundrel..."[5]

Approaching young adulthood and bursting with idealistic energy he hoped to direct towards the Church and Catholic youth, Karl chose a path along which he hoped to find the purpose and meaning he sought.

Catholic Youth Movement

In 1930 Karl decided to join the *Deutsche Jugend Katolische*, German Catholic Youth Movement, with the desire of widening his work with youth on a broader Archdiocesan level. In joining the DJK, Karl found a new and limitless world in which he could be a leader with an influential voice, as well as stay firmly connected with

---

[5] Bishop Heinrich Tenhumberg, "The Catholic World: A Prisoner for Christ – The Witness of Deacon Karl Leisner", Address on Radio Station Bavaria, Sunday, March 19, 1978. Translation by Reverend Marion Balsavich, O.S.B., p. 2.

Catholic clergy and laity who were struggling to defend the Church in an increasingly hostile and pagan environment. It was a cause that fired his blood and inflamed his passionate sense of history and romance.

Karl was consumed with the idea of the Christian Knight; the pure and fearless soldier of the Lord who, having vowed before the Altar to defend the Church who is Christ's Bride, placed himself under the protecting mantle of the Blessed Mother.

Were these the passing fancies of a German youth who was overindulging in the lives of the saints and heroic medieval literature? Perhaps, if they were merely dreams he grew out of as he passed from adolescence to young adulthood. As it was, Karl did, however, continue to build on his spiritual foundation to make his dreams a real and tangible dimension of his life.

Also remarkable was that while Karl arrived at this philosophy, this plan of life through an energetic encounter with nature and God indwelling in his soul, the same vision of Teutonic knighthood was being co-opted and paganized by the new Chancellor Hitler. The Führer's own version of a new youth bred of steel and flame to serve a new Reich would put his agents and Karl Leisner on paths that were soon to cross.

While time has a tendency to drag a lead foot when one is young, for Karl the days flew by too fast for him to accomplish everything he still wanted to achieve. Aside from the Kleve club activities, which were regularly taking the group throughout most of Northern Europe, other serious questions, decisions and responsibilities began presenting themselves to Karl with increasing regularity. In 1933, at the age of eighteen, two forces were to have a profound effect on him and the roads down which he chose to travel, namely the Nazi Party and the German Catholic Youth movement.

In that year of 1933, Adolf Hitler's National Socialist Party came to power in the Reichstag – the German national assembly – by bluffing, cajoling and bullying a weary and disillusioned populace still reeling from the humiliating Treaty of Versailles. Having already mastered the art of propaganda on a massive scale, the Nazis immediately set about politicizing all facets of life in the

Third Reich. From industry, agriculture and the military to the arts, religion and even motherhood, every element of human existence in Germany was re-oriented to serve and glorify the Reich and the Reich alone.

Certain elements, like Jews and communists, were by their nature incompatible and irreconcilable with the Aryan-centered doctrines of National Socialism, and therefore had to be isolated and ultimately eradicated from German culture. The first solutions were political and economic, 'final' solutions would be implemented in just a few years.

Recognizing the formidable voice of thirty million voting German Catholics under his authority, Hitler opted at first to corrupt the Church's power by stealth rather than destroy through a frontal assault. Though he was born and raised a Catholic in Austria, Hitler had abandoned all belief in the Church as a spiritual power, simply seeing German Catholics and a German Catholic Church that needed to be brought under the absolute control of the state. Hitler, however, did not want to repeat the mistake of Bismarck, Germany's "Iron Chancellor" who actively waged war against the Pope and Roman Catholicism during his *Kulturkampf*, or 'struggle for culture' in late 19th century Germany.

Inflamed by the fires of anti-clerical liberalism that swept through 19th century Europe, as well as by a genuine desire to finally unify the German empire, Bismarck declared war on the power of Church in Germany as well as what he perceived as the antiquated despotism of Rome. Following the example of Liberal statesmen in Italy following the *Risorgimento*, or unification of the multiplicity of Italian states and kingdoms, Bismarck enacted a series of laws in 1875 that he hoped would forever break the power of the Church over the lives and education of millions of Germans.

Named the Falk Laws, after Bismarck's Minister of Cults who helped formulate them, the laws mandated everything from compulsory civil marriage to the education of seminarians. These two examples were particularly oppressive for the Church for not only did the laws have a devastating effect on the Catholic concept of Sacramental marriage but placed the education of future priests for several years in the hands of 'enlightened' anti-Papal professors. Men and women religious were forcibly exiled from Germany by the thousands, and hundreds of priests and bishops were forced from their dioceses in poverty and homelessness with many ending up in jail for their beliefs.[6]

Far from having the effect Bismarck desired – namely of bullying Catholics out of their allegiance to Rome and into national or "Old Catholic" churches – adherents to the Faith stiffened their resolve to remain loyal to Pope and Church. Invigorated with the passion that can only come to those persecuted for their beliefs, German Catholics formed a unified front of faith that called upon the blood of the country's martyrs dating back to Saint Boniface, and within a few years the Iron Chancellor meekly began to sue for peace.[7]

Realizing that his greatest enemy was actually the Socialist party gaining seats in the Reichstag and not German Roman Catholics and their *Zentrum* (Centrist) Party, Bismarck negotiated with the nuncio of Pope Leo XIII and by 1888 the Falk Laws and Bismarck's *Kulturkampf* had all but evaporated into thin air.

The Growing Nazi Threat

A diabolical megalomaniac rather than a visionary statesman or deep thinker, Hitler nevertheless agreed with genuinely great minds like Socrates and Saint Thomas Aquinas, who knew the possibilities of changing the world by shaping a youth's mind.

One of the top priorities, therefore, of the new Chancellor and his henchmen, was winning the youth away from the Catholic Church and drawing them, singing and marching, into the dark ranks of the new German order.

While a great number of devout young Catholics were torn between their ancient, innate Christianity and the exhilirating,

[6] Anthony Rhodes, *The Power of Rome in the Twentieth Century: The Vatican in the Age of Liber*
[7] *al Democracies, 1870-1922* (London: Sidgwick & Jackson, 1983) p. 83-85.

patriotic call of their emerging national identity, Karl knew who he was and the gravity of the choices he was forced to make.

Karl was not a fence-sitter by any means, and his diary was filled with a growing distrust of the Nazi party as well as a fear for honorable Christian statesmen like Heinrich Brüning, the *Zentrum* chancellor who fell from power in his desperate but futile attempt to stem the nation's escalating economic and political woes in the early 1930's.

After Hitler's takeover in the elections of 1933, one of the Chancellor's first orders of business was to affect a *rapprochement* with the Catholic Church and the guise of legality under which the negotiations were conducted was the same which he employed a mere five years later at Munich.

Signing a Concordat with Rome in 1933 which supposedly guaranteed, among other things, freedom of worship, education and youth movements, the promised era of good relations with the Vatican actually resulted in an upsurge of anti-Catholic oppression, intolerance and even violence before the ink dried. Threats, intimidation and ultimately legal prohibitions were used by the Nazis to force Catholic parents and their children away from Catholic schools, and those parents who repeatedly ignored 'suggestions' to remove children from convent and parochial institutions came under the scrutiny of local party officials.[8]

On the pretext that they were politically inflammatory, Catholic youth groups in particular were forbidden to sing publicly, participate in sporting events or wave organizational banners; all sacred traditions of German Catholic youths. Catholic Youth groups, who like Karl thrilled to the excitement of marching and the comradeship of jamborees, were beginning to be harassed regularly by the brown-shirted S.A. (Stormtroopers), the *Hitler-Jugend* (Hitler Youth) as well as by police and private citizens. Groups of Catholic youths returning from pilgrimages abroad were routinely harassed by border guards, and gangs of *Hitler-Jugend* toughs began roaming the street looking for DJK members to rough up and bully.

---

[8] Ibid., p. 89-90.

The Führer wanted not only the minds and bodies of German youth, he wanted their souls too, and he demonstrated quite plainly that if they would not be surrendered he would come and take them.

At eighteen, Karl had no shortage of choices to make: the first being his plans for the rest of his life that would be in complete accord with the will of Almighty God. While approaching the crossroads that would decide the next plateau in his education, Karl committed himself even more to the Catholic Youth Movement. It was a decision that grew not so much out of a natural progression from local youth leader to diocesan youth leader as from well-pondered moral convictions.

Karl's diaries are filled at this time with not only references to his deepening love of the Eucharist and his increasing thirst for spiritual wisdom, but an admirable political savvy as well in regards to the sociopolitical climate of the time. With the noose tightening around the Catholic Youth Movement on a daily basis, Karl saw that a conscious commitment – fully cognizant of the inherent dangers – needed to be made either for God's Church or for pagan Führer Hitler.

A patriot who deeply loved his homeland, Karl nevertheless displayed a political perspicacity to be soon found lacking in professional statesmen of Europe, especially when he predicted "dark days" on Germany's horizon.

The dynamic young man rose quickly in the DJK, and his reputation increased, first on the parochial, and ultimately on a diocesan level. His primary function was to act as a sort of scoutmaster, catechist and big brother to the boys under his charge. As he had with his own friends in Kleve, Karl saw to it that the youngsters enjoyed the endless joys of the outdoors and the fellowship of faith as much as he did.

On an organizational level, Karl worked closely with pastors, diocesan officials and other youth leaders in coordinating programs and strengthening resistance to the threat of violence and oppression by the Nazis. His bicycle became his second home, and he was constantly shuttling back and forth between Kleve and the diocesan youth offices in Münster, where he ultimately came under the observation of the Bishop, August von Galen. A pugnacious, fiery champion of the Church and the people, Bishop Von Galen was soon to develop a reputation as one of the most virulently anti-Nazi bishops in the German episcopate. Impressed with the energetic, articulate young youth leader from Kleve, Bishop Von Galen kept his eye on Karl for greater service in the future.

As the DJK had been forbidden by the Party to camp on German soil after 1934, Karl would march the boys across the border into Holland. There, with the cross of Christ emblazoned on their banners and with spiritual hymns resounding through the fields, the young renegades would joyfully celebrate their faith and their homeland.

Aside from the energetic and raucous bonhomie of the jamborees, there was a catechetical dimension to the outings in which Karl delighted and excelled. Sharing with the youngsters his own deep love of prayer and scripture, of the Eucharist, the Pope, the Church and her richly textured history, Karl also explored relevant themes like chastity, integrity, honoring one's parents and devotion to one's country. As he did in his own diaries, Karl approached the subjects head-on with unvarnished frankness, and the honesty he brought to the discussions endeared him all the more to the boys.

Mostly, however, Karl talked about the supremacy of Christ in the life of a Christian. In a day and age where quiet, unswerving faith in God and the Church was replaced with a frenzied adulation of the Führer, Karl strove to keep the boys on the path of belief far from the diabolical allurements of the *Hitler-Jugend*. Threats, peer pressure or simply the swaggering glister of brown shirts, armbands and daggers proved too great an attraction for many of the Catholic boys, and by 1934 the ranks of the DJK began to thin and those of the *Hitler-Jugend* began to swell.

In Germany during the first heady years of Nazi power, vacuums of all sorts ceased to exist. As Hitler declared that all facets of life, culture, science and industry had to be directed to the glory of the Reich and the good of the German *Volk*, or people, one was either for the Nazis or against them. As a popular song went during the pre-Nazi political chaos, "Are you for or are you against?"

Loyalty, complete and total loyalty to the Führer and the Party was absolute, and if it were not present in the individual or the group, they were earmarked for what would soon come to be known as 'special treatment.'

Karl Leisner was, quite simply, *for* Christ, or as he would eloquently state as a leitmotif in his diaries and speeches, "Christ is my passion!" That simple choice, that eloquent summation of his beliefs, immediately put him at variance with the agents of the Third Reich. Herr Leisner, Karl's father, had already come under the suspicions of local Party officials for his anti-Nazi stance, which led the family also to be labeled as suspect.

As a high-profile district leader in the DJK, in military terms a regional commander for all youth leaders in the Münster diocese, Karl was now himself coming under the suspicions of the Hitler-Jugend as well as the local Party officials. By the very fact that Karl was a member of the renegade DJK, his every activity was considered a possible threat to the Nazification process of the area youth.

Along with several friends, likewise ardent young Catholics in the DJK, Karl was called in by officials of the local gymnasium, or high school, and forced to sign a document that pledged their abstention from any anti-Nazi activities in thought, word or deed. To drive home the point, several attempts were made to prevent Karl from graduating but, through a combination of wit and prayer, they all eventually failed.[9]

Freshly graduated and with his circle of experience and contacts constantly widening, Karl saw 1934 loom before him like a vast and infinite sea of possibilities. Socially, he continued to mingle freely with the young ladies of Kleve, and a few of the friendships blossomed into youthful romances. Yet, his internal struggles continued to revolve around the question of expectations, of his future and the true depths of his spiritual life. Having decided that he was either to be "a saint or a scoundrel," Karl now worked on which of those roads he was going to travel. If he was critical of the

[9] Anthony Rhodes, *The Vatican in the Age of the Dictators: 1922-1945* (New York: Holt, Rinehart Winston, 1973), p. 185-187.

German political system, of the Nazis, of Hitler and the weak statesmen allowing him to rule Germany, Karl was first and foremost critical of himself.

Along with his tender devotions and rich interior life, Karl also began at this time to confront the depths of his own brokenness and his capacity for sin. Neither a starry-eyed idealist nor a stern and dour Jansenist, Karl was, on the contrary, a realist whose crystalline understanding of original sin made him grasp even more the salvific mysteries of the Incarnation, the Passion and the Resurrection. In his torturous navigation of his seemingly endless capacity for sin and sanctification, however, Karl did stumble a bit into the same brambles of scrupulosity that have trapped many a saintly person in the early stages of their struggles.

What kept his interior balanced and his eye keen, however, was a constant turning and re-turning to the Cross, an almost overflowing sense of gratitude for Christ's sacrifice on Calvary, and the redemptive force it could have on an individual or an entire nation. It was this return to Christ, this passion for Christ, that he hoped by example he could help effect in his beloved country that was turning more and more to a diabolical, pagan tyrant. It was a cause for which, he said in his diaries, he was prepared to give his life.

Inflamed with this zeal both in the tumultuous, outward energy of his words and his deeds as well as in the quiet serenity of his soul, Karl decided to take the greatest step imaginable to make this sacrifice a reality. Though he had his doubts, confusions and faults, Karl placed himself squarely under the mantle of the Blessed Mother and asked Bishop von Galen for permission to enter the Theological Seminary in Münster.

Seminary

In April of 1934, Karl filed into the Collegium Borromaeum in Münster with ninety other young men intent on beginning their pre-theology studies for the priesthood. Attempts by the Party authorities in Kleve had been made to prevent Karl's admission into the seminary, but his diligence and cool tenacity, coupled with

Bishop von Galen' promise to become personally involved if the Nazi's persisted, triumphed in the end and he eagerly prepared for his first seminary year.

Even though he had agonized long and hard over the course his future would take, which was especially difficult as he truly thought he would have made a good husband and loving father, Karl's whole life had been lived in a preparation for spiritual fulfillment as either a spouse or a priest.

Besides his boundless energy, deep spirituality and winning ways with all people – especially the young – Karl possessed an unquenchable thirst for commitment, wholehearted commitment to an ideal and a vocation. His unshakable belief in what he called the "salvation of the Eucharist", and his filial devotion to the Blessed Mother were not segregated elements of piety, disconnected from the sum total of his being.

Karl's faith was linked like a series of arteries to every corner of his person. To integrate his spiritual life into every other facet of his life, to let his "passion for Christ" spread like ink in water through his every action, he sought visible guideposts by which he might find his way.

Through his friend Jupp Vermegen, Karl had been introduced to the Schönstatt Movement that had a deep and lasting influence on the direction of his spirituality and indeed all elements of his life. Centered on a shrine in the town of Schönstatt dedicated to the Blessed Mother, the Movement was geared towards the laity for the purpose of fostering an active contemplative life rooted in mortification and constant prayer.

The discipline, the sense of unity and spiritual comradeship while engaging the modern world in the home and workplace appealed to every instinct in Karl, and the Schönstatt Movement became a clarifying lens through which the young man saw his way in the world opening up before him. While he arrived at the Borromaeum needing shaping and guidance for the demands and the depths required of the priestly life, Karl also brought with him a wealth of maturity and experience which his superiors not only noted, but allowed to expand and flower.

Karl's room at the Borromaeum was like that of any overextended collegiate away from home for the first time. A seminary rather than a college, the room nevertheless reflected the multi-directional life of Karl Leisner in its fullest sense. Scattered about next to the requisite sports equipment were flyers, hymnals, booklets and of course his beloved guitar. A focused and hard-working student who took his studies seriously, Karl was given extraordinary privileges that allowed him to continue his work as a youth leader while pursuing his studies for the priesthood. Partly because of his excellent reputation and expanding leadership duties, partly because his superiors, like Bishop von Galen, realized the dire need for keeping as many youngsters as possible away from the evil allurements of the *Hitler-Jugend*.

Tearing from one town to the other on his bicycle, attending meetings and giving morale-boosting lectures, proved to be an exhausting endeavor and he began using a motorcycle provided by some priests in Münster. Aside from his break-neck pace on motorcycles and bicycles, roaring as he said, "like a raving maniac", other very real dangers constantly loomed over Karl in his DJK work.

The anti-Catholic violence that erupted through Germany following the Vatican Concordat with Berlin was steadily increasing, and the *Hitler-Jugend* was redoubling its war for the youth of the Fatherland. Groups of *Hitler-Jugend* would congregate outside DJK meetings, shouting raucous obscenities and intimidating those entering or leaving.

On one occasion, however, things were different when the speaker was Karl Leisner. Following one speech Karl made on the love of Christ, the Church and the true Germany, the DJK youngsters were so inflamed with zeal that they carried the speaker triumphantly on their shoulders to the grumbling chagrin of the *Hitler-Jugend* waiting outside the hall.[10]

---

[10] Pies, *The Victory of Father Karl*, p. 31.

Personal and Political Crises

The road down which Karl traveled to the priesthood was filled with the joys of growth, of revelation and deepening commitment to Christ and His Church. There were also numerous bumps and hidden snags, real and potential pitfalls that stretched his endurance to the limit and tested the strength of his already proven convictions.

During the winter semester of 1936/37, Karl went to Freiburg to take over the tutorial duties of a friend who fell ill. The family Karl tutored were good and devout Catholics who seemed to have a limitless supply of children running up and down the length of the house. The children took immediately to their new tutor and soon Karl was like a member of the family.

One of the daughters was close to Karl not only in age but in interests and temperament as well. An immediate friendship was formed, which led to a deeper friendship and soon, much to Karl's great joy and great agony, he was hopelessly in love with the young lady. Karl was, by this time, twenty-one years old, and years past the age of boyish infatuations. Outgoing, energetic and extremely insightful as to the depths of his own passions and often tempestuous nature, Karl sensed a deeper reality and bond in his relationship with the young lady that posed an immediate and serious threat to his priestly vocation.

By Karl's own account the young lady was not only charming and attractive but possessed an extremely kind and deeply spiritual center. It was more than merely a physical attraction that began throwing Karl into a state of profound and utter turmoil, it was a questioning of his very vocation to the celibate priesthood. His desire for a wife and children of his own suddenly electrified his whole being, but instead of simply walking away from the seminary and taking the girl for his wife, Karl tried to confront his vocational crisis in the same manner he confronted Nazi Party officials and Hitler-Jugend toughs; with courage, with honesty and with prayerful fortitude.

The agony, nevertheless, was atrocious, and each day seemed to plunge Karl deeper and deeper into confusion and darkness. Every fiber of his being seemed to cry out for the joys of marriage, children and home, yet the depths of his soul still resounded with the silent call of the Lord to follow him as a priestly shepherd of his people. If he could somehow have gone down both paths, he said, he would have found the means to do so. As that was impossible, he began to look for older and wiser hands to lift him out of his black pit of anxiety and confusion.

Karl went home to Kleve and opened his heart to his father, asking his advice on what to do to resolve this crippling conundrum. He also went to his spiritual father, Father Noppel, and likewise opened up the deepest recesses of his heart and soul.

Both his natural father and his spiritual father were sympathetic, gentle and understanding, and Herr Leisner stressed that whatever decision Karl made would have the wholehearted support of the family. Both men, however, agreed that the choice between marriage or the priesthood was ultimately a decision Karl himself would have to make and, once made, must remain permanent.

As he had in so many good and bad times, Karl went to the Blessed Mother and begged her guidance and protection. This was not the maudlin, sentimental affectation of a love-struck youth. Karl was literally being ripped apart by the emotional tangle in which he found himself, and in desperation he turned once again to his Thrice-Miraculous Mother.

"If I am to become a priest," Karl declared in his diary near the end of the crisis, "then let me know and obtain for me the strength to overcome myself. If I were to become a bad priest, then see to it that I die first."[11]

Having weathered the worst storm of his life so far, a peaceful calm that washed over him led Karl to believe he had an answer to his anguished dilemma. Quietly, he returned to the seminary and his studies. His head-on engagement of this question of vocation and marriage did, however, give him a new sense of himself as a man in every sense of the word. Like an athlete bursting through

---

[11] Tenhumberg, "The Witness of Deacon Karl Leisner", p. 2.

to new limits of endurance or a mountain climber achieving the next plateau, the pain of Karl's struggle gave him a deeper understanding of key truths hidden in life's obstacles. In Karl's particular case, it was a deeper understanding of love, sacrifice and the true essence of women whom he now respected in a more honest, holy and holistic way.

Despite Karl's renewed commitment to the priesthood and his studies, he had to interrupt his studies at the seminary to fulfill civic obligations demanded of every male over eighteen. A year in the Youth Labor Service, made compulsory by the Nazis, was something that Karl wanted to get out of the way before beginning his theological studies in Münster but the call from the seminary came first. In the spring of 1937, Karl arrived by train in the woods of Saxony, where he formally commenced his service to the Fatherland.

To Karl's surprise, the pre-war Nazi Youth Labor Service (RAD) was more like a work-oriented summer camp rather than a repressive military boot camp, and he quickly found his niche and settled in. While the camp was firmly under the political control of the *Hitler-Jugend* – themselves under the watchful eye of the Gestapo – the young men enlisted in the ranks there proved to be more raucous than idealistic. With his buoyant personality and magnetic leadership skills, Karl soon earned the respect and friendship of many of his camp comrades. His love of singing and his guitar playing skills served him well, and soon the barracks became a gathering place for the laborers following a day's work in the forest.

Despite the heavy handed doctrine foisted on the young men by the resident *Hitler-Jugend* functionaries, Karl deeply enjoyed the patriotic comradeship of the labor service. Seeing the time more as service to Germany rather than the Führer, Karl's time in the RAD also gave him an opportunity to engage in healthy, rugged work in the outdoors he loved so much. Clearing forests, draining marshes and paving roads from sunup to sundown, Karl was left exhausted but content in that he shared the lot of the common laborer. In his sweat, blisters and backbreaking toil he came to truly feel that he emulated Christ the carpenter and his fishermen friends from Galilee.

There was, however, a flip side to the warm comradeship and the boisterous *bonhomie* in the camp, which allowed Karl to experience firsthand the harsher side of human nature uncolored by the soft glow of seminary windows and sparkling alpine air. The young laborers – being just that – pursued more adolescent interests that had nothing to do with guitars or folk songs.

Saturday nights in the camp were specially reserved for drinking and carousing in the nearby town with the young female residents. Due to his status as a seminarian as well as his own deep moral convictions, Karl habitually stayed behind in the camp, playing his guitar, reading or enjoying the company of a few close friends. As the events of the past year proved, Karl's attitude was devoid of prudery or unhealthy ambivalence. On the contrary, his friendly and non-judgmental attitude towards those who did engage in behavior contrary to his beliefs was acknowledged and reciprocated by his comrades.

A key factor in Karl's spiritual growth at this time is that while not ostentatious and pietistic, he nevertheless was unashamed to practice his faith and lead an apostolic life of prayer and charity even in the officially pagan atmosphere of a Nazi youth camp.

Having made friends with the pastors of the churches in neighboring villages, Karl went regularly to Mass, often taking one or several friends with him. He prayed before meals, faithfully observed feast days and prayed with the Church in reciting the Liturgy of the Hours from his breviary. Karl was also by this time reading the Gospels and the epistles of Saint Paul quite deeply, seeing in the latter a wealth of spiritual insights on how to "run the race" and "fight the good fight" despite the onslaught of turmoil and temptation from within and without.

While the other young men respected and admired Karl for the depth of his beliefs and the sterling nature of his character, he came under the close scrutiny of the camp Party officials much the same way he had in Kleve. Being such an obvious Christian, as well as a seminarian prepared to push on to theological studies, Karl became a curiosity to the officials who after watching him from afar decided to engage him face to face.

Under the pretext of friendly chats and curious inquiries, the Hitler-Jugend leaders questioned Karl on his thoughts and beliefs on subjects ranging from the Führer and the Party to the Church, the Pope and the 'Jewish Question' that was coming to the fore of Nazi politics. When confronted with these questions, Karl neither equivocated nor provoked, but spoke his mind plainly and with honesty. By telling what he knew, without speculative embellishment or confrontational heroics, Karl was able to keep his heart concealed from those trying to pry it open.[12]

Convinced of his harmlessness, the Party officials at the camp allowed Karl to go his way, with Karl unaware that they were keeping notes on him and the officials unaware that Karl was carrying out a silent but extremely powerful apostolate of prayer and example among his comrades.

Nazi Attacks on the Church

By 1938 Karl was moving closer to his ordination to the sub-diaconate, the first stage of Holy Orders that would seal his bond with Christ forever as a priest. At the same time, the increasing hostility towards the Catholic Church on the part of the Nazi regime made Karl's spiritual commitment a genuinely hazardous undertaking.

While many bishops, priests and religious early on gave tacit support – or at least professed indifference – to Hitler and his programs on the basis that he was preferable to the Bolshevik menace to the east, countless more were bravely denouncing the Nazis in every available forum.

Pope Pius XI, called by the Italian dictator Benito Mussolini "that stubborn old man," had become more and more openly hostile to Nazism in theory and practice, and the pronouncements he made from the Vatican were straining the tenuous relations between Berlin and the Vatican. The pope's 1937 Encyclical *Mit Brenender Sorge* (" a denunciation of Nazi racial, human rights violations and

---

[12] Pies, *The Victory of Father Karl*, p. 67.[13] Ibid., p. 39-40.

blatant violations of the 1933 Concordat, had to be smuggled into Germany and clandestinely printed for publication.

The Nazi's were at first more stunned than infuriated by Pius' broadside – largely the work of Pius' Secretary of State Eugenio Cardinal Pacelli – and responded not so much with violence but with vicious smear campaigns and legal measures intended to break the moral and spiritual back of the Catholic Church in Germany. The Pope, as well as Secretary of State Pacelli – who would succeed him as Pius XII – were attacked in every foul organ of the Nazi propaganda machine with all manner of invective and insinuation.

Seizing every copy of the Encyclical that they could lay their hands on and shutting down all presses on which it was printed, the Gestapo then opened up a second campaign against the clergy that would outdo even old Bismarck and his *Kulturkampf.* "I shall open such a campaign of propaganda against them in the press, radio and cinema," Hitler said in Baden, "that they won't know what's hit them."[13]

True to the Führer's word, the Nazis began hurling slanderous accusations against defiant bishops, priests and religious that called into question everything from financial irregularities to moral improprieties. Having already convicted and imprisoned several nuns for transferring money out of the country, the Nazis then started on the priests whom they considered nothing but parasitic reprobates.

The morality of the priests, especially the religious who ran the primary and secondary schools throughout the Reich, were the objects of foul, obscene abuse in Nazi papers like *Volkischer Beobachter, Das Schwarze Korps* and *Angriff* and in propaganda films for the *Hitler-Jugend.* In 1937 alone, unsubstantiated charges of pedophilia were brought against 200 Franciscan friars.[14]

His heart broken with sorrow and just a few months from death, Pope Pius XI aptly prophesied that the furies of hell would soon be released upon all those who stood in defiance of Hitler and his

[13] Ibid., p. 39-40.
[14] Rhodes, *The Vatican in the Age of Dictators*, p. 207.

pagan Reich. "I tell you," the old Pope said in his 1938 Christmas address to the College of Cardinals, "in Germany today a full religious persecution is in progress."[15]

The priests, prelates and religious, exceptionally brave men and women who spoke out fearlessly against Hitler and the evils of National Socialism, became great influences in Karl's life and their example strengthened his own resolve to stand and fight for Christ.

While much has been said of the attitude of complacency, if not complicity, of many German clergy in the ascendancy years of Nazism – which is undeniable – what is not always acknowledged is the large and vocal majority of religious, priests and prelates who by the waning years of the decade were in open defiance against Hitler. Legions of unsung Christians paid for their defiance with imprisonment, torture and death.

With the mask off the evil visage of Nazis, priests began speaking out from the pulpit, in the classroom and in every available media. For this they paid a high price indeed and in Dachau alone, of the almost 3,000 priests condemned to the concentration camp, 500 were German. The *Domprobst* of Berlin's Saint Hedwig's Cathedral, Msgr. Bernhard Lichtenberg, spoke so vociferously against Nazi persecution of the Jews that the officials decided that he should share their fate. Sent to Dachau, Msgr. Lichtenberg died en route and was hailed as a martyr by Jews and Christians alike.[16]

Among the German episcopacy there was also a slow but nevertheless genuine change of heart as to the true nature of Nazism, and by the outbreak of the World War II many of them were bravely speaking out against Hitler. Cardinals Faulhaber of Munich, von Preysing of Berlin and even Cardinal Innitzer of Vienna – an early supporter of Hitler – began denouncing the evils of Nazism and in 1941 five cardinals and five bishops signed a joint pastoral letter in which they refused to put the German *Volk* before Jesus Christ.[17]

[15] Ibid., p. 208.
[16] Ibid., p. 209.
[17] Ibid., p. 198.

No bishop, however, was more fiery in his anti-Nazi denunciations that Karl's own ordinary, Karl August von Galen of Münster. Like Karl in that he was a patriot who loved the Fatherland, Bishop von Galen saw Hitler and his henchmen as a group of jack-booted gangsters who were perpetrating the greatest evil of modern times under the helpless noses of the world's leaders. A fearless orator and vigilant shepherd of his flock, Bishop von Galen attacked not only Nazi oppression of the Church, but violation of all civil and human rights of the nation's weakest citizens.

Bishop von Galen became a fierce opponent of the Nazi's use of euthanasia to eliminate increasing numbers of the aged, the infirm, the handicapped and the mentally ill. So vociferous and widespread were Bishop von Galen's attacks that Hitler and Reichsmarschal Göring had to deny the atrocities in the press and then began to slowly stand down the operations.[18]

While Hitler said that he wanted no martyrs among the Catholic bishops of Germany, propaganda minister Göbbels said that von Galen would be dealt with after the final German victory. The fact that von Galen was considered such a *bête noire* to the Nazi hierarchy is supported by an entry in the memoirs of Nazi party philosopher Alfred Rosenberg, author of the anti-Semitic, anti-Christian handbook of Nazi hatred, *Myth of the Twentieth Century*. The memoirs, published after Rosenberg's execution for war crimes at Nuremberg in 1946, contained the statement that Hitler's violations of the Vatican Concordat were justified in that the majority of German bishops had been antagonistic to Nazism as early as 1933. And the greatest enemy of Nazi Germany among the hierarchy, Rosenberg said, was von Galen.[19]

The Bishop was a key role model in Karl's life and the effect his considerable courage and faith had on the young seminarian cannot be over emphasized. More than hero-worship or surrogate fatherhood, Karl's admiration for von Galen was grounded in a cement-like bond of bravery and spirituality. Long before the Nazis openly

[18] Ibid., p. 296.
[19] Ibid., p. 295-296.

oppressed the Church in Germany, Bishop von Galen had impressed Karl with other qualities not associated with fiery orations and barricades.

Through the many contacts Karl had with his Bishop, liturgically as well as socially, Karl sensed a combined nobility of spirit and depth of character he rarely found in other individuals. He saw his Bishop's unhesitating stance against the Nazis as flowing from a firm center of faith, knowledge and an unequivocal sense of right and wrong.

Bishop von Galen was, in Karl's eyes, a living link to the Apostolic Fathers – the lone defenders of the true faith against onslaughts of heresy – and he truly came to reverence him with an affection and admiration that was boundless. "What clarity," Karl wrote in his diary about the Bishop, "clarity, peace of mind and saintliness. The philosopher becomes silent before the wisdom of the saint who roots himself firmly in faith."[20]

With such a shining roster of deeply spiritual and deeply courageous men and women before him, Karl moved slowly but joyfully toward his ordination to the sub-diaconate with a renewed desire to emulate them and give everything – even his life – unreservedly to Christ.

"This is the ultimate meaning of my life: to live Christ in these times," Karl wrote again in his diary, but as a private meditation. "Christ, if you do not exist, then let me not exist. You live-accept me, take complete control of me!"[21]

Ordination to the Sub-Diaconate

On the part of Bishop von Galen, the feelings of respect, admiration and affection were mutual, and with great joy he ordained Karl to the sub-diaconate on March 4, 1939. For Karl the day marked a

[20] Alfred Rosenberg, *Memoirs of Alfred Rosenberg*, translated by Eric Posselt (Chicago: Ziff-Davis Publishing Company, 1949), p. 97-98.

[21] Pies, p. 73.

joyful and wondrous watershed, the meaning of which he could
barely express in the pages of his diary. Robed and girded in white,
Karl pressed himself to the floor of the cathedral in prayerful obei-
sance, awed by the sacramental mystery that enveloped him yet still
unsure of his worthiness to be a priest. With his depth of feeling
and keen sense of the natural and the supernatural, Karl grasped
for the deeper meaning of his call in a way that penetrated the surface of his vocation.

Karl saw the ceremony as actually espousing his soul in a sacred
union with Christ's Bride, the Church. Why he had been called still
remained a mystery with which he energetically grappled. Sacred
Orders had not severed him from the passions and emotions that
still ran to the depths of his true self. Even in the weeks preceding
his ordination to the sub-diaconate, Karl openly confessed in his
diary the difficulty celibacy posed to his passionate nature and he
harbored no delusions about the desires ever ceasing with time.

After searching his entire youth for the meaning of his life, and
by that is meant how he was to spend it, Karl rejoiced in the revelation given him during this joy-filled time. Twisting and turning
in the tempestuous winds of youth, he had for years scrambled frantically – much to his father's exasperation and chagrin – to discover
what he was to do with his life. Priest? Husband? Youth Leader?
Something yet to be revealed?

The mystery to be resolved, the knot that needed untangling in
Karl's life was not so much what he ought to do, but what he ought
to *be*. The question that Antoine de Saint Exupery said in his book
Flight to Arras, "is the essential question, the question that concerns
spirit and not intelligence."

As Jesus gives Himself whole and entire in the smallest particle
of the Eucharist, so he had given himself entirely to Karl in the
guise of everything Karl loved so dearly. Everything, from his family, his friends and his youth groups to the mountains, forests and
lakes, and even the pangs of human love he so recently and deeply
felt, Karl came to see as bursting with the presence of Christ.

And now he wanted to give himself in the same fashion entirely
back to Jesus.

While he saw his ordination to the sub-diaconate as an unmerited grace, the greatest means through which Karl could return this gift was love. His diary at this time was becoming more intimate, more conversational and ultimately, more like a series of love letters in which he poured out his heart to God. The Master's call had been answered, and, seeing the profound essence of what it was he was doing in perfect freedom, Karl vowed he would return this love to God by loving all souls and accepting everything as a gift from the divine hands. In the end, it was this love that mattered; everything else was illusion and dust. Karl wrote in his diary as the ordination day approached:

God has given me so many gifts, so much strength and power, so great a richness in maturity and grace that there are no words to express – much less to measure – my gratitude. Now it is up to me to make answer for the great deeds of divine love. And in freedom. For God compels nobody – just as I myself cannot compel a beloved person to do anything. It must be out of love.[22]

Whether Karl sensed it or not, the crucible in which that love would be fired and purified was about to be ignited.

"Live Like a Plant"

The days that followed Karl's sub-diaconate ordination left him in a state of exhilaration that was rapidly followed by a tremendous state of exhaustion. The months leading to his ordination had been a non-stop charge through his studies at a break-neck pace, but the great weariness that settled over him was unlike anything he had ever experienced. Always proud of his excellent health and boundless energy, Karl was now sleeping for hours on end, even during classes, and he could barely find the strength to get out of bed in the morning or climb into it at night.

Karl's fatigue did not alarm anyone at first, least of all himself, until he started with a hacking cough that would not ease up or go

[22] Ibid., p. 64.

away. At the insistence of his family and the school officials, Karl
submitted to a chest x-ray that revealed a serious pulmonary lesion.
Confirming everyone's worst suspicions, the doctors informed Karl
that he had tuberculosis.

Only someone who has enjoyed nothing but robust health their
entire life can understand the shattering blow contained in the doctor's diagnosis. Never having been sick for more than a few days,
Karl suddenly felt very weak, frail and vulnerable, and the news of
his tuberculosis added a thorough depression to his fatigue. Making matters even worse was the potential danger this confinement
posed to his ordination to the Priesthood at the end of the year.
Like a child at Christmas, Karl had eagerly began counting the
days until he would truly be able to offer himself to Christ in the
totality of consecrated priesthood.

So close, and now this needless detour. What was God asking
of him? Having vowed every fiber of his being to God and eager
to join the increasingly heated fight for His Church, Karl was now
faced with the prospect of being quarantined with the sick and the
dying while his classmates proceeded to the Altar. He tried desperately to see God's purpose in the depressing drama unfolding
before him, but it was still with a heavy heart that he boarded the
train for sanitarium in St. Blasien.

Along with the blessings and best wishes of his teachers and
friends, Karl took along the advice of one professor in particular that
stayed with him over the next few months. "Live," the professor
said simply, "like a plant."

The sanitarium at St. Blasien was situated in the mountains,
where the crystal clear air worked as many wonders for the patients
as the doctor's medicine. Once settled into his room, Karl realized
just how exhausted he was and how badly needed was his rest. The
year's labor service in the swampy marshlands and damp forests of
Saxony – not helped by his punishing university studies – had
made Karl a perfect candidate for tuberculosis and the ailment had
simply worn him down to the point of total exhaustion.

At St. Blasien, Karl did indeed exist like a plant, and, like a living organism in the woods, he soaked up every bit of sun, warmth

and nutrition offered by the goodness of nature. Having become a less regular outdoorsman due to the intensity of his studies, Karl used this time to renew his deep friendship with the beauty and majesty of God's world. He slept endlessly, he read and dozed for hours in the sanitarium's solarium. He took long walks through the mountains and forests, prayed silently in the warm, healing sunlight and he dreamed about getting better and returning to Münster for his ordination.

There were some real and dangerous thorns among the roses at St. Blasien, however, and Karl became increasingly aware of the need for discretion among his fellow patients. Even in the sanitarium it still was 1939 Germany, and if one was not an ardent Nazi and fanatical follower of Hitler, one was just assumed to be the enemy. Hitler had, by this time, annexed Austria and the Czech Sudetenland, and the approaching clouds of war were crackling with tension and anxiety.

The young deacon from Münster was already being eyed with frosty suspicion by many of the patients, and several had no reservations in making their antagonisms known. Herr Leisner had warned his son during the Nazi's power ascendancy to beware of loose talk around "beer hall politicos," and Karl tried to remember that more than ever.

Despite this, the months passed by pleasantly enough until November 9, 1939, a day that was to change Karl's life forever. As the patients sat in the solarium, news excitedly began to circulate that a bomb had just exploded in a Münich beer hall that the Führer had just left. The news of the narrow escape of Hitler from the assassination attempt, which left several people dead and many more wounded, both terrified and astounded the sanitarium patients and staff.

Karl, however, was unmoved by the escape of the man he considered an evil tyrant, and hearing that several people died because of his presence said, "Too bad the Führer wasn't there."[23]

---

[23] Ibid., p. 77.

Regardless of what Karl's intention was or what meaning he attached to his comment, the words shot through the sanitarium like a thunderbolt. Like the words of King Henry II to his barons regarding Thomas Becket, "will no one rid me of this meddlesome priest?" Karl's words had an immediate and horrifying effect that were to set off a chain of cataclysmic events.

One patient, who had been continually antagonistic to Karl, went racing off to the party officials in the nearby town to tell what he just heard. The officials then called in the police who returned to the sanitarium and, despite a half-hearted attempt by the doctor's to mediate on Karl's behalf, bundled the young man off into custody.

Shaken and numbed by the horrendous prospects suddenly bearing down on him, Karl was interrogated for several hours on the precise meaning of his treasonous statement. Bullied by the Party official and disoriented by the threat of impending arrest, Karl simply could find no way to defend himself or explain his meaning to the official's satisfaction. Ordered to pack his things at the sanitarium, Karl was taken to the local jail and the next day was transferred to Freiburg Prison.

Arrest and Freiburg Prison

On November 10, 1939, Karl Leisner ceased to be a free man for all but a few months at the end of his life. At Freiburg Prison Karl left the custody of the police and the local Party officials and became the property of the Gestapo.

Aside from a handkerchief and a few tattered wool blankets, Karl was allowed absolutely no possessions in the prison. The cell, roughly nine feet by eight feet, contained a table, a chair, a bed and a corroded, foul-smelling toilet that polluted the already dank air. A guard brought Karl a meal three times a day but, aside from that, he was absolutely, totally cut off from the living world. He was allowed no communication with anyone inside or outside the prison, and he did not even know if his family was aware of his situation.

Slowly it dawned on Karl that he was terribly, utterly alone, sealed alive in a forgotten tomb and casually scratched off from the roster of the living. What had happened to his life? What did he do to deserve the horrible fate that had suddenly come crashing down on him? Most important, where was God in this terrible, unreal nightmare from which he could not wake?

Karl tried to pray, he tried to speak with God as he had his whole life, with a loving heart full of trust and hope and joy. He tried but he simply could not find the words. God had apparently vanished and returned to the mountains of St. Blasien and the churches of Münster, leaving Karl in the cold depths of Freiburg Prison.

In his feeling of total aloneness, Karl soon fell into a kind of existential no-man's land, a horrifying twilight between the worlds of reason and madness, where the temptation to simply scream and scream was barely controlled. The screams, echoing through the empty and silent corridors, would have done nothing but buried Karl deeper in the darkness that was slowly embracing his soul.

After a few days of wondering what had happened to the freedom, the security and the love he had known but a few days before, Karl's endless self-questioning and tangled thoughts began to drive him to the borders of a form of prison psychosis. The Nazi prison philosophy that sought to break the individual by robbing them of identity, dignity and ultimately hope, seemed to be concentrated in force in the dark cell in Freiburg.

This brutal, dehumanizing philosophy, the foundation of the entire concentration camp system, was beginning to affect Karl deeply and soon he was not only in a fight for survival, but a fight for his sanity as well.

To The Edge of the Abyss

In his temptations to despair, it slowly dawned on Karl that he had to either enter a great mystery or be swallowed by the darkness. If he entered the mystery it would require every ounce of the love he recently vowed to God with his whole heart. If he chose the darkness, he knew he would simply spin off into the endless night of hopelessness and madness. Karl chose the mystery.

Even though he had spent a lifetime speaking with God in prayer, Karl suddenly began praying as he never prayed before. His was no longer the prayer of the boy on the mountain, filled with exultation at the sight of nature, or the supplication of the love-sick youth torn between his heart's desire and his soul's longing. Karl's prayer now was reduced to the raw, naked scream of a man on the edge, and he howled it from the depths of his being for the simple reason he had no other choice left to him.

His prayer was followed by torrents of tears the likes of which he never shed in his life. Confused, bitter tears cried in helplessness and fear that seemed to purge him of the blackness that was desperately trying to take hold of his soul. When the tears subsided, Karl seemed to slowly regain his mental and spiritual equilibrium, and he began to assess his situation with a somewhat more level-headed and rational outlook.

The demons of gloom and doubt also began to evaporate, and soon it was evident to Karl that there were indeed people outside who not only knew of his whereabouts, but were trying desperately to secure his release. This was confirmed by the arrival of his mother, who had somehow managed to secure permission from the Gestapo to visit her son in prison.

Despite the overwhelming joy of this brief reunion between mother and son, it became clear that neither his family nor Bishop von Galen nor his professors or friends could do anything to secure his release or change the direction in which his fate seemed to point.

Had Karl's anti-Hitler statement come from a tubercular non-entity tucked away at a mountain sanitarium, it could quite possibly have been written off as a crank comment not worthy of the Gestapo's time and energy. While being interrogated in Freiburg, however, Karl's dossier arrived containing information which, in the eyes of his jailers, seemed to confirm his potential threat to the Reich's security.

Beginning with his work with the Catholic Youth Groups, to his well documented speeches exhorting young Germans to choose Christ over Hitler to his dubious Nazi loyalties evidenced by his pro-papal leanings while in the labor service, Prisoner Leisner's short life seemed to be one long series of anti-Nazi activities. And to dispel any lingering doubts as to his danger he posed to the Reich, it was pointed out that Leisner was currently studying for the priesthood in a diocese run by the fanatically anti-Nazi Bishop von Galen, who himself was high on the Party's 'special treatment' list.

With very little discussion and even less opposition, Karl's fate was irrevocably sealed. The Gestapo headquarters had, with Berlin's approval, labeled Prisoner Leisner a threat to the state and the Führer and ordered that he be held in "protective custody" in the concentration camp of Sachsenhausen outside of Berlin.[24]

In a cold aside, the Gestapo document also stated that the prisoner's mother was to be informed in Kleve that any attempts to secure her son's release would be futile, as his term of incarceration was indefinite.

With the knowledge that he was being sent to a concentration camp, Karl forced himself to accept the reality of his situation like the death of a loved one. The brick wall of darkness that he had hit when first confined in Freiburg had been surmounted by a titanic force of his spiritual and mental energies. Rather than succumb to the dark he instead reached into it and almost immediately began to feel the familiar touch of the Lord hiding within

Fully committed to stepping into the darkest, most uninhabitable regions where no one wanted to go, Karl began to understand that it was there, in total aloneness, that the Christ of Gethsemani and Golgotha was to be found. Having pleaded with God to be allowed to join Christ at the Altar, it slowly began to dawn on him like sunlight in a sleeper's eyes that he was instead being asked to join Him on a solitary climb to Calvary.

Though fearful and unsure of what the next hour would bring let alone the day, Karl set off into the unknown once again feeling the healing calm of God's presence. This presence was clearly manifested by a gift received by Karl during Christmas of 1940. Smuggled into Freiburg Prison, the gift was the only consolation Karl received during that time when he was supposed to have been finally ordained to the priesthood. Inside the package was a cincture; the

---

[24] Tenhumberg, "The Witness of Deacon Karl Leisner", p. 4.

knotted cord symbolizing celibacy with which the priest girds himself for Mass.

What made the gift so precious to Karl was that it was from a particular young lady with whom he had been acquainted in the recent past. In fact it was the same young lady with whom he had fallen so desperately in love with there in the same city several years back. He was, after all, not alone by any means. The young lady, like so many friends, had heard about Karl's arrest and imprisonment and wanted to offer some sign of support and solidarity.

Upon the cincture were words that seemed to not only confirm Karl's destiny as a priest but also began to give some measure of meaning and purpose to his journey of suffering. The words stitched upon the cincture were, quite simply, *Vinctus Christi*: Prisoner of Christ.[25]

Sachsenhausen

Soon after the visit by Karl's mother, the guards informed him that he was being transferred to Sachsenhausen Concentration Camp. Officially now a political prisoner of the Reich, Karl was relegated to the status of a criminal, and was treated as such during the two-week rail journey back towards Berlin. Chained and herded into a police truck and driven to an iron-barred police train, Karl endured two weeks of claustrophobic fear, hunger and cold before being unloaded like cattle at K.Z. Sachsenhausen.

Built by prisoners of other camps in 1936, K.Z. Sachsenhausen was designed by Reichsführer SS Himmler as a model munitions factory to serve the growing Nazi war machine. By this time in full preparation for aggressive war, Germany still needed vast amounts of aircraft, tanks, and ammunition to bring the Wehrmacht to a level of superiority over the other European powers.

---

[25] Copy of the original Gestapo document, dated October 17, 1940, regarding transfer of Karl Leisner to Sachsenhausen Concentration Camp. Given to the author by Blessed Karl's brother Wilhelm and translated by Reverend Marion Balsavich, O.S.B.

To accomplish this massive undertaking, Himmler worked in concert with other Party leaders to marshal great numbers of slave laborers from among the Germans quickly populating the concentration camp network as well as from the millions of Jews, Slavs and refugees being sent from the conquered provinces of the east.

While categorized as a labor camp and not an extermination camp like Auschwitz and Treblinka, Sachsenhausen nevertheless did contain the mechanisms of mass destruction, used primarily to exterminate the Soviet POW's who began to arrive in the thousands after 1940. To this end, the SS installed torture and execution bunkers, a crematoria and a gas chamber disguised as a shower that was fortunately used only once or twice.

Regardless of its status as a labor and not an extermination camp, by the time the Red Army liberated Sachsenhausen in April of 1945, 200,000 human beings had been imprisoned in the camp and ultimately 30,000 of them perished from execution, torture, disease, exhaustion or suicide.[26]

When Karl arrived in the camp, he was forced to endure the dehumanizing rituals of initiation that severed every connection between the prisoner and previously known concepts of legality, decency and morality. Bombarded with kicks, blows and screamed obscenities by truncheon-carrying SS men the moment the train arrived, the prisoners were herded into the reception area. Forced to undress, the men were shaved, deloused and registered with a number that from that day forward would replace their name.

Prisoner Leisner was now Number 22,356, which he had to use when responding to a command or when addressing a guard or officer. The traditional speech of 'welcome' by the Kommandant informed the prisoners that, having no more identity, rights or freedoms, were simply objects to be used for the good of the state and then burned like rubbish when that service was no longer possible.

His body still weak from the tuberculosis and his mind still reeling from the shock of his arrest and imprisonment, Karl

---

[26] Tenhumberg, "The Witness of Deacon Karl Leisner", p. 4.

nevertheless tried to maintain his renewed sense of calm and prayerful optimism in the face of such overwhelming misery and madness.

Like the other camps throughout Germany and the eastern provinces, Sachsenhausen was a Babel of men and languages, and to survive meant seeking out as quickly as possible compatriots, confreres or comrades among the prisoners. Fortunately for Karl, there was a growing number of priests in the camp, primarily Poles sent from the east following the September invasion by Germany. Unfortunately, however, the "black vermin" as the clergy were called by the SS, were singled out for particularly foul abuse, and priests regardless of age or nationality, could expect nothing but blows and assignments to the worst possible work details.

Despite the risks entailed in being associated with the clergy, Karl sought them out not only for spiritual support but to maintain basic links of human survival. Although joined by a common thread of desperation and injustice, the prisoners nevertheless were often reduced after a short time to base, often brutal, instincts to simply survive – a psychological condition no doubt fostered by their SS jailers. The overcrowded, vermin-ridden barracks that the prisoners found themselves in generally seethed with all forms of asocial, criminal and even psychotic elements.

Companionship was never a problem for the dynamic, outgoing Karl, and the prisoner priests gladly took the young deacon under their wing. While they could advise the younger man on how not to stand out, make eye contact or beware of certain guards or *capos*, the most vicious adversary he found impossible to avoid was hunger. While the constant exposure to torture, execution and mass murder as well as the filth and barbarity of camp life either broke a man or filled him with regenerative hate, the interminable, gnawing hunger could quickly destroy even the sturdiest of prisoners.

The diet of a few potatoes, watery soup and a pat of margarine a day could barely keep an animal alive – let alone human beings pressed into slave labor – and the effects were soon manifested in Karl as the tubercular abscesses ravaged his chest.

The fact that he was a deacon, freely associating with hated Polish priests to whom the guards meted out severe punishments and onerous work details, made Karl's predicament even more precarious. The best way he decided he could keep from 'going under' – the term used by inmates for prisoners who gave up and gave in to hunger – was to keep himself physically fit. Karl placed himself on a regimen of exercise, and through this he was able to keep himself reasonably healthy and fit for a longer period than expected for someone in his medical state.

After four months in police jails and almost eight months in Sachsenhausen, Karl had been in prison for nearly a year. He had not broken or gone under, yet he was still uncertain as to what each day would bring and whether he would see the end of it. In December of 1940, an answer in part was received when Karl was informed that he was being transferred to another concentration camp.

When he heard that the camp was K.Z. Dachau – the oldest and one of the most infamous of concentration camps in Germany – he desperately pleaded with God to protect his path and give him the strength to live or die according to His will. When the day arrived for the transport to Dachau, he knew his prayer had been heard. The day was December 8, 1940, the Solemnity of the Immaculate Conception. Six days later Karl arrived in Dachau and was assigned to the camp's Barracks 26.[27]

Reichsführer-SS Heinrich Himmler, probably the most feared figure in the Nazi hierarchy and himself an apostate Catholic, would have been greatly amused to learn that Karl Leisner attributed his transferal to Dachau on a Marian Feast to the intercession of the Blessed Mother. Himmler most certainly would have claimed all the credit for himself, and declared that heavenly intercession had nothing to do with it.

In the winter of 1940, Catholic clergy of all nationalities that had been steadily pouring into camps throughout Germany and the east, were suddenly transferred en masse to K.Z. Dachau.

---

[27] *Encyclopedia of the Holocaust*, Volume 4, (New York: MacMillan Publishing Company, 1990), p. 1321.

Reichsführer-SS Himmler, in a rare display of political acumen over brute savagery, had crafted the relocation policy as a means of defusing the mounting outcry over the arrests of priests and religious who stood in opposition to Hitler and the Third Reich.

The German Episcopal Conference in Fulda had mounted a vociferous campaign against the Nazis for the mass imprisonment, and demanded humane treatment be accorded them. Himmler, surprisingly, gave in to the demands – presumably as a mollifying display of Nazi 'humanity' for a worldwide Catholic audience – and for a time the clergy were absolved from hard labor and arbitrary punishment.

Resettled in Dachau, the clergy were concentrated in several barracks, primarily Barracks 26, and even given certain privileges. After January, 1941, the priests were given a crude chapel and allowed to use the space for daily Eucharist as well as private devotions and liturgy. Even though certain liturgical appointments had been smuggled in over the course of the years, for the most part the furnishings were improvised by a somewhat disparate group of artisans.

There was a hand-crafted Altar, Tabernacle, candlesticks, Stations of the Cross as well as a crude yet serviceable monstrance; an elaborate standing repository used for adoration of the Blessed Sacrament. This last was hand-made by an Austrian communist who, though an atheist, was justifiably proud of his artistic contribution to the chapel interior.

These meager privileges, however, were intended for the 500 or so German priests in Dachau, and were not for the 2,000-plus clergymen from other countries crammed into the overcrowded barracks with their confreres. All other priests, primarily Poles, were forbidden from even entering the barracks chapel, which was cordoned off and patrolled by armed guards.

The reprieve granted to the clergy, however, was crafted as a well-publicized propaganda stunt, and, as soon as Himmler felt that the pressure was off, he revoked all privileges. By 1942, while limited use of the chapel was still allowed, clergy were once again assigned to brutal work details and were subject to torture, beatings and executions. They were also, under pain of severe punishments, forbidden to carry out any priestly functions, including giving Communion and hearing confessions to administering Extreme Unction and preaching.

Undaunted, the priests organized a highly efficient sacramental network, where the Blessed Sacrament could be transported through the camp, in glass cases, cigarette packs and even scraps of paper, and given to the sick and the dying without the guards or *capos* even suspecting.

Not only were the Sacraments clandestinely administered, but untold acts of charity, heroism and sacrifice were made at great risk for comrades of all faiths and nationalities. The comportment of the priests was a magnificent display of faithful ingenuity over the worst possible form of oppression, and many priests who survived Dachau chronicled the works of charity by their brothers. German priests Otto Pies, SJ, Franz Goldschmitt and Johannes Neuhasler – later auxiliary bishop of Munich – attest in their works to the pervasive spirit of a pure, catacomb Christianity there in the hell of Dachau.

Dachau

Karl Leisner's arrival in K.Z. Dachau on December 14, 1940, however, coincided with the official reprieve and he was allowed to settle into camp life, at least in terms of practicing his faith, under a somewhat better cloud that those who came before or after him.

Having been through several prisons and one concentration camp, Karl was painfully aware that he would have to yet again be subjected to the brutal and dehumanizing initiation procedures. In Dachau, it was several weeks of back-breaking, non-stop work meant to test the fitness of the prisoner and determine their level of usefulness to the Reich.

For the twenty-five year old Karl, the vigorous, athletic young deacon, the punishments and the privations should have posed no serious threat to his physical or mental well-being. The problem was that the vigorous, athletic Karl was rapidly becoming an idealized image of the past and replaced by the increasingly real image of a very sick man.

The tuberculosis, acquired during his service in the RAD, was hastened along considerably by the unhealthy miasma hovering over marshy bogs around Dachau. Even though he struggled to maintain his physical health and stamina, the odds against his weak lungs were simply too great to fight.

The real threat Karl faced was not what his condition would cause him, but what it could cost him: namely, his life. While Bishop von Galen's denunciation of the Nazi euthanasia programs had succeeded in stopping the en masse gassing of the terminally ill and handicapped in hospitals and institutions, murder of the ill and infirm in concentration camps proceeded with impunity.

Had the extent of Karl's illness became apparent to the guards or infirmarian, chances were quite good that he would have been sent to the gas chambers of Schloss Hartheim a grim castle of death outside of Linz, Austria. To insure that this did not happen, friends began a hide-and-seek game in which Karl was shifted around and hidden for almost five years.

While relatively safe in the barracks, Karl would be sent to the infirmary for crude medication and treatment and then pulled out and placed on a work detail when sympathetic orderlies put the word out that selections were being made among the worst cases for transport to Hartheim.

Like the other prisoners, Karl was living in an atmosphere not only of brutality and horror, but of squalor and filth on an unimaginable level. While prisoners were forced under pain of severe beatings to keep the overcrowded barracks spotless and absent of even the slightest footprints, the Nazis succeeded in keeping hygiene and basic sanitary precautions at sub-human standards.

Karl's zebra-striped prison uniform, like his wooden clogs, were ill-matched hand me downs generally from men who had died from disease, execution or exhaustion. The only time the filthy, rotting clothes would be washed was often when the owner stood for hours in the pouring rain, then keeping them in a state of almost constant dampness.

Although completely shorn of hair, Karl, like his confreres, fought a continual and ever-losing battle with the vermin that swarmed like a pestilence in the straw beds and tattered blankets. Typhus, dysentery, influenza and deadly diseases of all sorts swept through the camp, killing off large numbers of persons already weakened by hunger, overwork and physical abuse. With even the healthiest men being reduced in a short time to physical wrecks, Karl's worsening tuberculosis made his situation dire indeed.

The winter of 1941, coming in the wake of Karl's arrival in Dachau, was one of the coldest in memory, and the prisoners of the camp seemed to experience the nadir of human wretchedness and misery. Karl was in no way capable of withstanding the rigors and privations of the cold, and in March, 1941, his health finally broke.

His persistent, hacking cough resulted in a burst blood vessel that caused him to bleed profusely from the mouth. Realizing that if he did not get some form of medical attention he would soon be dead, Karl's priest friends in Block 26 spirited him away to the camp's TB ward. The danger did not end in the infirmary with the possibility of gassing, but extended to the treatment as well. In the Dachau TB ward, the 'surgeon' was in actuality a locksmith by trade, who used his singularly inappropriate skills in finding ways to drain fluid from the lungs of his patients.[28]

The fact that so many of his fellow inmates, mainly priests, were prepared to sacrifice so much for Karl amply proves the powerful effect he had on all who met and came to know him. Despite his worsening physical condition, Karl had, from his arrival, exuded a curious mixture of peace and joy that immediately affected those around him, priest or layman. Though his body was failing him, Karl managed to keep a sense of humor and adolescent playfulness that helped to lighten the oppressively grim atmosphere.

Never was this playfulness more evident than an episode involving his beloved guitar, which had been secretly transported with Karl from Freiburg Prison to Sachsenhausen and ultimately to Dachau. Upon arrival it was, however, locked up in the storeroom containing the prisoner's pilfered possessions. Undaunted, Karl

---

[28] Klaus Kreitmir, "Ihr Mut is Vorbild", Weltbild, Nr. 7 vom Marz 1996, p. 12.

sauntered off to the storeroom armed with several cigarettes for bribes and returned to the barracks, smiling broadly, with his guitar slung jauntily over his back.

Karl's deeply rooted joy was not that of a buffoon or a simpleton, oblivious or unconcerned about the day to day unfolding of his fate. Karl's joy, though ineffable, was solid, steady and rooted in the depths of an intense and constant state of prayer that the brutality of concentration camp life was unable to snuff out or strangle.

Sanctity, normality and strength were not guaranteed to anyone, especially the clergy, and a tremendous amount of focused energy and will was required to survive on a daily basis. Though several members of the clergy 'went under' out of sheer hopelessness and despair, according to many eyewitnesses – Catholic and non-Catholic alike – the behavior and spiritual comportment of the majority of priests and religious in Dachau was exemplary. For Karl, as for the other priests, there was simply one way of staying on the path.

As he knew that he had to align himself with friends and good companions in order to physically survive, so Karl renewed his commitment to continually root himself in God's presence in order to spiritually survive. The primary source of strength for Karl was, as it had been his whole life, the Eucharist. Arriving in Dachau at a time when the Nazis had granted German clergy access to the chapel and permission to celebrate Mass, Karl immersed himself daily in the mystery of Jesus present on the Altar in the midst of such horror and despair.

In this way he was able to not only derive spiritual nourishment from the Body and Blood, soul and divinity of Christ, but able to see in the Passion and death of the Lord a slowly evolving purpose and meaning to his own suffering. The depth of his love was tested by the revocation in 1942 of the privileges previously granted to the German clergy. Prevented from visiting Jesus in the chapel tabernacle, Karl joined the other priests in shepherding the Blessed Sacrament throughout the camp with an audacity matched only by a deep and tender devotion.

Concealing the consecrated hosts in an aluminum tin, Karl was able to bring communion to sick and dying prisoners who would otherwise have suffered, or often died, without the consolation of the Eucharist and the presence of a caring deacon.

The nature of Karl's sacrifice, the depths to which it was taking his spirituality, became never so clear as at the passing of yet another Christmas in a concentration camp. Christmas of 1941 saw Karl's first year in Dachau and second year of imprisonment. It also marked yet another anniversary of the ordination that never was. He was, however, granted an inestimable consolation by being allowed to chant the Epistle at the Christmas Eve High Mass the priests of Barracks 26 managed to celebrate.

Of all the pangs that seared Karl's heart, one of the worst was the agony he felt in being so close to Christ in the dignity of the priesthood, and yet having to stare at his goal from across a seemingly vast and insurmountable abyss. Prevented from advancing to ordination, prevented from serving Christ as an *alter Christus* – another Christ – consumed him with almost as much agony and helplessness as his turberculosis.

More than just the honor and the dignity the sacerdotal state conferred, the priesthood represented to Karl his true identity and the secret self to which God had called him from all eternity. Being separated from the Altar as a priest, Karl felt, not only separated him from his vocation, but from his very self.

Like Another Stephen

Karl's genuine, unaffected spirituality was by no means confined to ministrations of the Sacraments and long hours in solitary prayer, but was manifested in countless practical and compassionate ways among fellow inmates of all faiths. Not only was Karl able to make friends with a vast array of individuals, but he was known to always have a quick smile and ready word of encouragement and support for everyone he met. He also was in the habit of passing on to other prisoners more needy than himself a portion or sometimes all of his own meager rations.

In Dachau, showy, demonstrative displays of sacrifice and heroic self denial ran the risk of calling to one's self the notice of the dreaded guards and *capos*. Although with Karl it usually took the form of a slice of bread here, and a chunk of dubious sausage there, this constant yet unassuming form of self-giving to others became one of the deacon's most distinguished traits. This constant and total giving characterized Karl to the point where his fellow clergy had to constantly warn him that giving away food placed his own health in danger and jeopardy. "Don't worry," the young deacon would invariably say, "the Lord will give back twice as much."[29]

After 1943, when the SS butchers and priest-hating communist doctors and nurses were replaced by more humane infirmarians in the Dachau infirmary, it became somewhat safer to go to the camp hospital for treatment without fear of becoming a human guinea pig. After that year, Karl had become a more frequent patient in the hospital, not only because the conditions were indeed better but also because his health was gradually getting worse and worse.

It was during this time also when Karl realized the seriousness of his condition and his improbable recovery that he was taken to the very depths of his soul and raised up again in a night of purification. Black periods of melancholy and depression attacked Karl on a regular basis, a common side effect of tuberculosis, usually as he lay for days in the icy and the foul smelling barracks. Often, he pulled the blankets over his head and began to weep silent, bitter tears over his shattered health and his wretched, interminable imprisonment.

Though protected and cared for by a loving cadre of confreres and appearing to all as a joyful, outgoing paragon of hope, deep inside, Karl often felt his life devolving into a gray, gloomy dance of death. While this side of his personality was rarely revealed to his friends and confreres, who saw only the sparkle and the vivacity of the joyful deacon, the gloom that attacked Karl's soul was all too real and needed to be fought with God's grace and sheer force of will.

Not helping this were the brutal marks of illness and concentration camp privations that now began to manifest themselves in

---

[29] Pies, *The Victory of Father Karl*, p. 136.

his appearance. The skin stretched a bit more taut over the shaved skull, the cheeks began to hollow out and the zebra-striped uniform hung increasingly baggy over the emaciated frame. Karl's eyes, however, remained clear and filled with a radiant peace that, despite his occasional periods of gloom, remained a source of awe and wonder to his fellow inmates.

It was clear, though, that by late 1943 a transformation was taking place in Karl in, of all places, the horrid camp hospital. Karl's silent, solitary questioning of his fate and almost certain doom seemed to fade and be replaced with an apostolate of hope and love among his fellow patients in the ward. Having descended into the depths of his being tangled in a morass of questions and confusion, he entered a new light of sorts only when he once again emerged from himself into the presence of others.

Going from bedside to bedside, Karl became a calm, reassuring presence in the hospital that could be relied on for sympathy, advice or just a silent ear. He wrote letters to and read letters from home, shared jokes, played cards and did what he could to ease the physical and emotional pain of those desperately ill or on the verge of death. Wherever he saw a need, Karl rushed to fill it like a soldier rushing to a breach in the defenses, and to his friend, fellow Dachau inmate and future biographer Father Otto Pies, SJ, Karl had literally been transformed into nothing less than a new Saint Stephen. Like Stephen, deacon and first martyr of the young Church, Karl carried Christ to his brothers either in the Blessed Sacrament or in simple acts of charity and kindness.

While everyone in need received his love and caring attention, certain groups attracted Karl out of the shear hopelessness of their condition. After the Jews, Nazi rage was directed at the Russian prisoners of war that streamed by the tens of thousands into concentration camps from the Eastern Front. Considered sub-human rubbish, Nazi policy was to exterminate as many Russians as possible without the slightest tinge of mercy or common decency. The numbers executed in cold blood were frightful.

Moved by the plight of the young Russian soldiers, characterized by the invariable look of terror in their eyes, Karl endeavored to communicate with them in some way. He learned basic Russian phrases and was able to offer a few words of comfort to the lads, many of who were hearing about God and Christ for the first time, dying far from their mothers and their homes. He also learned phrases in Italian, French and Polish to speak with sick and dying prisoners from those countries as well.[30]

The genuine spirituality of the young deacon was not lost on the priests of Barracks 26, who saw manifested in Karl a unique and deeply prayerful presence that went beyond surface piety and a kindly disposition. The constant gift of self that Karl continuously made to everyone in need – despite his own considerable pain and declining health – gave evidence to the fact that he truly understood the concept of 'sacrifice' as inextricably linked with the word love.

It was a sacrifice that, seen by itself in the bitter, naked harshness of Dachau, seemed a blunt and pointless end unto itself. Seen from the heights of the Cross, however, the sacrifice became a sublime, magnificent and ultimately life-renewing act of love subsumed into the Mystical Body of Christ. The great paradox of Karl's life, which everyone knew was coming to an end, was that the deeper he pressed into the cold humiliation of hunger and the darkness of suffering, the clearer became the lines and the subtle shadings of the image of the crucified Christ.

Karl's identity as a deacon, his aspirations for the priesthood, his love for his fellow prisoners and even his charity towards his jailers, reflected a true self that was slowly emerging from the darkness of pain, confusion and fear. It was a Eucharistic self of sacrifice and thankfulness that was centered on the ultimate gift of Christ on his Cross. Drawing nearer each day to the foot of the Cross, the next and most logical step would have been to call Karl to actually touch Him.

While the thought of ordination burned brighter in Karl than ever before, and though he had the full confidence and support of his fellow clergymen in Dachau, the actual mechanics of the

---

[30] Ibid., p. 127.

ceremony were nearly impossible to carry out. To ordain a deacon to the priesthood, the key ingredient is a bishop; a successor of the Apostles who is canonically empowered to lay his hands upon the candidate. Unfortunately, the only bishop imprisoned in Dachau, Bishop Kozal of Leslau, had died there in the camp in 1943 and the chances of another arriving in the near future were remote, if not impossible.

God, however, had plans of His own, and in the summer of 1944 trainloads of prisoners began arriving in Dachau from camps scattered throughout France. Included in the hundreds of soldiers, members of the Resistance, politicians and workers, was His Excellency, Bishop Gabriel Piquet of Clermont-Ferrand.

After the obligatory waiting period, Bishop Piquet – who was to become a beloved and centrifugal force among the imprisoned clergy – was approached by the priests of Barracks 26 and queried about the possibility of a secret ordination.

With the celebration of the Eucharist severely curtailed after the 1943 revocations, any sacramental or liturgical function was considered a severe breach of regulations. An ordination of a deacon to the priesthood, never before attempted in Dacha, would most certainly be looked upon as a flagrant act of defiance and subversion.

For Bishop Piquet, however, the Eucharist constituted the central element of the priestly life, and by his presence he hoped to be instrumental in re-establishing the Mass in the daily rhythm of camp life. An ordination in the brutal, punishing hell of a concentration camp seemed to symbolize more than a gauntlet slapped in the face of their Nazi oppressors. It proclaimed the mastery of the Lord over the vicissitudes of time and the circumstances of place. It proclaimed the presence of the Holy Spirit, the continuum of the visible Church, and the eternal freedom of the individual despite the outward imprisonment of the body.

Yes, Bishop Piquet said, he would gladly and wholeheartedly consent to the ordination.

The presence of a bishop, however, was merely the first of numerous obstacles that needed to be surmounted in order for the historic – and risky – ceremony to proceed. Aside from the episcopal laying on of hands, there were the proper vestments, books and chrism (holy oil) needed for the Sacrament to be administered validly. Complicating matters even further, Karl was legally attached to the diocese of Münster, and Dachau fell under the ecclesiastical jurisdiction of the Archbishop of Munich.

Permission would therefore be needed by Karl's ordinary, Bishop von Galen, as well as by Cardinal Faulhauber of Munich, in whose archdiocese Dachau lay. While it all sounds like so much distracting legalese – especially given the desperate and unusual circumstances – they were necessary guidelines needed to insure that no illicit ordinations could be performed.

Another pressing need were the dimissorial letters. By definition, dimissorial letters are documents "by which a proper ordinary (e.g. a diocesan bishop) permits another bishop to ordain one of his subjects and presents a recommendation of the candidate's worthiness to the ordaining bishop" (CLSA Commentary).[31]

In other words, knowing little of Karl other than that he had spent almost five terrible years in a concentration camp far from any focused instruction in theology and the sacraments, Bishop Piquet was vouching for the deacon's preparedness in ordaining him a priest of the Church. In fact, the bishop was quite moved by the prospect of the ceremony and having given his consent, the pace of events began to quicken considerably.

The Ordination Plot

While contact was secretly established through an extensive underground network between prisoners and local townsfolk, preparations were underway in the camp itself for the upcoming event. It was a miraculous triumph of organization and secrecy, which ran not only the length and breadth of Dachau, but also several cities throughout Germany.

The bishop's crozier – or staff of office resembling a shepherd's crook – was carved out of wood by a Benedictine monk, Father

---

[31] Ibid., p. 138-139.

Spitzig, who himself was a prisoner in the camp. Carved into the base of the cross centered in the swirling Gothic top piece of the staff were the words "Victor in Vinculis" ("Triumphant in Chains"). A Russian communist personally designed and executed a beautiful bishop's ring, and the silk for the vestments, pilfered by the SS from Jewish merchants in Warsaw, was secured from the camp store and fashioned into a chasubles, stoles and even a bishop's miter.[32]

Through the camp store an outside link, a 'door to life' as it was called, had been established with friendly civilians, and through it passed a never ending flow of intelligence, contraband, medicine and food. Maintained by a young priest assigned to the store, the 'door to life' was absolutely leak proof and secure for transmitting and receiving verbal and written communications. It now became a conduit to and from Cardinal Faulhauber using a most unusual but extremely courageous go-between.

In nearby Freising there lived a young but very brave young lady who went by the alias Madi, so needed due to the danger involved for all in the unfolding plot, was living in a convent in the town while discerning a vocation to the religious life. Sent by the mother superior to Dachau to buy seeds from the camp spice plantation, Madi soon showed herself to be calm, quick thinking and cool-headed when stopped or questioned by the SS guards. When Madi established herself as a regular camp customer after several uneventful trips, the mother superior then began sending food, medicine and supplies to the prisoners concealed in the packages.

When the SS no longer inspected the packages of the familiar young girl 'buying' spices and plants, the priest in the camp store quickly pressed Madi into service as a secret courier between Barracks 26 and Cardinal Faulhauber in Munich. Had the actions of one or the other been discovered, it would have meant certain imprisonment for Madi and possible execution for them both.

---

[32] T. Lincoln Bouscaren, S.J., et al, *Canon Law: A Text and Commentary*, Fourth Revised Edition (Milwaukee, WI: The Bruce Publishing Company, 1963), p. 426-427. Pies, *The Victory of Father Karl*, p. 150.

Convinced of her total reliability, the priest gave Madi several documents for the Cardinal, one requesting permission for the ordination of Karl Leisner to the priesthood and the other listing all the items needed for properly carrying out the ceremony. The cool Madi personally delivered the documents to the Cardinal at his residence and, having been given everything requested, returned to Dachau with the official documents of approbation and all the mandatory liturgical appointments.[33]

For Karl, the expected day was awaited with a liberating, almost healing sense of elation and peace. It was apparent to all that Karl was seriously ill, a fact that added a touch of urgency as well as poignancy to the whole upcoming drama.

Confined almost entirely to bed, Karl nevertheless threw himself into the preparations and his final studies as though he were in the pink of health. Lying in bed, Karl immersed himself in the Gospel of Saint John, especially the Last Supper Discourse in which the Lord unfolds the redemptive mystery of the Eucharist for the Apostles he now calls 'friends'. After speaking at length to His friends of love for one another, of humble service and the stilling of troubled hearts in the face of fear, Jesus goes on to compare Himself to the vine, telling them to remain faithful branches close to the source. The world will hate you, Jesus tells the friends who in a few hours will abandon Him, but always remember that "it hated me before you" (John 15:18). You are not alone, the Lord tells them, because even though He must suffer, die and be seen by them no more, it is only in this manner that the Advocate, the Spirit of Truth, will descend on them and remain with them forever.

The Last Supper Discourse ends with the priestly prayer of Jesus, where He declares that His work for the Father has been completely and perfectly fulfilled. Returning to the Father, Jesus will consecrate those given to Him, to be sent into the world even though they do not belong to the world. "Father," Jesus prays, "I want those you have given me to be with me where I am, so that they may

[33] Internationaler Karl-Leisner Kreis Rundbrief, Nr. 34, Dezember 1996, p. 13-15.

always see the glory you have given me because you loved me before the foundation of the world" (John 17:24).

Despite the poetry and the majesty of the Lord's intimate revelations to his friends that touch upon the very meaning of life, death and suffering, the Apostles do not comprehend the mystery.

For Karl, immersing himself in the depths of Saint John's Gospel did not merely present a pedagogical requirement to be fulfilled. The last chapter before the Lord's Passion seemed, in fact, to encapsulate in one magnificent, sweeping arc Karl's own journey through fear, loneliness and suffering to charity, sacrifice and a unitive love far beyond even his own powers to comprehend.

The Day of Ordination

The day chosen for the ordination was December 17, 1944, the third Sunday of Advent known as Gaudete Sunday. Miraculously, secrecy had been maintained up to and throughout the day. Despite the presence of nearly one hundred priests, religious and even seminarians in the block chapel, neither the SS nor the hostile *capos* had the slightest inkling of the historic event transpiring under their noses.

Karl himself, roused into a feverish yet joyful state of mind, was brought into the bishop's presence in the chapel wearing his long white alb and deacon's stole. Despite the wretchedness of the surroundings, the liturgy proceeded as solemnly and as properly as if it were being conducted at the high Altar of the cathedral in Münster. While the priest choir intoned the awesome strains of the ancient chant *Veni Creator Spiritus*, the congregation awaited in awestruck silence for the moment when the hands of the bishop would bring down the Advocate, the transforming Spirit of Truth, upon the head of their brother Karl.

Prostrate on the floor, head pressed firmly against the floor and eyes closed in intense prayer, Karl awaited the call from Bishop Piquet to arise. To distract the SS guards from the activity proceeding secretly in the chapel, a Jewish prisoner sat in front of the building playing his violin. When called, Karl arose and knelt before the bishop, who now laid his head upon the deacon's head. The transcending nature of the moment must have made the assembly forget they were in a concentration camp, a fact brought back to them only by the sight of the zebra-striped uniform visible below the hems of Bishop Piquet's and Karl's white albs.[34]

With his hands extended over Karl's head, the bishop transformed the deacon Karl Leisner, by the power of the Holy Spirit, into a priest, a servant of God and His sacramental instrument, forever. *"Thou art a priest forever."* Trembling with a joy that sparkled in his shining eyes, Karl arose and, with his hands still wet with Holy Oil, proceeded to the altar where he joined Bishop Piquet in the celebration of the Eucharist.

Though Karl was indeed translucent with joy, it took every ounce of his failing strength to make it through the lengthy ceremony. Offering the traditional first blessing to his absent mother and father, the new priest then blessed all those present in the congregation.

The ceremony had emotionally drained all those present but physically drained Father Karl. He had to be physically carried back to his infirmary bed where he collapsed out of sheer exhaustion. The massive expenditure of energy required of Father Karl to make it through the day seemed to echo the motif and words of the card designed especially for his ordination. A simple line drawing showed manacled hands lifting up the chalice at the moment of consecration, and below the image was the words *Sacerdotem Opertet Offere* – *"a priest must offer!"*[35]

Nine days later, on December 26, 1944 – the Feast of Saint Stephen, the first martyr of the Church – Father Karl celebrated his first Mass. The cold, dismal privations of yet another Christmas in Dachau were warmed and mingled with the ineffable joy of the young priest's first Mass, and it was for all present a splendid and radiant day. Taking as the theme of his first sermon the sacrifice of the martyr-deacon unjustly persecuted and condemned, Father Karl quoted Stephen's words from the Acts of The Apostles as he was

---

[34] *Christ in Dachau*, (Westminster, MD: Newman Press, 1952), p. 80-81.
[35] Tenhumberg, "The Witness of Deacon Karl Leisner", p. 1.

stoned to death by the angry mob. "Lord Jesus, receive my spirit," followed by "Lord, do not hold this sin against them," as he fell asleep in the Lord (Acts 7:59-60).

Father Karl was almost nearing his own final consummation, and the same spirit of love and forgiveness that animated the deacon saint animated him as well.

Following the first Mass, the priests had put together without Father Karl's knowledge, a wonderful spread of pastries, cakes and real coffee with which they could celebrate the momentous day. It was a generous and gracious outpouring of love that washed over the new priest, and everyone seemed to revel in the day as though it was they who were being honored. The spirit of joy and celebration was not limited to the Catholic clergy in the camp, and a similar meal held in the evening was orchestrated and hosted by a Protestant minister who scrounged, bribed and bought every delicacy he could find to honor the young priest.[36]

What added such poignancy and depth to the day was that, although few could have actually known at the time, Father Karl's first Mass was also to be his last. Desperately ill, forced by circumstances to keep his ordination a secret from the camp authorities, and in the grips of a historical conflagration about to radically alter direction, Father Karl was destined to celebrate the Eucharist on earth only once.

Liberation

By the early months of 1945, it was clear to both the inmates and their Nazi masters that the war would soon be coming to an end. The Allied forces of the United States, Britain and France, pushing inland from the Normandy beach heads won the previous summer, were slowly closing in on Hitler's Reich from all sides. In the east, the Soviet Red Army was sweeping victoriously across the Nazi's former territorial outposts east of the Oder River.

---

[36] Rene Lejeune, *Wie Gold im Feuer geläutert: Karl Leisner (1915-1945)*, (Hauteville, Switzerland: Parvis-Verlag, 1991), p. 257.

For the inmates in Dachau and other camps throughout the Reich, it was a time for neither cavalier bravado nor undiluted hope. As the winter dragged slowly into spring the prisoners hung in a state of anxiety and daily uncertainty. As it became clear that the spring was going to bring with it a massive Allied thrust to the heart of the Reich, rumors abounded that Himmler planned to destroy all camps as well as inmates in a desperate attempt to eradicate all evidence of Germany's most barbaric national crime.

As the nightmare of the Dachau inmates began to draw to a close, the conditions of the camp deteriorated to a state of utter horror and insanity that was literally like something out of Dante. The winter of 1945 saw a plague of vermin in the camp that turned the barracks into a crawling, swarming nest of lice. Despite the nearly freezing temperatures outside, the prisoners were herded naked into delousing centers, where they were hosed down or simply thrown *en masse* into disinfecting pools where many drowned. Those who could barely walk were carted in wheelbarrows but many more who could not were left in their bunks, covered with lice, to die in their own filth.[37]

This unspeakable horror continued literally up to the day when advance tanks of the U.S. Army emerged from the woods into the body-strewn streets of the camp. The day was April 29, 1945.

Stürmbahnfuehrer Weiss, the camp commander of Dachau, had ignored all of Himmler's orders to destroy the camp and all the inmates, and prepared for the capitulation of Dachau to the U.S. Army. For the most part, the SS and the brutal *capos*, sensing the approaching end, had quietly deserted their posts and fled into the woods. The empty watchtowers and fluttering white flags encountered by the American soldiers gave ample testimony to the fact that Hitler's 'thousand year Reich' had not ended with a bang, but with a pathetic and cowardly whimper.

Still, the advance guard was a small force and singularly unequipped to handle the vast, teeming city of the dead, the dying

---

[37] Neuhasler, *What Was it Like in the Concentration Camp in Dachau?*, p. 65.

and the starving that Dachau had become. Thirty thousand prisoners were suddenly and uncomprehendingly free and, though hundreds had come forward to assist the troops in medical, feeding and administrative operations, the chaos was staggering.

An international committee was quickly formed, and it took it upon themselves to minister to the most pressing needs of the inmates as well as rounding up their former captors to await Allied justice. While the Americans did what they could to bring food, medicine and order to the beleaguered ex-inmates, the situation was too overwhelming and certainly not helped by the daily discoveries of crematoria, torture instruments and boxcars loaded with corpses.

A handful of Father Karl's friends, hearing of the camp's liberation, made it their immediate priority to get the dying priest out of Dachau as quickly as possible. A purulent wound on the side of his chest confirmed the fact that the tuberculosis had spread through his lungs and into his intestines. If medical attention was not received soon, Father Karl would be dead in less than a week.

The pastor of the church in the town of Dachau had been instrumental in the underground network between the camp and the outside world. Knowing all about Father Karl's desperate condition through the role he played in the secret ordination, he became intent on spiriting his brother priest out of the camp at all costs. Armed with a suit of clerical clothes and an Allied travel permit, the pastor was allowed into the camp where he made his way to the hospital and the bed where Karl lay.

Telling the emaciated young priest to dress quickly, the pastor had to spend some time in allaying Karl's fears and hesitations about leaving. When he assured Father Karl that this was his one and only hope of getting out of Dachau alive (the Americans kept all the sick and dying inmates in the camp wards until they could be slowly transported to other hospitals) the pastor succeeded in finally getting him up and dressed. The two priests then walked unsteadily but quickly across the main yard of the camp, out the gate and into a waiting car.

The deacon who entered Dachau as prisoner 22,356, left as Father Karl Leisner. He was a free man for the first time in almost six years. Tightly clinging to the Blessed Sacrament concealed in his jacket, Father Karl wearily climbed into the car, sunk into the back seat and broke down in torrents of tears.

Planegg and Death

Father Karl was driven immediately to the sanitarium at Planegg, where a warm bed was found for him in a private room. On the way to the sanitarium, Father Karl had glimpsed through the haze of his pain and the blur of his tears the horrific torrents of devastation that had rained down upon Germany.

Crater-pocked fields, bombed-out cities and endless heaps of smoking rubble proclaimed the price Germany was paying for Adolf Hitler and twelve years of National Socialism. Passing through the choked roads and actually finding a bed in a private room while the defeated nation collapsed in chaos, Karl's escape was nothing less than miraculous.

Lying between clean sheets and attended by real doctors and endlessly fussing nuns, Father Karl began his final journey in a reverie of incomprehensible joy. While the staff did what they could to make him comfortable, it was clear to all that the young priest would soon be dead. Despite shortages of almost everything and the privations endured by everyone, friends were able to smuggle in bits of food, supplies, and religious articles that became priceless treasures for Father Karl. One of his greatest joys was that, weak as he was, he was able to once again jot down a few lines in his journal.

Father Karl welcomed the smallest gift with the deepest gratitude, and the most common everyday event became a source of joy and wonder. The melding of these two feelings was clearly manifested in the entry for May 28, 1945. "I made my confession: Holy Oil, Viaticum through Otto (Pies, SJ, his priest friend from Dachau also liberated), medicine from the pharmacist in Weilheim (a great benefactor). Pray for him! There was a terrible hailstorm on Corpus Christi Day! Too bad, but we must make amends and atone and not trumpet false victories."[38]

---

[38] Pies, *The Victory of Father Karl,* p. 194.

What began to run through Father Karl's writings as an under-tone was not only a sense of gratitude and peace, but an over-whelming sense of love and forgiveness for everyone and everything that had taken his life down this tortured path. On June 8, Feast of the Sacred Heart, he wrote "Everything for the Sacred Heart, for priests and candidates for the priesthood. Heartfelt atonement. Metanoia!. Repentance!"[39]

While he longed to once again celebrate the Eucharist, Father Karl's declining health simply would not permit it. Instead, he lis-tened to daily Mass over the radio, read scripture, wrote short entries in his journal and lay for hours on in silent prayer looking at a picture of the Blessed Mother tacked on his wall. While Father Karl was unable to say Mass, permission was granted by the Cardi-nal for the Eucharist to be celebrated in his room. It was for its day an extraordinary privilege that filled Father Karl with a tremendous sense of peace and strength for the journey ahead.

One of the greatest joys of his last days was to be reunited with his parents and siblings, who in June had somehow managed to get to Planegg over the bombed out roads and through Allied road-blocks. It was a joyous reunion that seemed to rally Father Karl for a short time from his pain and occasional stretches of semi-con-sciousness. It brought about, however, a short-lived hope. Rapidly reduced to child-like helplessness, Father Karl was washed, dressed and fed by his mother.

Surprisingly, he clung to life for several months after his flight from Dachau, but by August the end was truly at hand. In incred-ible pain and barely able to speak, Father Karl whispered some-thing to his mother that confirmed his nearness to God and his anticipation of eternity. "Mother", he whispered, "I must tell you something, but you must not be sad. I know that I am going to die soon; yet at the same time I am happy."[40]

On the evening of August 12, 1945, after kissing a crucifix and raising his hands in a silent, farewell blessing to his family and

[39] Ibid., p. 195.
[40] Ibid., p. 206.

friends, Father Karl quietly died and entered finally into the immensity of God's love. He was thirty years old. The last entry in his diary, a prayer that echoed the words of the martyr/deacon Stephen he emulated so nobly, summed up his passionate and Christ-centered life. "Bless my enemies too, O Lord," went his final journal entry. "'Lay not this sin to their charge.'"[41]

On June 23, 1996, Pope John Paul II beatified Father Karl Leisner along with Monsignor Bernhard Lichtenberg in a ceremony in Berlin's Olympic Stadium, built by Adolf Hitler for the 1936 Olympic Games. The Holy Father carried the same crozier carved in Dachau fifty-two years earlier by the Benedictine monk Father Spitzig for Blessed Karl's secret ordination. In the vast throng were Blessed Karl's younger brother Wilhelm and his family, as well as friends and former inmates in Dachau. Also present was an elderly nun named Sister Josefa Imma Mack who, as the brave young courier Madi, had risked her life so that a young man she never met could be ordained in secret to the eternal service of the Lord.

[41] Ibid., p. 204.

Chapter IV
"We Are Heading Toward the East"

Saint Teresa Benedicta of the Cross
(Edith Stein)

On August 7, 1942, a young woman standing on the station platform in Schifferstadt, Germany was surprised to hear someone calling her name. Most surprisingly of all was that it was a woman's voice, originating from the window of a standing transport train. Into the third year of the Second World War, most Germans were used to the sight of trainloads of Wehrmacht troops and enemy prisoners chugging in and out of stations throughout the Fatherland.

Most Germans were probably aware of the existence of concentration camps, often near large German cities like Dachau near Munich and Sachsenhausen near Berlin, into which disappeared Jews, Communists and dozens of racial and religious groups deemed dangerous by the Reich hierarchy. Their knowledge of the horrors inflicted within, which re-defined the concept of genocide for the twentieth century, cannot be gauged with any measure of certainty.

However, since July of that year, when SS and Party officials met in Wansee outside Berlin and formulated what was called the 'final solution' to the Jewish question, increasing numbers of boxcars loaded with Jewish men, women and children had pressed through Germany to unknown destinations in the East. Where they went and what happened to them when they got there was not a mystery a great majority of Germans cared to unravel. After all, there was a war on and the day carried enough troubles for each citizen of the Reich.

While most citizens looked away, this particular young lady actually looked toward the dark transport boxcar. The woman in the window, small but by no means tiny or fragile looking, was dressed in the dark clothes that immediately identified her as a Carmelite nun. Her large, warm intelligent eyes and her small, sad mouth were framed by a white coif and black veil that hung down over a brown tunic and scapular. Fastened incongruously to the scapular was a yellow cloth Star of David, in the center of which was printed the word *Jood*, Dutch for Jew, which by law all Jews in the Reich and its conquered provinces were forced to wear.

The young lady recognized the nun in the window as a teacher she had had while a student at the Dominican convent school of Saint Magdalena in Speyer, just a few miles away from Schifferstadt. Known then as Fräulein Edith Stein, the nun now bore the religious title of Sister Teresia Benedicta a Cruce, or literally, Sister Teresa Blessed by the Cross.

A warm-hearted, friendly, though somewhat solitary teacher at Saint Magdalena, Fräulein Stein was known to have been an atheist in her youth who converted from Judaism to Catholicism in her thirties. Having been a glowing light in the field of German philosophy, Fräulein Stein studied in Gottingen and Freiburg under the 'Master' of Phenomenology Edmund Husserl and, having earned a doctorate, moved in the finest intellectual circles.

Fräulein Stein was reputed to possess one of the most gifted philosophical minds in Germany and, were she not a woman and a Jew during the Nazi's political rise, would have certainly ascended to the pinnacles of academia.

Instead, having entered the Catholic Church, Fräulein Stein became a teacher at a girl's school in Speyer and, living a life of recollection and solitude with the Dominican sisters who ran it, became a noted and highly sought after author and lecturer throughout Europe. Finally, after having waited many years to fulfill her heart's desire, she was granted permission by her spiritual director to enter the Carmel in Cologne.

That was the last the young lady had heard of Fräulein Stein, who now stood in the window of a reeking, filthy transport train, packed with Jewish citizens from Germany as well as from the countries of conquered Europe.

Despite the ominous atmosphere of uncertainty and doom surrounding the dark transport, Sister Benedicta conveyed the same peaceful affability she did for years as a teacher at Saint Magdalena. Exchanging pleasantries and inquiring after old friends, Sister Benedicta's happy reminiscences were suddenly cut short by the abrupt jerk of the train as it started to rumble out of Schifferstadt station.

Asking the young lady to remember her to the good sisters at Saint Magdalena, Sister Benedicta then asked her to pass on a message to her mother superior at the Carmel in Echt, Holland. The message from Sister Benedicta, which was indeed relayed back to her superiors, was simply: "We are heading toward the East."[1]

While the deeper meaning of Sister Benedicta's final communication can be endlessly plumbed and pondered over, her immediate meaning was geographical. Having been held for several days in the concentration camp in Westerbork, Holland with her sister Rosa, who also had converted to Catholicism, it was apparent that they were being taken, not to Germany, but somewhere beyond its eastern frontier.

As the train bumped and jounced its terrified passengers across Germany, the horror mounting in the hearts of every person intensified with every spent mile of the journey. The hunger, the thirst, the filth and the sheer crush of horrified humanity soon made the boxcar interior indistinguishable from the suffocating depths of a sealed tomb. With the passengers already robbed of freedom, dignity and legal rights, the further privations of everything from food and water to ventilation and sanitary provisions mercilessly shattered minds and bodies alike. Many simply went insane and not a few found ways of ending their agonies before the hellish journey was finished.

And yet, the God of Israel, the Almighty, was invoked and called upon by the endless intonations of countless voices deep within the cars. Even in this horrendous, surreal nightmare, God's promise that He would care for His chosen people and that under His wings

---

[1] Hilda Graef, *The Scholar and the Cross: The Life and Works of Edith Stein* (Westminster, MD: The Newman Press, 1955), p. 230.

they would find refuge went with them towards the East. A few of
the passengers, who miraculously survived the transports, remember
the woman in the dark clothes, who tenderly cared for her fellow
passengers and victims. They especially remembered the tenderness
of the nun towards the children of mothers who went mad with
horror, washing them, dressing them and feeding the little ones
what bits of food she could find. By all accounts, Sister Benedicta's
was a silent yet remarkably powerful and peace-filled presence that
was remembered by all that came into contact with her.

The Eastern destination was arrived at two days later, on August
9, 1942. It was the southwestern Polish city of Oświęçiem, or, as
it was called in German, Auschwitz. Details of Sister Benedicta's life
get hazier and more vague after her arrival. Unloaded like cattle,
the passengers were separated by gender and age, with the old, the
children and the infirm being sent off to what they were told were
delousing baths before receiving work assignments.

It was a masterpiece of diabolical efficiency and factory-like precision. The Jews were told by the SS guards to remember where
they placed their neatly separated clothes, shoes, glasses and valises
so they could get them again when they emerged from the baths.

The showerheads, of course, did not spout forth water upon the
people, but the poisonous gas Zyklon-B, which killed all in the
sealed chambers in a matter of minutes. When the operators of the
gaskammer were certain all were dead, the corpses were then carted
off to pits where they would be burned at a later date. According
to documents made available after the war by the Red Cross of the
Netherlands, Sister Benedicta, formerly Edith Stein, was killed in
this manner most likely a short time after she arrived on August 9.
She was fifty years old.

Birth and Childhood

Edith Stein was born on October 12, 1891 in the city of Breslau,
Germany (now Wrocław, Poland), the capital of the German Eastern province of Silesia. Edith's birthday was the Day of Atonement,
the highest of all Jewish Holy Days, in which the high priest

traditionally entered the 'Holy of Holies' to offer himself as sacrifice of expiation for the Jewish people. The profoundly religious significance of Edith's birth date was not lost on her devoutly pious parents, Siegfried and Auguste Stein.

Siegfried, Edith's father, came from a background of Silesian merchants and minor industrialists whose fortunes waxed and waned with the mercurial temperaments of war and commerce in Imperial Germany. Herr Stein had inherited the family lumber business in Breslau and, despite the wealth of timber in Silesian forests, was struggling to keep the firm afloat when he married twenty-one year old Auguste Courant.

Despite the French-sounding family name, Auguste likewise came from a solid middle class lineage of Silesian merchants, small business owners and even a few artists. Despite, or probably because of, her cool tenacity and unswerving solidity in all things practical and spiritual, Auguste was a firm favorite in both her own family and that of her new husband, and she eventually developed something of an awe-inspiring matriarchal reputation.

From 1872, when the first child, Paul, was born until Edith's arrival in 1891, Auguste gave birth to a total of eleven children, four of whom would die in infancy and four of whom would perish in Nazi concentration camps.

In July 1893, when Edith was barely two, Herr Stein set out one day to examine trees in a nearby forest and never returned home. Suffering a stroke in the heat, he died by the side of the road, propped up against the trunk of a tree. Though shattered by the death of her beloved husband, Frau Stein forced herself through sheer willpower to learn the lumber business and somehow keep it going. She had a house full of young mouths to feed and her poor Siegfried, good man that he was, had left the firm in something of a financial jumble. Putting on the black of mourning, which she never took off, Frau Stein then set off to work.

By a combination of acumen and bone-wearying work, Frau Stein was able to keep the business not only afloat, but managed to make it turn a profit as well. Despite her pronounced traits of thrift, discipline and Prussian-like efficiency, Frau Stein possessed a fervent soul and warm heart that was manifested in many practical ways to friend and stranger alike. She routinely bought surplus lots of lumber for distribution among the poor in the harsh Silesian winters, she gave money generously and she seemed to be forever playing hostess to endless streams of displaced relatives and troubled friends.

Regardless of her twelve-hour days put in at the lumberyard, Frau Stein would keep the Sabbath and attend without fail every Holy Day service at the synagogue. With the children growing and going their own ways, her baby Edith, who looked with awe at the immensity of her mother's faith, invariably accompanied her. Frau Stein's Jewish faith was not observed with indifference or looked upon as a social obligation. It was, on the contrary, a well spring, and a conduit that ran to every fiber of her being. She saw to it her children were raised firmly in their faith, and told them that since God gave much, much was to be expected of them in return.

Life in a Jewish Family

A highly detailed picture of Edith's childhood and young adulthood, rendered in lush tones and rich texture, has been left by Edith herself. *Life in a Jewish Family*, begun shortly before her entrance into the religious life and worked on sporadically until her 1939, is Edith's tale of her family life from before her birth in 1891 to her university days in 1916. Frank, lively and unflinching when it comes to the foibles and faults of herself and her family, *Life in a Jewish Family* is not only a recall of youth and young adulthood in a devout Jewish home but an almost photographic record of life in the twilight of Imperial Germany.

The hard work and business sense of her mother paid dividends and, though ends did not often meet, Edith presents a picture of a relatively well-off Jewish family effortlessly ensconced in the starchy Prussian middle class. Mantles are covered with family photographs and the requisite Victorian bric-a-brac, and the inevitable piano, upon which are played the works of Schumann, Schubert and the popular tunes of the day, stands upright in the corner.

Teas and afternoon walks are taken, children are well groomed and raised to love the Kaiser and commit to memory large chunks of Schiller and Goethe. On the whole, *Life in a Jewish Family* portrays a middle class German Jewish family that mingles freely in commerce and on the streets with their Catholic and Protestant neighbors. To be sure, the ravenous dogs of anti-Semitism, to be loosed in a few short decades, are growling as always but during these times of peace and prosperity remain relatively under control.

There are dark parts to life in this Jewish family as well, and Edith does not refrain from full disclosure in regards to family skeletons and shameful secrets. Aside from the love, support and devotion she finds in her immediate and extended family, there is also bankruptcy, mental illness, divorces, feuds and even a few tragic suicides mixed in together. Edith's early life and young adulthood, though extraordinarily observed, is, in the end, like so many ordinary families of the day.

With the loss of her father Edith grew extremely close to her mother, and a bond was formed that would continue to deepen and grow with the passage of time. Frau Stein doted on her baby, and both mother and daughter seemed to speak a silent language all their own that linked them to their very depths. The older children adored baby Edith and treated her as a cross between a fairy tale princess and a porcelain doll. She was a wide-eyed, curly-headed moppet who, if she did not get her way in all things, would let forth with screaming fits and temper tantrums of titanic proportions. Edith was, by her own account, by an early age a precocious and thoroughly spoiled child.

There were, however, glints and glimmers of the intellectual future shining through the tears and tantrums, and through the great works of German poetry and literature read aloud to her by her brother Paul, Edith developed a fascination with books at a very early age. Far from being a dreaded specter, the prospect of school became an eagerly awaited event for Edith, much in the same way other children would await the arrival of Christmas and Santa Claus.

Her precocity grew with her, however, and, as the time came for her to be registered for kindergarten, Edith vociferously protested the injustice. She did not want to go to the 'baby' school, but with her sister Erna to the Viktoriaschule for 'big people'. While her overindulged behavior shows that she still thought of herself as the center of everyone's world, subtle undertones and patterns of her mental development began to show that Edith was beginning to grasp concepts and ideas in regards to the thought process.

What in the six-year-old was a child-like fascination with the classroom, with theater and music and the infinite world of possibilities found in books, in a decade would become what Edith herself would term a search for Truth.

As older brothers and sisters married and had families of their own, the appearance of nieces and nephews slowly removed Edith from the center of the familial universe. The flames of her temper cooled, her responsibilities in the bustling household increased and in a few years Edith had mellowed into an introspective, quiet and almost shy girl. While Frau Stein continued to work endlessly at the lumberyard, her youngest daughter took on the role of aunt, nanny and mother hen to the toddlers of the growing Stein family.

Edith, though almost a child herself, assumed the mantle of aunt easily, and her gentle, fun-loving and genial rapport with children deepened in her as the years went by. Edith continued to do extremely well in school, and her reputation for being a precocious prodigy had solidified into an amazing thirst for knowledge. Her brother's recitations to her as a child impressed her deeply, and she voraciously devoured books on German literature and poetry. This was no passing fancy of childhood, and Edith's sister Erna said that "she began to get a grasp of literature when she was between four and five years old."[2]

While she received plaudits from family and teachers alike, Edith did become acquainted with the uglier reality of life in twentieth century Europe. In 1904, when she was thirteen, Edith was passed over for a school prize that she clearly deserved. When the class protested the injustice, the headmaster nervously tried to defend his

---

[2] Sister Teresia de Spiritu Sancto, ODC, *Edith Stein*, translator Cecily Hastings (New York: Sheed & Ward, 1952), p. 12

choice. Despite their ages, the children knew the real reason was the omnipresent, though occasionally dormant, anti-Semitism that was rampant in all strata of German society.

Another unpleasant reality was unfolding in Edith's life as well during this time, one which was to color her life for the next fifteen years. Despite her rigorous religious upbringing and the example of her devout mother, the thirteen-year-old Edith had ceased to believe in God. Basing all her beliefs on that which could be proved by logic, science and reason, Edith casually dismissed God from her life when she realized that she could not intellectually conclude His existence.

While she continued to accompany her mother to the synagogue for the Sabbath and Holy Days, Edith sat empty and devoid of prayer or belief of any kind. She had become self-sufficiently intent on journeying to truth by the power of her own mind, and as the new century began Edith chose the intellectual paths blazed for it by the likes of Darwin, Marx, Nietzsche and Freud.

Atheism and Intellectual Growth

For a time following her loss of faith, Edith grew sullen, withdrawn and was often plagued with maladies of one sort or the other. Sensing that a change of scenery coupled with increased duties and responsibilities would do her good, Frau Stein sent Edith in 1906 to stay with her eldest sister Else in Hamburg following her daughter's decision to leave school. Married and busy with the raising of three small children, Else welcomed the arrival of her younger sister, who was to help with the household chores and the care of the children.

The sea air of the large harbor city, the loving care and friendship of her sister and the myriad responsibilities assumed by her in running the house matured Edith considerably, and after a few months everyone saw in her a noticeable and pleasant change. Ready again to pursue her goal of entering a university, Edith returned home and began a vigorous tutorial program in Latin, Mathematics and other vital subjects.

Edith's years in the *Gymnasium*, or German equivalent of high school, was a time of serious application towards her studies which she hoped would ultimately take her to the university. Her fellow students looked up to her, her family beamed with pride and her masters were awed – and sometimes outshone – by the clarity and subtlety of her mind. Her curricular studies, like the question of God's existence, was washed through a mind that computed data, turned it into information and stored it as usable knowledge.

Her thought process was a fascinating procedure of machine-like precision; best described by Edith herself in her autobiography. "My decisions arose out of a depth that was unknown even to myself. Once a matter was bathed in the full light of consciousness and had acquired a definite form in my thoughts, I was no longer to be deterred by anything; indeed I found it an intriguing kind of sport to overcome hindrances which were apparently insurmountable."[3]

Despite the seemingly Prussian nature of her will and mental fortitude, Edith was quite ordinary and natural in her family and social life. While the endless stream of nieces, nephews and cousins threatened to burst the seams of the orderly Stein house on the Michaelisstrasse, Edith began spending more and more time with her growing circle of friends. Not all time was spent in the study hall or after-school tutoring sessions. Edith and her friends played tennis, rowed in park lagoons and engaged in typical adolescent pranks while on picnics or extended train excursions throughout the surrounding countryside.

It was, however, her intellect that raised her far above everyone else at school or at home, and to no one's surprise Edith graduated from the gymnasium with flying colors following a difficult examination process. Her first choice of university was Heidelberg, the fabled Gothic town of drinking songs, student princes and dueling scars that appealed to Edith's deeply patriotic nature. She was to go there with her sister Erna, a medical student, but when the plans fell through she registered at her hometown university in Breslau.

The path to heights of her own choosing spread before Edith like paved gold, and everyone predicted great things for her future.

---

[3] Edith Stein, *Life in a Jewish Family 1891-1916*, translation by Josephine Koeppel, O.C.D.,(Washington, D.C.: ICS Publications, 1986), p. 152.

Even one of her gymnasium masters felt as much when he inscribed the back of Edith's program following her graduation. Playing on the all too obvious pun of Edith's family name – Stein is German for 'Stone' – he nevertheless said more than he possibly knew. "Strike the Stone," he wrote, "and treasures will gush forth."[4]

The four terms Edith spent studying at the University of Breslau were focused on German language and literature, with a heavy leaning towards the psychology seminars offered by two eminent professors in the field: Stern and Hönigswald. From these two genuinely brilliant men, Edith learned the rudiments of the psychology of thought – an area of great interest for her – as well as the realities of academic politics and specters of the anti-Semitism still very much alive even in the realms of education. Professors Stern and Hönigswald were Jews, and as such were prevented from rising too high in the ranks of academia.

Edith, however, soon made it clear that she was someone to be reckoned with, regardless of racial origin. As a woman and a Jew Edith was more handicapped than they in the academic field were, but she let everyone know that she would not be deterred by interfaculty backbiting nor frightened by externally imposed limitations. "My primary interest," Edith said in looking back on her Breslau days, "was acquiring knowledge."[5]

While lost in the voluminous reading list for Professor Stern's winter lecture in 1912, Edith repeatedly crossed paths with references to the *Logische Untersuchungen* (*Logical Investigations*), the magisterial two-volume exposition of Phenomenological tenets written by the great philosopher Edmund Husserl. Husserl, a Moravian Jew who had converted to Lutheranism, was by Edith's time the preeminent German philosopher who had given life to Phenomenology as a full-fledged philosophical movement.

Something of a revolutionary time bomb lobbed into the ranks of Kantian thought, Husserl's Phenomenological philosophy was based on the premise that there *is* such a thing as objective Truth and

---

[4] Ibid., p. 179.
[5] Ibid., p. 187.

that there does indeed exist a 'knowable' world. This contradicted the thought of Immanuel Kant, the 18th century Prussian considered by many to be the dominant philosopher of the modern age, who claimed that while knowledge of 'things' is possible, knowledge of the ultimate realities beyond their appearances is utterly impossible. Worse than impossible, it is pure folly, for proof of realities beyond appearances cannot be proved intellectually or scientifically. God, therefore, is reduced from source and prime mover of space and time to an excuse for one's inability to rationally grasp what lies beyond sense experience.

Bored by the conventional educational atmosphere at Breslau, Edith was increasingly electrified by this bold philosophical movement that explored the experience of sensible things, or phenomena, in all their wonderful diversity and infinite subtlety. It seemed to lead her in the direction of the Truth for which she had been seeking since she was thirteen. Fascinated with the psychology of thought, Edith had nevertheless considered the disciplines and methodology of psychology to be in its infancy. Phenomenology was, however, a movement as old as thought and as new as the day's sunrise, and it was attracting some of the most promising young intellects in Germany.

Husserl, known as ' The Master', was *the* philosopher of the day, and to sit at his feet Edith needed to go to the universe of thought of which he formed the center. If Husserl was the person, Göttingen was the place.

About the same time Edith's restlessness at Breslau was fermenting, she was shown a letter addressed to her mother from the wife of her cousin Richard Courant. Richard, a mathematics tutor in Göttingen had brought many male friends into their lives, but as a young bride the wife said that she needed the companionship of young ladies as well. Couldn't Aunt Gustel send Erna and Edith to Göttingen for their studies? The letter convinced everyone, especially Edith, that a transition from the respectable halls of Breslau to the rarefied heights of Göttingen was meant to be. Though broken hearted at the prospect of being separated from her beloved child, even Frau Stein consented and gave Edith her blessing.

When Edith arrived at Göttingen in 1913, the inner corridors that led to the presence of the Master, Husserl, were vigilantly guarded by a coterie of handpicked assistants – often renowned scholars themselves – whose job it was to screen the applicants on the basis of merit and intellect. Edith was fortunate to have her path to the Master first take her to Adolf Reinach.

One of Husserl's most respected and distinguished assistants, Reinach was also, in himself the opposite of everything that Husserl was and represented. Young, generous, warm-hearted and genuinely interested in people, Reinach welcomed Edith into his home and encouraged the pursuit of Phenomenological studies at Göttingen. Impressed with the depth of her intellect and the seriousness of her academic convictions, Reinach organized an informal meeting between Husserl and a handful of prospective students; including Fräulein Stein.

The first meeting between Edith and the Master was direct, easy and surprisingly unremarkable. Fifty-four at the time, Husserl was every inch the professor of the old Viennese stamp. With his spade beard, spectacles and briar pipe, the handsome and dignified Husserl conveyed a lofty yet non-threatening presence. Throwing out random inquiries to the assembled students, Husserl asked Edith which of his works she had read.

"The *Logical Investigations*," Edith responded.

When he asked if she had read all of it, Edith said she that she had read all of volume two.

Impressed, the Master smiled and announced "Why, that's a heroic achievement!" Drawing such an ebullient response from the normally reserved Husserl, Edith clearly demonstrated that not only had she done her homework well, but that she could hold her own against one of the towering intellects of her age.[6]

Husserl

A professor at Breslau had told Edith that at Göttingen one doesn't simply discuss philosophy, but eats, sleeps and breathes it

[6] Ibid., p. 249-250.

day in and day out. For Edith, this total immersion into the heady realms of higher thought was an invigorating experience that challenged her already considerable intellect. She wasted no time in making herself known in the social and academic circles in the university and soon she was a key member of the Göttingen Philosophical Society – no mean feat for a newcomer and a woman.

The formidable array of minds that constituted the philosophical world at Gottingen was an impressive roster indeed, and Edith came to know many of them intimately during her years at the university. They included Max Scheler, a Jew by birth but a convert to Catholicism whose on-again, off-again relationship with the Church implanted in Edith's mind the first ideas of Catholic 'phenomena.' There was the liberal Lutheran couple Theodore Conrad and his wife Hedwig Conrad-Martius, and the dashing young Hans Lipps, who would capture the heart of Edith but ultimately find death fighting for the Fatherland in the Second World War.

It was, however, Husserl's assistant Reinach and his wife Anna who were to play such inspirational roles in Edith's life and faith journey. Newly married and in the full bloom of young love, Reinach was at the time being drawn deeper into a journey that would in a few years culminate in his and his wife's baptism in 1916. Even though he was still several years from embracing Jesus as Lord and Messiah, Reinach was beginning to evince a disinterest for philosophical disciplines and a marked inclination towards the study of purely spiritual questions. Aside from his profoundly spiritual dimension, Reinach's practical generosity and spontaneous affection showed Edith the human face, the beating heart of what could have easily become for him a dry world of philosophical ideas.

While coming to be an intimate part of this tightly knit bond of friends who spent their time pondering but more of ten than not hotly debating great philosophical thoughts, Edith was still an outsider in one great respect. For many of the Gottingen Phenomenologists, the belief in objective truth and in the ability to know what lies beyond 'the thing' led not to intellectual satisfaction but to embrace the reality of a personal and loving God. For some, like the Conrad-Martius' and Dietrich von Hildebrand, it led to a more cerebral pursuit of a cradle religion, but for others like the Reinachs and Max Scheler the pursuit of Phenomenology meant a radical break from what they were into something they hoped yet to achieve. In fact, Husserl once said half-jokingly that he should be canonized for leading so many people to the Faith.

While impressed and curious, Edith was still for all intents and purposes at this time an atheist. While she still considered herself a Jew, it was by way of identifying with a particular cultural heritage and not by a faith in the God of Abraham, Isaac and Jacob. It was simply a way to say where she had come from but not who she was in her deepest self.

"She didn't believe in anything," says Sister Waltraud Herbstrith, OCD, a Carmelite nun at the Edith-Stein-Karmel in Tubingen, Germany who has written extensively on the life of Edith Stein. "You can be a good Jew, a baptized Catholic, a Protestant, but suddenly you say 'I don't believe in God.' So it was with Edith Stein. She did not separate from Judaism. She saw a great awe and a love for God in her mother, but she could not imitate it."[7]

Though respectful of her friend's faith, Edith was not so much interested in pursuing matters of the spirit as in making sense of her increasingly complex relationship with the Master.

With a reputation for surrounding himself with brilliant disciples, Husserl sized up Edith's intellect and clearly saw someone who could be of inestimable value to him in the future. From her earliest days in Göttingen, Edith was granted rare intimacies in Husserl's academic as well as family circle and, being the same age as his daughter, was even doted on by the Master's matriarchal wife. For Edith, however, her status as a young Göttingen philosopher in a field dominated by men and the considerable talents that took her there represented something of a double-edged sword. While her male counterparts and their wives treated her like a younger sister, Edith also became cognizant of an implicit agreement of boundaries that had barred her ascent in the academic world.

---

[7] Interview with Sister Waltraud Herbstrith, O.C.D., conducted by the author at Edith-Stein-Karmel in Tubingen, Germany in April, 1999.

The towering figure, the formidable intellectual lion of the philosophical world who could have removed many obstacles posed by Edith's gender and Semitic blood was none other than Edmund Husserl. As Edith moved closer into the Master's world, first as student and later as assistant went Reinach served in World War I, it was quite justifiably assumed that he would do what he could to advance her career. After all, if Husserl helped disciples like Reinach, who would give up pure philosophy for matters of the spirit, or Martin Heidegger, who would later distance himself from the Master as a Nazi university rector, he would certainly help a loyal and kindred spirit like Edith Stein.

Edith would come to be disappointed, even hurt, by Husserl on many levels.

Academically, Husserl saw Edith's talents merely as an efficient and precise set of tools that could help focus him in his own numerous projects, and not as a gift to be developed and allowed to bloom. Within a few years, after she had become the Master's assistant, Edith's suspicion that she would never be a collaborator with Husserl had become transformed into a resigned fatalism. In a letter to Polish Phenomenologist Roman Ingarden, Edith wrote that Husserl declared that she should assist him until she married; "then I may only accept a man who will also become his assistant."[8]

While Husserl admired Edith and Edith regarded Husserl with an affection bordering on veneration, the relationship between the two was a tangle of complex emotions that caused a great deal of confusion and even pain to the young philosopher.

"There were professors who were good to their students but Husserl was not," says Sister Waltraud Herbstrith. "He just liked using Edith's philosophical gifts to help himself. "[9]

---

[8] Edith Stein, *Self Portrait in Letters 1916-1942*, translated by Josephine Koeppel, O.C.D., (Washington, D.C.: ICS Publications, 1993), p. 6.

[9] Interview with Sister Waltraud Herbstrith (see 7).

Friends and Growing Reputation

If Edith's relationship with Husserl was wending down a rocky path, other relationships at Gottingen were flowering with health and vigor. This entailed relationships with men as well as with women. The daughter of a widowed mother who struggled against unimaginable odds to succeed in the male-dominated world of business and the sister of a brilliant young woman pursuing a career in the male-dominated field of medicine, Edith was intent on carrying on the family tradition in academia.

Neither coldly antagonistic nor cynically jaded in regards to love and marriage, Edith was, however, from her teen years fully committed to the highest level of success and personal achievement based on her own merits. Edith knew she was intelligent, gifted and capable of achieving great thing in the field of philosophy, and she did not see the need to be defined or confined by a male presence in her life. Edith's feminism, however, was neither radical nor politically guided during this time; it was merely a manifestation of her belief in the individual's worth and basic human rights.

At Göttingen, Edith was exposed to solid marriages that bonded together many of her intimate philosophical acquaintances. Aside from Adolf and Anna Reinach, there was Theodore and Hedwig Conrad-Martius and even the lofty Master and his tolerant wife Malwine. These were not servile, unilateral unions based on oppressive and chauvinistic Victorian dictates. On the contrary, they were healthy, giving partnerships in which love, respect and friendship seemed to be the mortar.

"She had friends who were happily married, the Conrad-Martius', her sister Doctor Erna Biberstein and Anna Reinach," says Sister Waltraud Herbstrith. "These couples loved each other tenderly. Edith Stein saw that and she was very happy to see it. She had no broken marriages before her eyes, and so she hoped herself to be married in this fashion."[10]

---

[10] Ibid.

It was very healthy for Edith because it showed the possibility of continuing with one's life and work while bonded for life in matrimony, but also the first fleeting glimpses of love on a deeper and entirely ineffable level. Seeing the natural union of man and woman began to open her eyes, even though she did not see it clearly yet, to the mysterious and infinite return of love resulting from the total self-sacrifice of the lover to God, the Beloved.

While Edith cared for Husserl as a father and loved Reinach like a brother, she was by no means devoid of the feelings of romantic love. Despite her cool façade and even her own reticence in regards to serious suitors in her life, Edith indeed fell in love and even began to nurture hopes of marriage.

Hans Lipps, a twenty-three year old soldier/philosopher from her Gottingen circle of friends, became for some time the object of Edith's quite ardent attentions. A baby-faced dragoon whose passion for Phenomenology was tempered by a delicate love of art and antiques, Hans Lipps captured the heart of Edith Stein and would ultimately be the source of yet another hurt in her life. Independent feminist though she was, Edith nevertheless did not totally exclude from her life the idea of the marriage that for Jewish people is as natural as breathing and walking.

"She loved Hans Lipps and would have married him if he would have agreed," says Sister Waltraud. "But when she sensed that he had another person in mind to marry, it was a hard blow for her. For a Jewish person, marriage is a form of theology. It is God's wish that man and wife are happy together and praise God in the marriage. That is old, good Jewish theology and Edith Stein knew nothing else. She had a very positive attitude toward marriage."[11]

Even after Hans married, Edith kept a small photo of him on her desk until told by her good friend Hedwig 'Hatti' Conrad-Martius that it was unhealthy to do so. Though the picture came down and Dr. Conrad-Martius said the cynical would claim that the monumental hurt accounted for Edith's ultimate conversion and

[11] Ibid.

baptism, she added that one cannot discount the often surprising methods employed by Divine Providence "in order to draw near the persons who are called."[12]

If things were somewhat fragmented in areas of love, in other areas of Edith's life things were actually coming together quite nicely. It was clear that, despite a few feeble thoughts given to returning to Breslau to finish her school, Göttingen was to be Edith's home. While completing requirements for her third subject, history (the first two being philosophy and psychology), Edith had the good fortune to become a star pupil of the celebrated professor Max Lehmann. Like Husserl a respected giant in his field who did not suffer academic fools gladly, Lehmann was a Hanoverian liberal dedicated to the parliamentarian ideas of that particular German province that gave England a line of monarchs that reigned for several centuries. Though his liberalism made Edith retrench her heels deeper in her patriotic Prussian attitudes, the professor and student developed an intense awe and respect for the other and under Lehmann Edith's writing and research skills were considerably honed.

In fact, a particularly difficult essay completed by Edith for Lehmann, entitled *The Realization of the Party-Programmes in the Proposed Constitution of 1849*, was so brilliantly executed that the professor was prepared to let it stand as Edith's *Staatsexamen*. These were the exams that, approximating the test for an American B.A., qualified the graduate for State posts. Edith, however, had her heart set on getting her doctorate first and only then taking her *Staatsexamen*. Husserl advised her to do the State test first, declaring it academic suicide to become too strong in one philosophical area before mastering other academic disciplines. Though the advice was sound indeed, Edith was thoroughly depressed at the prospect of being kept from her doctoral destiny. Husserl, however, offered to soften the blow by helping her select a proper subject for her *Staatsexamen* that could later be reshaped into a doctoral thesis.

---

[12] *Never Forget: Christian & Jewish Perspectives on Edith Stein*, edited by Waltraud Herbstrith, O.C.D., translated by Susanne Batzdorff (Washington, D.C.: ICS Publications, 1998), p. 266.

Edith had been fascinated with a subject Husserl had examined in one of his courses, which dealt with the objective world as being knowable intersubjectively, or, by individual 'knowers' who can share what they know with each other. Husserl, walking in the footsteps of philosopher Theodor Lipps, called this experience 'empathy.'

Having passed her *Staatsexamen* with flying colors in January 1915, Edith then began an intensive course in Greek to prepare her for her doctoral examinations. In the meantime, Edith was apparently losing the battle she had been waging with Husserl to get him to read her doctoral thesis. Having just been granted a professorship at Freiburg University, the Master was extremely busy and procrastinated every time she asked him for a read.

When he finally broke down and read it, Husserl professed profound admiration for its depth and intelligence, going so far as to somewhat condescendingly call her a "very gifted little girl." Taking her orals in August 1916, Edith passed her examinations without a snag, and was ultimately awarded her doctorate *summa cum laude*. While out walking with the Master before he left for Freiburg, Edith obliquely hinted at the possibility of becoming his assistant; this to replace Reinach who was in uniform on the Western Front. Husserl thought it a wonderful idea and said the position would be waiting for her when she finished her post-doctoral work at Gottingen.[13]

At twenty-five, Edith was already considered one of the brightening lights of German philosophy and, at ease in the highest intellectual circles was just awarded a doctorate with the highest possible honors. It was with great joy and ebullient confidence that she set off to become, as she thought, the 'right arm' to one of the great modern European philosophers.

World War and Red Cross Service

In the meantime there was also unfolding in Edith's life a parallel world, one that would ultimately set in motion her journey towards

---

[13] Stein, *Life in A Jewish Family*, p. 410-411.

faith. The path down which that journey would wend its way was hidden, however, and being hidden, it would take her through the darkest possibilities of human experience that now seemed to encroach on Edith's orderly world from all sides.

Edith had known suffering to be sure, and she had known great disappointment, but the nature of these two experiences were in the nature of the normal ebb and flow of daily life and the seasons of an individual life. There was the loss of her father, of relatives and the pains and hurts that inevitably accompany life in a large family. Professionally, Edith was becoming increasingly aware that despite her acknowledged brilliance in her chosen field, as a Jewish woman she would be allowed to go only so high and so far. Emotionally, there were scars as well, particularly those left by the unrequited love she felt for Hans Lipps that would take a long time to heal.

Nothing in her realm of experience, however, was sufficient enough to prepare her for the horrors of World War I that she experienced up close and first-hand. Fiercely patriotic and eager to do her part for Germany, Edith quit her studies in the spring of 1915 and volunteered as a Red Cross nursing sister. To the horror of her family – and under violent but futile protest from Frau Stein – Edith completed her basic medical training and was sent to a lazaretto (infectious disease hospital) in what today is Hranice, The Czech Republic.

While she had been a devoted and diligent nurse to ailing cousins, nieces and nephews at home, the worst ailments there were an infinitely better sight than the diseased and shattered men that poured into her ward from Galicia on the Eastern Front. Dressing ghastly wounds, gently tending delirious and dying typhoid victims and bathing filthy soldiers who hadn't seen soap and water for up to months at a time, Edith calmly tended the victims of the wholesale human destruction that was to characterize the new century.

Though warned that 'reputations' as well as cholera generally followed women who tended wounded soldiers in army hospitals, Edith performed her services splendidly with a maternal solicitude and tenderness that was remarked upon by all who observed her. Her nursing duty was completely devoid of any hint of romance and glamour, and after six months of non-stop, backbreaking work among the dead and the dying, a burnt-out Edith requested permission for a discharge from Red Cross service.

Reinach's Death and Questions of Faith

Returning to Göttingen, where she finished the thesis she was preparing to defend in Freiburg, Edith quickly resumed the pace of her hectic academic life with a sense of relief as well as duty. Beginning in 1916, with the war still raging on both fronts, Edith went to Freiburg to assume her duties as assistant to Husserl. It was an enviable position but a thankless task. What awaited Edith was not an intimate partnership with the Master, a collaboration of minds in which hers would eventually be allowed to shine, but something of a titanic house cleaning job.

Edith's main chore as Husserl's assistant was to sort out the thousands, if not tens of thousands, of notes, manuscripts and various bits of scribblings written by the Master and to put them into some form of coherent and printable order. For a man like Husserl, whose staccato, rapid-fire thought exploded like fireworks across countless reams of paper in Gabelsberger shorthand, clerical organization and discipline was an entirely foreign concept.

With her dauntless discipline and brisk efficiency, however, Edith proved equal to the monumental challenge and she actually succeeded in bringing order to Husserl's vast yet chaotic *oeuvre*. So well was the task accomplished that the collection of Husserl's papers in the University of Louvain in Belgium, one of the greatest repositories of philosophical thought in Western Europe, is largely due to the silent yet invaluable work of Edith Stein.

While the job of assistant proved infinitely beneficial to the Master, for Edith it soon became a monotonous, interminable task that did not bode well for her own future. It was a sort of professional malaise that was compounded by yet another and this time truly terrible, blow for Edith and the philosophical world as a whole. Adolf Reinach, the gentle philosopher who had always been such an inspiration and a support, was killed in Flanders in November

1917. Having been baptized a Christian the previous year with his wife – who was ultimately to enter the Catholic Church – Reinach had come to represent for Edith so much that was good and true and possible in the world of philosophy. His death shook Edith deeply and, having been asked by Anna to come and help organize her husband's papers, it was with fear and uncertainty that she went to visit his widow.

Expecting to see a shattered and broken woman bathed in grief and unable to go on with life, Edith was awestruck to find exactly the opposite when she encountered Anna. Though she felt the loss of her beloved husband to her core, Frau Reinach exuded a peace and joy that amazed and unsettled Edith in a way she remembered until her death. In the gaping hole of sorrow opened up by Adolf's death, Anna Reinach felt an inflow of certainty that her husband was alive in Christ, at peace and awaiting reunion in eternity. At a loss for words since her atheistic beliefs did not embrace the possibility of life after death, Edith found *herself* consoled by the bereaved woman.

For Edith, the death of Reinach pointed out a deeper reality in her life that had been increasingly gnawing at her for some time past. Namely, that her days as a rational, dispassionate atheist were coming to a close. Edith was always aware that so many of her Gottingen circle of friends were Christian, but up until now she indifferently respected their faith rather than sought its source.

The Reinachs, the Conrad-Martius', Max Scheler, even the Master himself, were all living lives of faith of varying denominations and intensity. The unifying factor in their lives, however, was that their philosophical endeavors had led them to a divine presence, sustaining and guiding humanity and indeed the universe, Who was the source of all reality and experience. For Edith, who had dismissed, or rather seconded, the possibility of God's existence in favor of her own considerable intellectual powers, faith began not so much as a thunderbolt but as delicate flames flickering in the periphery of her vision.

Reinach's death and the peaceful sense of joy and hope manifested by his widow began to bring faith closer to the center of her vision, and in sharper focus. Edith was struck by the overpowering sense of Christ and the power of his Cross that was so strong it literally bridged the infinite chasm of darkness and pain that separated the living from the dead. The Cross, therefore, as it appeared in Edith's life for the first time, represented not agony and wretchedness, but an immense and ineffable love.

"At that moment my unbelief was utterly crushed," Edith wrote of the experience years later. "Judaism paled before my eyes, and the light of Christ poured into my heart – the light of Christ in the mystery of the Cross."[14]

Despite the fact that the seeds of belief had been planted in her soul, Edith still had a long and arduous journey ahead of her before she would come to freely embrace Christ in the waters of Baptism. Increasingly curious and open to questions of faith and spirituality as never before, Edith still remained headstrong and obstinate in her methodology of acquiring and processing knowledge. She knew no half-measures in any facet of her life, and if she were to accept Christianity it would have to be an unequivocal and total immersion into a wholly other Being who would reveal to Edith her true self and the mystery of her existence.

While she struggled to find her professional way in the academic world, Edith began to quietly live life of faith in a sort of twilight world; neither fully denying nor fully accepting but observing the movement of belief in those closest to her. Max Scheler, with his merry-go-round relationship with the Catholic faith he would ultimately and permanently leave, was brilliant but too mercurial to give Edith a solid example to follow. Husserl, devout Bible-reading Lutheran though he was, was using a totally rational approach in regards to the question of God's existence in his writings that failed to ignite in Edith the sparks of passion she needed at this time. He was, as it were, trying to find God without God's help.

Reinach probably came closest to Edith's own single-minded and devoted ideal of the pursuit of God as objective Truth. In his writings, Reinach seemed to grasp the concept that acceptance of

---

[14] Spiritu Sancto, ODC, *Edith Stein*, p. 59.

Christ is not a qualifying act, done partially and with certain conditions, but an embrace followed by a consummation of love. "When we call Jesus' teaching beautiful," Reinach wrote, "when we laud and magnify His doctrines, we do so absolutely."[15]

With Reinach dead, a key example and major source of inspiration for the spiritual path that was slowly emerging from the fog of Edith's disbelief was her dear friend Hedwig Conrad-Martius, the progressive Lutheran wife of Theodore Conrad and a brilliant philosopher in her own right. In 'Hatti' Edith found a soul companion, who not only understood the uncertainties and fears of this seminal spiritual period of her life, but could also counsel and advise her on the right directions in which to go. In fact, for some time Edith considered joining her friend in the Lutheran faith. A deep and abiding restlessness and sense of being unfulfilled, however, prevented her from settling neatly into any niches just yet.

Edith's whole life, as has been stated repeatedly, was a search for truth. Increasingly consumed with finding answers to questions that arose not only from her studies but from the pain, suffering and sense of purposelessness all around her, Edith's journey allowed for no sham or artifice.

Her answers had to be as genuine as the nature of her questions, and if her intellect and soul did not move in tandem towards the goal, her search for truth would be reduced to a dry and futile academic problem. Without that unity of mind and soul, belief in God would not take root in Edith's heart. In his book *Edith Stein*, Jean de Fabregues said "man's existence is a unity; and Edith threw herself into the quest for the whole man."[16]

Husserl's Restless Assistant

Edith's role as 'intellectual housekeeper' for Husserl took on the unwanted dimension of nursemaid as well, and it was not long

[15] John M. Oesterreicher, *Walls Are Crumbling: Seven Jewish Philosophers Discover Christ* (New York: Devin-Adair Co., 1952), p. 131.

[16] Jean de Fabregues, *Edith Stein: Philosopher, Carmelite Nun, Holocaust Martyr* (Boston: St. Paul Books, 1993), p. 31.

before the association began to wear thin. After nursing the Master through a serious bout with influenza during the deadly outbreak in 1918, Edith decided to leave Freiburg and return to Göttingen, where she hoped to receive habilitation as a professor in the university. Though Husserl wrote Edith a sincerely glowing recommendation, it was not enough to overturn deep rooted traditions that held out against female habilitation and anything that would "unseat" psychology as it was traditionally taught at the University.[17]

Göttingen denied Edith the post of professor; in fact they ignored her application and refused to even look at her thesis. Once again a heavy blow fell on Edith, this one made worse by the fact it was so unnecessary to deny her access to a profession for which she was obviously more than qualified. Instead of receiving habilitation in Göttingen, Edith returned to Freiburg where she once again assisted Husserl while concentrating on her own philosophic writings as well. One of these papers, dealing with phenomena of the psyche such as fatigue and vitality, ended up being published in Husserl's philosophical and phenomenological yearbook; quite a prestigious honor for the young doctor.

In an examination of the phenomenon of vitality, Edith describes what she calls a "state of resting in God, a complete relaxation of all mental effort, when no one longer makes any plans or decisions, where one no longer acts but abandons all the future to the Divine Will."[18] In going on to describe a quieting of the discursive powers and a passivity of the will as a child-like repose in the arms of God, Edith came extraordinarily close to a near-perfect description of the mystical experience of God.

The fact that Edith, who up until a short time before was a confirmed atheist, was using language suspiciously approximating Saint John of the Cross' image of the soul as a "still house' and a nursing baby, shows how receptive she was becoming to the working of grace in her life.

[17] Stein, *Self-Portrait in Letters*, p. 35-36.
[18] Waltraud Herbstrith, *Edith Stein: A Biography*, translated by Father Bernard Bonowitz, OCSO (San Francisco: Harper & Row, 1985), p. 26-27.

While navigating an interior sea of thoughts, emotions and experiences resulting from her gradual spiritual awakening, Edith outwardly continued to pursue her academic career and lend her invaluable assistance to the Master. While renewing her commitment to sort and organize Husserl's papers, Edith initiated a course that would give students an introduction to phenomenology rather than going headfirst into it as she had.

It was a brilliant and even solicitous gesture on her part that demonstrated a genuine sense of concern for young students following the same intellectual path that she had. It was, like assisting Husserl, more rewarding though for the person on the receiving end rather than Edith, and asked if it was true that she was conducting philosophical seminars Edith good-naturedly replied "No, I am running a philosophical kindergarten."[19]

In her private life Edith continued to be active and found excursion, picnics and hiking trips to be good ways of letting the intellectual steam out of her head. Despite the intensity and natural reserve of her personality, Edith was far from a glum, asocial egghead interested in books and theories. She retained her deep love of nature, and she would regularly accompany her friends on mountain hikes and impromptu getaways. Edith had an eye for natural beauty as well as intellectual beauty, and friends recalled her exultation over a field of flowers, butterflies in the sunshine and even the thrill of being able to see the lights of Basel in a valley below while tucked into the bed of a mountain hotel.

While Germany – which had been defeated by the Allies in 1918 – fell into postwar chaos, civil war and ultimately a debilitating depression, Edith even found reasons for great celebrations at her home in Breslau. Her sister Erna, now a doctor, had fallen in love with her fellow medical student Hans Biberstein and was married to him in 1920. It was a wonderful event that was celebrated with much happiness by the Stein family, and Edith even composed commemorative poems to mark the happy day.

---

[19] Spiritu Sancto, ODC, *Edith Stein*, p. 60.

Though restless and unsure of where her academic career was
going, Edith's actions and persona conveyed the image of a person
who was calm, centered and in no way disposed to frantically chas-
ing spiritual rabbits that happened to pass her way. She was, as it
were, herself, but with her true self about to be revealed.

Faith

Edith never completely revealed the details of her conversion experience. Indeed, when once asked for full disclosure on the how and
why of her receiving the gift of faith, Edith simply quoted the
prophet Isaiah: "secretum meum mihi" ("my secret is my own".)
As Edith's quiet and intense personality were often mistaken for
aloofness and iciness, so can this remark be mistaken for reticence.

On the contrary, it only goes to show the tremendous spiritual
force behind the process of Edith's conversion. God did not speak
to Edith in the higher part of her intellect, where she could rationally deal with thoughts, experiences and ideas.

One would think that a woman of Edith's awesome intellect would
discover the truth of faith in lofty philosophical tomes written by the
great minds of the Church; Augustine, Aquinas and the towering
intellects of the Patristic Age. That would presume, however, to know
the workings of the Holy Spirit who blows where He will.

In speaking to Edith's heart, God spoke to the most hidden
recesses of her soul using a language unfathomable to anyone but
the object of His love. These words of love were not whispered in
the active, higher part of the intellect and will where Edith was so
firmly in control, but in the passive quietude of the soul in that
state of complete repose which she struggled to articulate in her
study of vitality and fatigue. Hence, the word 'secret' is used not
secretively, but by default since no words can adequately explain her
experience of God.

What we do we know about Edith's conversion comes from details
supplied by Edith herself. Her dear friends Conrad and Hedwig
Conrad-Martius had a farm in Bergzabern in the Palatinate, where
Edith had a room set aside for permanent use. Attached to the

farm was an orchard where Edith would help pick and pack fruit not only for physical and mental relaxation, but to help defray the costs of her room and board with her friends.

In the summer of 1921, while staying alone at Bergzabern Edith found herself flipping through the Conrad-Martius' considerable collection of books. At random she picked out *The Life of Saint Teresa of Avila, Written by Herself*, the celebrated autobiography of the dynamic 16th century foundress, reformer and mystic of the Carmelite Order. In the course of one night Edith finished the entire book. As the first rays of light dawned on the farm, Edith finally put the book down and exclaimed, "This is the Truth!"[20]

Grace builds on nature, and the laws of nature dictate that a closed or filled vessel cannot receive anything. From the intensity and the permanence of Edith's experience of grace, we can gather that it was simply not a reaction to or a running from or even an explanation of the disappointments and lack of fulfillment in her life. Like Teresa, Edith's acknowledgement and ultimate embrace of the Cross was indeed a open wound, but far from an object of pointless pain and suffering, the wound would be a point of inflow of the love of Christ crucified that is both mysterious and without end.

Whatever transpired between Edith and the Holy Spirit was so powerful that her first action of the new day was to go to town and buy a Catholic catechism and missal. Devouring the catechism and missal with the verve and determination she had applied to her phenomenological studies, Edith soon felt confident enough to attend her first Mass, there in Bergzabern. Feeling completely at home and at ease, she followed the liturgy without losing the rhythm or order of the service.

After Mass she went into the sacristy and asked the priest – whom she remembered as a kindly – faced old man – for the Sacrament of Baptism. When asked how long she had been receiving instruction Edith responded "please Father, test my knowledge."

---

[20] Graef, *Edith Stein*, p. 32.

Amazed at her lucid grasp of the Catholic faith, the priest agreed and began making the formal preparations for her baptism.[21]

With her dear friend Hedwig Conrad-Martius standing as her godmother, Edith Stein was baptized a Catholic on January 1, 1922. It was what in the pre-conciliar Church calendar was called the Feast of the Circumcision, the first shedding of Christ's blood. For Edith, who was to lose her life in the Shoah twenty years later, the date of her spiritual birthday was as portentous as her human birthday on the Day of Atonement. A month later Edith was confirmed by the Bishop of Speyer in his private chapel in the Cathedral.

Though her baptism had brought about a marked change in Edith, who seemed to her friend Hedwig radiantly happy, there was a large and painful obstacle that needed to be surmounted before the young convert could begin honestly living her faith. Edith knew that she needed to tell her beloved mother about her Baptism and reception into the Catholic Church. She knew that her mother needed to be informed in person rather than through the cold formality of a letter. She also knew that the news was going to shatter the old woman she loved so tenderly.

Returning to Breslau, Edith summoned all the courage and moral fortitude of her being, and knelt before Frau Stein.

"Mother, " Edith quietly said, "I am a Catholic."

While it is not entirely clear how the ensuing scene unfolded – doubt has been cast on the oft-told story that both mother and daughter broke down and silently wept together – it must have been a painful and heart-wrenching moment for the two women.

Frau Stein was in no manner Jewish in name or cultural identification only; on the contrary, her faith ran to the very core of her being. Auguste Stein was a deeply religious woman of genuine spiritual convictions, and the practice of her Jewish faith was an expression of her trust in the God of Abraham, Isaac and Jacob as well as identification with the chosen people Israel.

While not seeing it as betrayal, *per se*, Frau Stein saw Edith's conversion as an incomprehensible leap into an unfathomable

---

[21] Ibid., p. 65.

world infinitely removed from her sphere of experience. Her youngest daughter was an exceptionally brilliant and rational woman with a promising future in the concrete world of education and philosophy. Her embrace of a faith that the Stein family saw as comprised of mysterious rituals, a powerful hierarchy and superstitious peasants seemed to them a monumental leap backwards. Frau Stein's feelings toward her daughter's conversion were complex and, while Edith trod as soft a spiritual path as possible around her mother, the unbreakable bond of love between them would be forever edged with an unspoken yet heart-rending pain.

The pain, however, was not without paradox, and in a mysterious way, the separation of faith between Edith and her mother actually brought them closer together in prayer. Whenever home in Breslau, Edith as always accompanied her mother to the synagogue on the Sabbath and all Holy Days. Presenting what must have been a singularly curious sight, Edith would sit and pray the Psalms in Latin from her breviary while the cantor intoned them in Hebrew.

"When she went with her mother to the synagogue – impossible for a Christian at that time – Edith Stein broke with an old taboo in Catholicism," says Sister Waltraud Herbstrith. "Edith Stein was a very modern person in this respect, a very ecumenical person. She was a prophet and such a personality that her baptism did not distract her from her Jewish origins."[22]

Even in her tremendous agony of heart and confusion over Edith's baptism, her mother was genuinely amazed by the prayer of a daughter who just a year before had been a confirmed atheist. "I have never seen such prayer as Edith's!" the astonished Frau Stein said to a friend after several visits to the synagogue together.[23]

Edith had found Truth, but far from being a culmination her discovery was more of a catalytic agent that was constantly drawing her deeper into the heart of the source. The immediate means through which God called Edith to Himself in His Trinitarian life was the writings of Saint Teresa of Avila. Teresa's audacity, determination

---

[22] Interview with Sister Waltraud Herbstrith (see 7).
[23] Spiritu Sancto, ODC, *Edith Stein*, p. 67.

and dynamic mixture of faith and common sense helped ignite torches in Edith's mind and heart, and her life and lifestyle appealed greatly to the energetic young convert. To be enmeshed in the fullness of the world's reality and problems as Teresa had been, to be keenly aware of the vicissitudes and subtle shadings of the human condition, and yet remain hidden with God in prayer and contemplation was to Edith the highest possible idea of fulfillment. Almost from the earliest days following her conversion, Edith expressed a deep desire for the religious life in which she felt she could best serve God.

Her sails full of wind and her heart aflame with a convert's zeal, Edith was nevertheless also in need of a wise and moderate guiding hand. Her spiritual director was Canon Schwind of the Diocese of Speyer, a very holy yet very practical priest who was to play an integral role in Edith's growth and maturation as a Catholic. The Canon, aware that Edith's intellectual gifts needed cultivating as much as her fervor needed direction, counseled prudence and told her to remain in the world.

The defeat of Imperial Germany and the devastation of Europe in World War I had resulted in more than just economic depression and a wounded national pride. The systems, the philosophies, the power structures and the very beliefs that had governed Europe for centuries had literally vanished in the first salvo of the Guns of August. Social revolution, the eradication of numerous monarchies and the capability of mass destruction utilizing technological advances were some of the changes resulting from the severed bloodline with the old world.

The disenchantment and the disorientation that followed the Great War created a void that was filled with chaotic expressions of confusion and terror in every facet of human existence. Music, painting literature, were but a few of those facets that conveyed the sense of a lost people wandering through a ruined wasteland.

Canon Schwind, appreciating the depths of Edith's mind, told her that lay Catholic intellectuals were desperately needed to counteract the waves of pessimism and doubt that were washing over the shattered remains of European civilization. While good people were sorely needed behind convent and monastery walls, they were needed just as badly in the midst of the world when God had given them particular talents to use in His service.

Respecting Edith's desires for a more contemplative atmosphere while remaining in the world, Canon Schwind arranged for her to live with the Dominican Sisters of Saint Magdalena in Speyer. These sisters, who ran a convent school for girls, had recently lost several of their number when they opened a daughter house. An instructor in the teaching school was desperately needed and, in exchange for room and board, Edith could live in the prayerful silence of the convent and keep the horarium – or prayer schedule – with the sisters.

This was a rare accommodation that in normal circumstances probably would not have been granted to a laywoman so recently converted to Catholicism. As Edith's spiritual father, however, Canon Schwind had a fairly lucid grasp of her spirituality and sensed in her a genuine call to a life of action and contemplation that she could best find at Saint Magdalena. Although Edith was now ensconced with the Dominicans with their rich legacy of academic and intellectual excellence, she was probably a better model of the Benedictines, whose motto of 'Ora et Labora' ('Work and Prayer') she came to embody so well. Taking a sparsely furnished room, eating her meals with the nuns and living a life of material simplicity, Edith was, for all intents and purposes, living the life of a vowed religious.

The most extraordinary feature about Edith's life at this time, however, was neither the silence nor the simplicity but the intensity of her deepening life of prayer. Taking literally the words of Jesus and the Apostles to pray constantly, she became absorbed into a deep and rhythmic spiritual communion with God that no exterior force could disturb.

Edith would pray, sometimes for hours at a time, kneeling perfectly still before the Tabernacle in the convent church. Often she would pass entire nights in silent prayer and, despite her regular fasts and habit of sleeping just a few hours a night, would be the first person in choir for morning prayer. Her desire for solitary, undisturbed communion with God was so respected by the Sisters that they even allowed her to place a chair off to the side of the Altar, hidden from the community as well as the congregation, in the sanctuary of the church. There, tucked away behind a column, Edith could sit or kneel for hours either absorbed in the Mass or private prayer.

Far from being lost in an ethereal realm of mystical prayer, Edith was slowly being drawn closer to those around her through a greater awareness of and participation in the Church's cycle of prayer and liturgy. Most of all, Edith loved the Eucharist. From the first Mass she attended in Bergzabern, it was as though the beauty and essence of the Eucharist was revealed to her and locked deep into her heart. While faithful to her vocal and mental prayer, it was ultimately the Eucharist that would come to form the center of Edith's life.

For Edith, the Eucharist was not a liturgical obligation to which she had to be obedient and faithful. On the contrary, the Eucharist represented a sacred mystery that was central to the life of the Church in a way that transcended liturgy. In becoming personally present on the Altar under the species of bread and wine, Jesus suspends the laws of time and space in a way beyond far beyond the power of mortals to grasp. The immensity of that mystery contains the immensity of love manifested by Jesus' sacrifice on Calvary, and His presence on the Altar nourishes not only those who receive Him but all of creation.

"This is where the life of the Church begins," Edith would later write. "The things that serve to sustain human life are fundamentally transformed, and the people who partake of them in faith are transformed too, drawn into the unity of life with Christ and filled with His divine life."[24]

St Magdalena's

Even though Edith was living a quiet life of prayer and recollection, she was not a wraith-like recluse who stalked the shadowy corridors

---

[24] Edith Stein, *The Hidden Life: hagiographic essays, meditations, spiritual texts*, edited by L. Gelber and Michael Linssen, translated by Waltraut Stein, (Washington, D.C.: ICS Publications, 1992) p. 8.

of a convent cloister. Though respecting their boundaries, Edith interacted daily with the Sisters, the students and the outside world, even going so far as giving classes to the postulants and helping out with household chores around the convent. She also continued with her phenomenal output of letters, corresponding regularly with old friends, family and numerous religious and laity throughout Germany.

Edith also maintained an active apostolate to all those in need of material help, and she was known to be extremely generous to the poor and the underprivileged. Although she asked a salary that would just cover her needs, any extra she had would be given away to the poor and Christmastime would find her room stacked with presents she had bought and hand-wrapped for distribution to needy families. While deeply spiritual, Edith's life was not one of private religious theatrics but a constant self-offering enriched by love of God and a practical concern for her neighbor.

Edith's primary function at Saint Magdalena's, however, was to teach. As an instructor in the secondary school for future teachers, Edith presented a remarkable if initially curious picture to her students. Completely at ease, unruffled and in total control in the classroom, she brought to the classrooms of the school a level, a standard of excellence, to which many of the girls had not been held. Edith had not matriculated at the normal schools that prepared teachers for their careers. On the contrary, she came from the intense, rarified academic atmospheres of Göttingen, Breslau and Freiburg where she had already made quite a name for herself in philosophical circles. Teaching young women full of energy and fun necessitated something of a re-orientation, a restructuring of her whole teaching methodology.

It was difficult at first, and to many students Fräulein Doktor Stein was an intimidating, remote and unapproachable figure. Edith held the girls to university standards in their schoolwork and behavior, and since she tolerated no mediocrity in herself she expected the same from them. If it was difficult for the girls at the beginning of their school year it was because it was difficult for Edith at the beginning of her life of faith. Despite the intensity and depths of her religious beliefs, she was still trying to wholeheartedly respond to the grace at work in her soul and translate that grace into a pragmatic application to her everyday life.

While she had not completely shut out the world, Edith was struggling to find a way to integrate love of God with immersion in worldly activity. To those who did not understand this, Fräulein Doktor was a perfect, brilliant but remote teacher who kept to herself and prayed for hours in the dark corners of the church.

Though the girls found Edith a bit cool and unapproachable in the beginning, her reserve and discretion was never mistaken for disinterest. She demonstrated to the girls from the start her concern and care for them as well as a personal investment in their future as Christian professionals. Having been so firmly enmeshed in the philosophy of thought and education during her undergraduate and post-graduate studies, Edith now was face to face with the means by which pedagogic cause and effect could be experienced directly.

No longer studying these problems from a phenomenological standpoint, Edith was now conveying knowledge by the light of faith and in the shadow of the Cross. Like a priest at the Altar, Edith saw the teacher as an *alter Christus* – other Christ – who needed to truly embody His spirit if they were to impart wisdom and truth. While those who taught needed to be doctrinally sound, they also needed to be cognizant of the new sociopolitical dynamics of the new and violent century of which the girls had already seen too much.

"The younger generation of today has passed through so many crises that they cannot understand us any more," Edith wrote to a nun during her time at Speyer. "But we must try to understand them, and then perhaps we shall be able to help them a little more."[25]

Forty years before the term became popular, Edith was prophesying that a 'generation gap' was going to alienate disillusioned youth from parents seen as warmongers and spoilers. The older generation did not need to simply 'hold on' to youth, but needed to close the gap as well. The only way to do that was with love.

---

[25] Stein, *Self-Portrait in Letters*, p. 123.

To this end, Edith desired not only to understand the problems, needs and anxieties of the young women, but to demonstrate a pragmatic, genuine sense of empathy and common courtesy as well. When permissible, she joined in their outings, their jokes and their celebrations. Her door was always open to any of the girls who needed academic advice or just a sympathetic ear, and soon Edith was respected as a friend and confidante by a great number of students. Despite the exhausting pace of her teaching schedule and the demand her extracurricular activities made upon her prayer life, the years at Saint Magdalena rolled peacefully and fruitfully along.

Catholic Scholar

In 1925, Edith was introduced to Father Erich Przywara, a prominent Jesuit author and theologian with whom she would work and correspond for the next several years. Father Przywara was in the process of translating into German the complete works of England's Cardinal John Henry Newman and, knowing of Edith's scholarly reputation – as well as her command of English – asked her to contribute to the massive project.

The story of Newman (1801-1890), the nineteenth century Anglican Tractarian and member of the Oxford Movement whose study of Patristics and history helped to lead him into the Catholic Church, was a journey of faith close to Edith's own heart. Newman, like Edith, was a brilliant intellectual whose conversion brought about a considerable amount of controversy in university circles but was destined to be a great and leading light in his nation's spiritual history. Like Edith, the catalyst for Newman's conversion was not lofty debate and disputation, but spiritual truths whispered through solitary individuals of great personal sanctity: for Edith it was Saint Teresa of Avila, for Newman it was an Italian Passionist priest, Blessed Dominic Barberi.

Appropriately, Edith's translation of Newman's *Letters and Journals: 1801-1845* was followed by his classic *The Idea of a University*, which in turn was followed by Edith's serious introduction to a figure of even more magnitude in secular as well as sacred history.

Edith's commendable translation of Newman's work led Father Przywara to ask her to undertake a translation of the works of Saint Thomas Aquinas. For a Phenomenologist such as Edith Stein, delving headfirst into the unity of faith and reason that was the hallmark of Scholastic philosophy was a brave undertaking indeed. Still finding her way as a newly baptized Catholic, Edith now had to reverse her intellectual direction and proceed down an entirely different route that relied on faith as opposed to direct observation of 'phenomena'. Instead of investigating subjects like 'empathy' and 'exhiliration' she now began exploring the nature of angels and the ordering of the will.

The work recommended by Father Przywara was Saint Thomas Aquinas' *Quaestiones Disputatae de Veritate (Disputed Questions on Truth)*, the Angelic Doctor's introduction to Scholastic Philosophy. The translation was demanding in terms of time as well as in terms of re-ordering Edith's well-honed mind to an entirely faith-based school of thought. While Saint Thomas borrowed much from the great philosophers of the Christian as well as Pagan eras (truth, according to Saint Thomas, was truth regardless of who it is that speaks it) but rooted his ideas in key words like beauty and love in regards to knowledge of God. God is love, and that love cannot be grasped or fathomed without the cooperation of the soul with the workings of grace. The natural inclination of the soul, therefore, is to seek the happiness which can only be found through, with and in God.

For Edith, the translation of Saint Thomas' Quaestiones was not only an enriching mental exercise, but it reinforced the power of God's grace in her own search that had led her through so much darkness before the light of faith illuminated her soul. While not perfect, Edith's translations received widespread recognition and even the most dogmatic philosophes of contemporary academia were awed that the work was the achievement of a Jewish woman recently converted to the Catholic faith.

In 1927 Canon Schwind, Edith's beloved and wise spiritual father, died of a stroke while hearing confessions in the Speyer cathedral. The blow was especially hard for Edith, not just because of a deep personal bond between them, but also because of the intense nature of Edith's life and the many directions in which she seemed to be going during this time. Aside from her teaching, writing, translating and ever-deepening spiritual life, there was still the question of a vocation to the religious life that had relentlessly pursued Edith from her baptism.

It was going to take a hand as firm and wise and loving as Canon Schwind's, but stronger, given the crossroads that Edith seemed to be rapidly approaching. At Father Przywara's suggestions, Edith visited one of Germany's most famous abbeys where such a person was apparently in waiting.

Beuronese Idyll

The Benedictine abbey of Beuron is home to one of the greatest liturgical traditions in Europe. The Benedictines have always been great leaders in the area of liturgy and liturgical renewal, and at the magnificent abbey worship was simply one of many threads of a richly textured spiritual tapestry. Aside from the liturgy, Beuron was also home to a relatively new fresco and mural style that would be exported to Benedictine abbeys around the world; a highly colored meld of Byzantine, Egyptian and Art Deco form that bore the abbey's name.

Presiding over the community during Edith's time was the abbey's energetic and prayerful young abbot, Dom Raphael Walzer OSB. A personal friend of Father Przywara's, Dom Raphael and Edith hit it off immediately and soon the abbot was Edith's new spiritual father and a worthy successor of Canon Schwind. Despite being a key center in the liturgical revival movement, Beuron represented for Edith more than merely a forum in which to hold forth on the subjects of private piety and communal worship. At the abbey, Edith was able to lose herself totally in an environment of contemplative prayer with like-minded individuals who saw God's praise – not teaching or missionary activity – as their primary purpose.

Edith's time at Beuron brought her further down a road of balance, of integration of private prayer with a communal celebration with strangers united in the bond of faith. While Edith had always taken the fruit of her prayer and contemplation to all those she encountered, Beuron gave her the opportunity to truly experience faith as an act of worship on a wider scale and thereby allowed her a more honest vision of the Church as a whole people.

The abbey of Beuron was for Edith "the silent corner where she could draw breath. It was there that the substance of her being came most clearly into the light."[26]

Going to the abbey for retreats, holy days and private spiritual direction with Dom Raphael, Edith soon became a much-loved figure among the monks and the local townsfolk with whom she lodged during her time there. Like she did at Saint Magdalena's, Edith fasted, prayed with the community and spent long hours in front of the Tabernacle speaking silently to God. What was different was that Beuron was Edith's desert, a place of retreat and solitude to which she could withdraw for spiritual refreshment and renewal. Unlike many people who walk gingerly and with uncertainty around monks and things monastic, Edith felt very much at home at Beuron and moved with ease around the community.

Whether she was praying alone, chanting the Liturgy of the Hours in choir with the monks or taking part in the Eucharist, Edith was totally present to the moment and so absorbed that she often mirrored the mood of the particular service. Lost in the painful journey of Christ to His passion and death during Holy Week, Edith was then observed to be almost radiant on Easter Sunday morning with a joy that continued to glow for weeks.

While the bond between Edith and Dom Raphael was deep and intensely spiritual, there was an area of his directee's life in which the abbot remained unmovable. Like Canon Schwind, Dom Raphael was convinced that God was calling Edith to service outside – not inside – the walls of a cloistered convent. Furthermore, the dynamic young abbot felt that it was time for Edith to end the recollected life with the sisters and schoolgirls of Saint Magdalena and take the

---

[26] Spiritu Sancto, ODC, *Edith Stein*, p. 85.

'good fight' more determinedly into the crucible of the modern world.

Edith's tremendous gifts as a lecturer, essayist and Catholic intellectual were at best seen by Dom Raphael as not being fully utilized and at worst as blazing lights hid under a bushel.

Adamantly refusing to give Edith permission to enter the religious life, the abbot encouraged her to step up her lecturing and writing activities in high-profile forums throughout the country. Edith was disappointed at being yet again held back from the cloister but, like her adopted patroness Saint Teresa of Avila, she obeyed the counsels of someone she trusted as a wise spiritual father.

Privately Edith felt much the same, having matured considerably in her ability to remain in God's presence while in the midst of frenetic worldly activity. It was a balancing act for which she no longer needed absolute silence and solitude; in fact she found she needed nothing more than a heart open to whatever and wherever God's will led her. After Christmas, 1930, Edith told the mother superior at Saint Magdalena's of her decision to leave Speyer at the end of the next term. Her decision was warmly supported by the superior but sadly regretted by a great number of the sisters and students who let Edith know how much she had meant to them and how sorely she would be missed.

Re-Engaging the World

As early as 1927, Edith had begun speaking throughout the Rhineland on lecture tours organized by Father Przywara. Her topic, the role of women in modern society, was a subject of vital concern for Catholic women as well as the Church and the immense, riveted crowds that Edith began to draw attested to the fact that she had her finger squarely on the pulse of the issue. During and after the time of World War One, women had gained socioeconomic footholds in previously male-dominated power structures that had begun to revolutionize their role in society.

The political upheaval caused by the Great War and its devastating aftermath – not to mention the massive drain of manpower from Germany's working and ruling classes – had allowed women to step more and more into new positions of authority and self determination. The question for Edith Stein was not how to continue the revolution, but to view it through the clarifying lens of the Catholic faith.

For Edith, the feminist philosopher turned Catholic intellectual, women could no longer be pigeonholed as either wife or mother no more than they could be recast as a radically independent sociopolitical species disconnected from God or Man. As with every subject Edith tackled, the questions asked and the solutions offered were neither facile nor pat, but extremely complex ideas in want of great thought and reflection.

Having committed herself to re-engaging the world and confronting the problems of the modern Catholic woman, Edith sought a base of operations from where she could launch herself back into the mainstream. A whirlwind of activity soon arose in Edith's life as she struggled to choose the best of many professional roads that seemed to be opening up before her.

Before leaving Speyer, Edith applied for a lecturing position at the University of Freiburg. The director of the Institute for Educational Theory in Münster had offered Edith the position of lecturer on the subject of women's education and a prominent Catholic theologian pushed her to apply for a lectureship at the University of Breslau. While any of these positions would have had a distinguishing effect on her career, in the end both Freiburg and Breslau came to dead ends and Edith accepted the Münster post in 1932.

Whether or not the dead ends were due to either her gender or her Jewish heritage cannot be accurately determined but more or less guessed at. However, with the Nazis still a year away from becoming the legal ruling party in Germany, the ugly head of anti-Semitism was quietly but steadily being raised once again in the land.

Indeed, far from separating herself *in toto* from her Jewish faith and heritage, Edith continued to identify with God's chosen people and their common journey of belief through history. Her embrace of Christianity and belief in Jesus as the Messiah may have hurt and confused a great number of individuals precious to Edith, but in bound her in spirit ever closer to the Jewish people as a whole, as a nation consecrated to God.

While in Paris for a conference entitled *Phenomenology and Thomism*, Edith went out walking with philosopher acquaintance from her Göttingen days Professor Alexander Koyré. On top of Montmartre, whenever the subject of Jewish philosophers was broached, Edith inevitably referred to them as "one of our people."[27]

Although Edith Stein had been publicly speaking on the role of Catholic women since 1927, it was after her well-received 1930 lecture *The Ethos of Women's Professions* – given at Salzburg, Austria – that she really began to focus her attention more clearly on the wider and deeper implications of her subject.

Speaking about the problems and questions of women in contemporary life, Edith was not simply presenting lists of do's and don'ts as though she was presiding over some Catholic finishing school for girls. On the contrary, she dove into the heart of the matter, tunneling and digging into the essence of woman, her nature and identity vis a vis God and her fellow species Man. Although by today's standards she could be seen as startlingly conservative in certain areas of the woman's role and vocation, in other areas Edith displayed a surprisingly progressive, almost prophetic acumen in grasping the problem and offering a solution.

Basic to her philosophy of Woman is that she is, in the final analysis, biologically, psychologically and spiritually different from Man. That difference translates into a difference of ability to perform the fundamental functions that sustain and nurture life. Women are created by God to re-create life, and therefore they are life-givers by their very nature. This, however, does not relegate women to a second-class status of breeding machines. On the contrary, this role of life-giver and life-nurturer raises them up to not only a prominent position in society but a co-redemptive position in God's plan for humanity.

For Edith, this role is not a nebulous vision, but is firmly anchored in the prototypical role of the Blessed Virgin. Mary, in

---

[27] Graef, *Edith Stein*, p. 73.

Edith's estimation, represents the purest ideal of Christian womanhood and, being a *Theotokos* (God-bearer), bears the solemn responsibility of shaping and preparing the God-Man for His ordained role as Redeemer of the world. As the Blessed Mother plays an integral role in the carrying and forming of Jesus inside and outside her womb, so do all women when they carry and form the children of the Church that is His Mystical Bride.

The following comes from her 1932 lecture *The Church, Woman and Youth*, in which she expanded on her concept of the connection between Mary and women. "Those women who wish to fulfill their feminine vocations in one of several ways will most surely succeed in their goals if they not only keep the Virgo-Mater before their eyes and strive to form themselves according to her image but if they also entrust themselves to her guidance and place themselves completely under her care. She herself can form in her own image those who belong to her."[28]

In the professional world, Edith saw the prevention of women from holding positions of authority and power in the male domain as sheer prejudice and ignorance. While created for the biological role of mother and companion, Edith saw nothing in natural or God's law that prevented women from competing in a previously all-male workplace if she possessed the skills and talents to do so. She did not, however, see the professional and economic equality of women from a Utopian standpoint divorced from the realities of the technological age in which she lived.

In joining the workforce and balancing career and family responsibilities, the modern woman runs the risk of burning herself out physically and spiritually, which leads to the jaded ennui that has washed over post-War European society. For Edith, not only is education and self-knowledge necessary for balance and preservation in the world, but, more important than these is a firm rooting in the Eucharist.

---

[28] Edith Stein, *Essays on Woman*, Second Edition Revised, Translated by Freda Mary Oben, Ph.D. (Washington, D.C.: ICS Publications, 1996), p. 241.

The modern Catholic woman must have the sacramental presence of Jesus at the core of her life and, if the Blessed Sacrament is not the point from which her life originates and to which it moves, she will lose her purpose, her way and ultimately her source of strength. "To have divine love as its inner form," Edith said in her 1930 address, *Ethos of Woman's Professions*, "a woman's life must be a Eucharistic life. Only in daily, confidential relationship with the Lord in the Tabernacle can one forget self, become free of all one's own wishes and pretensions, and have a heart open to all the needs and wants of others."[29]

In other areas, Edith is remarkably progressive for a female Catholic intellectual of her age, and the subjects she began to broach in her lectures often appear thirty to forty years ahead of their time. Edith felt, for instance, that Catholics were lagging far behind in the area of sex education for girls, and that a thorough re-evaluation of the issue was desperately needed if they intended Catholic women to meet the world's challenges with the proper intellectual and moral equipment. A genuinely Catholic approach to the subject of sex education was central to the development of the whole woman, Edith felt, and it needed to be grounded not only in doctrine but in an appreciation for human love as well as an understanding of consecrated celibacy.

On the more touchy, if not taboo, subject of women in ministry, Edith was similarly prophetic and truly Conciliar thirty years before the Second Vatican Council was called. With the drain of hundreds of thousands of men from all strata of German life following World War One, it was natural that the area of ministry would feel the depletion as much as the factory, the office and the shop. As she did in regards to women in the secular world, Edith believed that there could be no turning back the clock for the role of women in the Church.

Drawing on her considerable knowledge of Patristics, the Apostolic and the Sub-Apostolic ages, Edith cited the decidedly non-passive role of women in the liturgical and apostolic life of the early Church.

---

[29] Ibid., p. 56.

Deaconesses, consecrated virgins, martyrs and holy women of great faith were, according to Edith, actively engaged in liturgical and charitable services to their fellow Christians from the earliest days of the faith and displayed a participatory zeal that a whole new generation of women needed to emulate and re-define.

The stereotypical role of women in ministry, by which Edith meant passive pedagogues, needed to be replaced with the authentically traditional role of the proactive participant in the fields of scholarship, charitable works and pastoral care. Engaged in some form in all these fields and balancing them with a punishing lecture schedule and demanding professional life, Edith proved it was possible for a woman to be faithful to her feminine nature as well as the apostolic exhortations of the Gospels.

Despite her seemingly progressive stand on the role of women in ministry, the one area in which Edith remained staunchly dogmatic was in the exculsively male Catholic priesthood. In a daring intellectual move for her day, Edith did not dismiss the question of female ordination outright or bow meekly to the orthodox party line. On the contrary, she examined the question closely by the light of her conscience. At the close of her lecture entitled *The Vocation of Man and Woman According to Nature and Grace*, Edith weighs the pros and cons of the question of women's ordination. Declaring that nothing actually prevented the Church from taking a radical step in that direction, a certain logic does not support any belief that the Holy Spirit was moving the Church in that way. The answer for Edith ultimately lay in the person of Jesus Christ as High Priest and Victim.

"The whole tradition speaks *against* it from the beginning," she said in the lecture. "But in my opinion, even more significant is the mysterious fact emphasized earlier – that Christ came to earth as the *Son* of Man. The first creature on earth fashioned in an unrivaled sense as God's image was therefore a man; that seems to indicate to me that He wished to institute only men as His official representatives on earth."[30]

[30] Ibid., p. 84.

"incompetent for this world"

As she had while teaching in Speyer, Edith sought a suitably quiet and contemplative place in which she could live after taking the lecturing position in Münster. She took a room in the Collegium Marianum, a woman's residence run by the Sisters of Notre Dame, which allowed her to live in relative recollection and simplicity.

Though she maintained as always a warm, friendly and accessible persona toward the students and faculty alike, Edith was being led deeper into an interior stillness, a waiting upon God that on the surface seemed to take her far from worldly events and activities. To some extent this was true, but in a way that still kept her very much a part of daily life despite her ethos of living a simple but practical lifestyle. In appearance, Edith remained proper and immaculately groomed, though her plain, almost dowdy, handmade clothes were mended and re-mended to the point of despair.

Taking her meals with the Sisters, Edith was observed to avoid all meats and to eat and drink everything else in moderate portions. To no one's surprise, Edith was in the chapel before the Sisters in the morning and could usually be found there in silent prayer before the Tabernacle late into the night.

Edith maintained a much too punishing and active work schedule in the world to be accused of leading a reclusive and eremitical life. There is a wide and substantial line between active contemplation and self-serving escapism, and Edith never fell into the trap of confusing the one with the other. She did, however, occasionally stray a bit to the latter side, but was wise enough to not only notice the list but quickly put it right. While visiting Vienna for the first time during a lecturing tour, Edith shut herself in her room to review and correct her notes while totally ignoring the glories of one of Europe's most magnificent cities outside her window. Realizing that she had foolishly put blinders on when she could have enjoyed a day of rest and recreation, Edith asked her hosts to take her on a whirlwind tour of the city the day of her departure.

The fact was that, past forty and wearied from ten years of nonstop work in the exacting fields of pedagogy, translation, lecturing and writing as well as being continually denied permission to enter the religious life she so desired, Edith was mentally and physically tired.

While grateful for her position at Münster, she felt in her heart that she was on a path diverging from that of her colleagues and the field in general. Feeling that her profession had lost sight of the true nature of pedagogy and that she could no longer play along, Edith confided in a letter Hatti Conrad-Martius how professionally anachronistic she felt she had become. "Now that I am in constant contact with people who are totally caught up in their life's work," Edith wrote, "who have been educated for it with technical thoroughness and have grown up in it, I notice that, actually, I have lost connection with it on all sides, and am generally incompetent for this world."[31]

Instead of maundering about and pondering lost years and new directions, Edith proposed a new field of thought in which she would like to move. In the same letter, she tells Hatti of a new idea of metaphysics she is contemplating, theologically based grasp of reality based on "the inclusion of revealed truth." This movement is ample testimony of how much the phenomenologist had mastered Aquinas' thought: Edith was confident to the point where she hoped to break it open to get new kernels possibly hidden within.

Although resigned, as she told Hatti, to remain at her post as long as God willed it and to abandon herself entirely to His will, many burdens began to weigh Edith down. Aside from the professional dissatisfaction she felt, the religious tension with her family was in danger of increasing with a recent development known to her alone.

Edith's older sister Rosa, the serious, hardworking and devoted housekeeper for their elderly mother, had secretly embraced the Catholic faith as well after a long and hidden discernment process. Having discussed her conversion at length with her sister as well as priests and several close Catholic friends, it was decided that Rosa should postpone her Baptism, out of respect, until after her mother's

---

[31] Stein, *Self-Portrait in Letters*, p. 126.

death. Frau Stein's perceived inability to handle a second blow like this coupled with the secrecy with which Rosa had to practice her newly accepted faith was a silent burden of pain that bonded Edith with her quiet, devout sister.

Edith herself never moved from under the shadow of Mount Carmel, cast by the sunburst of Saint Teresa's autobiography which had helped move her to conversion almost ten years before. Despite her strong and intimate bonds with nuns of the Dominican and Benedictine orders – including friendships that would last her entire life – it was increasingly clear to Edith that it was the heights of Carmel she was being called to ascend.

Edith was reading more and more works by Carmelites and non-Carmelites that dealt with the history as well as the spirituality of the order, including works by her good friend Father Przywara and the novelist Gertrude von Le Fort, who was becoming a friend as well as a regular correspondent.

While, like her conversion, Edith could say in regards to her attraction towards Carmel that *"my secret is my own,"* certain patterns can be looked at in her life that help illuminate and clarify her choice of direction. While her prayer life was suffused with an air of deepening mysticism, it was clear that mystical prayer was not her attraction. While her life of simplicity and moderation in food, clothing and money approximated the poverty of Discalced nuns and friars, it was probably not this either that attracted her to Carmel.

The answer, if such a thing is possible, to why Edith sought the intense, contemplative solitude of Carmel was most likely – and paradoxically – other people. Edith astounded all who observed her with the ability to remain in prayer, motionless, for hours at a time, absorbed in Jesus's presence like a child at its mother's breast. Her silence and solitary life of prayer, work and study gave her the focus and energy needed to leave her room and engage the world and its problems at the highest intellectual levels. Like Saint John of the Cross' commentary on the *Ascent of Mount Carmel*, Edith was even able to achieve great capacities for knowledge, only to let it fall like dross as she reached higher for a God who is beyond limited human reason and concepts.

Technically speaking, Edith did not need a convent to live the
ideal of Carmel, and as a professional laywoman – and a very successful one at that – she could have easily continued at her own pace
to emulate Saint John and Saint Teresa while pursuing a career in
the world. What was missing for Edith, however, was other people.
For Edith, to try to seriously live the ideals of Carmel without the
help and support of other like-minded individuals on the same journey was like sailing a magnificently sleek boat without a compass.

"Edith Stein could not live alone, she was absolutely not a hermit," says Sister Waltraud Herbstrith. "Up to the conversion she
was very active and outgoing. After her conversion (Polish philosopher) Roman Ingarden said she was always in search of a community with people, with friends. Then, she writes that when she read
Teresa's book she felt she must live in the Carmel, she must live
with women who live like Teresa. That was her ideal. After this
she said yes to Baptism and converted."[32]

The 'yes' to Baptism was followed by a 'please' for the religious
life that continued for nearly ten years. Despite the continual
refusal of her spiritual fathers to allow her to enter Carmel, Edith
continued to obey in perfect love and obedience and return again
and again to the world. Like the psalmist, Edith's heart was ready,
and full to the point where nothing would be able to prevent her
from fulfilling its desire. By a set of strange circumstances, brought
about for the most part by the worsening political situation in
Germany, that desire was indeed about to be fulfilled.

The Dogs of Anti-Semitism

In his book *Tyranny on Trial*, Whitney R. Harris, a naval officer and
eyewitness to the Nuremburg Trials who helped prepare the case
against Gestapo and SD chief Ernst Kaltenbrunner, succinctly
summed up a primary goal of the Nazi hierarchy. "The elimination
of German Jewry – and of world Jewry – was fundamental to Hitler's
program and philosophy," wrote Lt. Commander Harris. "Jews

---

[32] Interview with Sister Waltraud Herbstrith (see 7).

were absolutely unacceptable in any state or empire ruled by Hitler. In his mind there was always the determination, when opportunity provided itself, to annihilate the Jews of Germany, and of Europe."[33] The persecution and ultimately the genocide of European Jewry was not a political backlash that snowballed with the growth of Hitler's blitzkrieg warfare on the continent. Nor was the Final Solution – the decision made in 1942 to systematically eliminate Jews from the continent using factory style means of liquidation – a horrific operation clandestinely executed beyond the Reich's frontiers without Hitler's knowledge.

As Lt. Commander Harris pointed out, elimination of the Jews was a fundamental tenet of Nazi philosophy. Hitler offered something of a blueprint for the Holocaust in his rambling, hate-filled autobiography *Mein Kampf* when he called the Jewish people the "true enemy" of civilization. Anti-Semitism was also written into the bylaws of the fledgling Nazi party program, when it declared that Jews could not be considered members of the German race. When Adolf Hitler assumed control of the nation as Reich Chancellor on January 30, 1933, Anti-Semitism became a twisted doctrine that was stealthily worked into the national consciousness.

With the military, political and judicial branches of the government working in tandem, the Nazis began a multi-phased operation intent on ridding Germany – and then Europe – of the hated Jewish race they considered to be the architects of the world's political, social and economic ills. Propaganda campaigns were followed by segregation, exclusion from positions of authority, confiscation of wealth and property and ultimately, outright persecution.

In less than ten years, with emigration both slow and costly and Hitler's war machine steamrolling unopposed across Europe, the Nazis no longer needed to hide their original intentions in regards to the 'Jewish Question.' By 1942, with the mechanisms of mass genocide nearly in place, Hitler began to make good on his evil

---

[33] Whitney R. Harris, *Tyranny on Trial: The Evidence at Nuremberg* (Dallas, TX: Southern Methodist University Press, 1954), p. 281.

threat against the Jews of Europe and by 1945 six million of them – including Edith Stein – would be murdered.

In 1933, Edith had felt the impact of the first wave of the Party's Anti-Semitic philosophy first hand. In that year the Jews of Germany were forbidden under Reich law to hold any position of authority or power, a decree that took in the field of politics, medicine, jurisprudence and education. Edith was therefore unable to remain in her teaching position in Münster or, for that matter, lecture or publish pedagogic works intended for the education of German youth. While her name was officially removed from the lecturing roster of the upcoming semester, Edith was promised by the Institute that she would be kept on the payroll for as long as possible.

While being a baptized Catholic offered her a buffer for a somewhat longer period of time, Edith was primarily a Jew and as such was considered liable to the laws and restrictions beginning to choke her Jewish brothers and sisters throughout the nation. Siblings, relations and friends of Edith began to be dismissed from various posts and their businesses reflected a marked decline in sales and patronage. Among those affected were her sister Erna Biberstein and her husband Hans, both well-respected doctors, who would ultimately be forced to flee to the United States where, despite many hardships, heartbreaks and setbacks, they managed to re-establish their practices.

Edith had no illusions regarding the rising tide of Anti-Semitism in Germany and she looked for ways in which she could use her voice to call attention to the plight of Jews in the Third Reich. Edith was intelligent enough to know that the injustices, the harsh legislation and the increasingly open violence against the Jews were not merely reactionary paroxysms of a humiliated German people scrambling for socioeconomic scapegoats. The Anti-Semitism was not simply going to peak and then quietly trickle off into grumbling indifference.

Edith obviously saw beyond the present events and rightly recognized them as the opening acts of a more horrific drama yet to unfold. In the spring of 1933, she wrote to Pope Pius XI in Rome expressing her hope to personally apprise him of the increasingly ominous situation in Germany. Going through local ecclesiastical channels, Edith was told that while a private audience was impossible, she had a good chance of getting a semi-private, or group, audience. The Pope, while not indifferent to the concerns of the eminent German philosopher, was much too preoccupied with secular and spiritual affairs of the Holy Year to grant any audiences. While he sent regrets he did, however, also send his Apostolic Blessing to Edith and her family.

Though Edith did seem to presage the course of events in Nazi Germany, she typically expressed less concern for herself than for her family and friends around the nation. Of particular concern was her aging mother in Breslau who, like the rest of German Jews during this time, lived in a state of growing anxiety and uncertainty as to the future. "I will stay her for the time being until the situation is clearer," Edith wrote to a friend after her Münster lectureship was cancelled. "Don't worry about me. The Lord knows what he has in mind for me."[34]

Actually, the situation was becoming clearer for Edith and she was increasingly sure of the direction in which the Lord wanted her to go. While feebly casting about for various employment options after Munster, including an offer to teach in South America, Edith felt more than ever the call to enter the Carmel in Cologne and pursue the religious life for which she so ardently longed. While the political circumstances at the time did play a factor in Edith's timing for a vocational re-direction, to strip it of the supernatural dimension and the role of God's divine economy would be a serious case of spiritual myopia.

Edith's abandonment to divine providence, and her total childlike trust in God had guided her down a path on which few people could have stayed with similar diligence and devotion. If she did not express fear for her own future and career, it was not because of ennui or foolhardiness. For Edith, the freezing over of one professional road

---

[34] Stein, *Self-Portrait in Letters*, p. 141.

meant that the one leading to Carmel was thawing like icicles in the sun.

In fact, Edith confided to Hatti Conrad-Martius that, having been accepted by the Carmelites in Cologne, she would remain with them for several months as a guest and then enter as a postulant in October. Conveying the impression to everyone else that she was going to simply live with the nuns until new plans had been formulated for her future, Edith returned home for an extended stay with her mother in Breslau. Before leaving for home, however, she set out to receive the unequivocal approval of the single most important person in her life. Entering a church for services, Edith knelt and pledged that she would not leave that spot until she felt the Lord had revealed to her heart his approbation for her entrance into Carmel. As the final benediction was being pronounced, Edith said at that moment "I felt the Good Shepherd giving me his consent."[35]

Content that the Lord's approbation had been revealed to her heart, Edith then began for the means by which she could break the heartbreaking and potentially devastating news to Frau Stein.

The Ascent Begins

There never has been such a thing as a 'good' time for a child to tell parents about a vocation to the contemplative life. Even for good Catholic parents, familiar with the tradition of sons and daughters going into the priesthood and active teaching orders, the idea of a child living a hidden life behind the walls of a silent monastery is a difficult, often agonizing fate to bear. In the case of Edith Stein it was a certainty that no matter how she revealed her decision, her mother's heart would not simply break, but shatter. Auguste Stein was much too wise and perceptive not to know that something more lay behind her daughter's decision to 'stay' with the nuns in Cologne. When Frau Stein asked her daughter the simple

---

[35] Spiritu Sancto, *Edith Stein*, p. 120.

question of what she planned to do when she was there, she received the equally simple answer that she intended to join them.

At eighty-four, Auguste Stein had reached a time and an age in her life when she should have been resting on laurels won after leading a full life devoted to God, her family and the values of hard and honest work. Instead of enjoying the quiet pleasures of faith and home in the twilight of her life, surrounded by children and grandchildren, Frau Stein was forced to contend with an array of crises closing in on her from all sides. With the Nazi government stepping up a brutal and unrelenting persecution of German Jews, the word that her daughter had chosen this time to enter a cloistered convent was simply too much to bear.

While Auguste said she did not mean to show disrespect towards Jesus, she simply could not see Edith's attraction to "that man" whose claim that He was the Son of God had caused their people so much suffering through the ages.

While Frau Stein retreated into a heavy silence, her children attempted to get the answers to help solve the riddle of brilliant youngest child. Edith's siblings did not so much try to dissuade her from entering as try to *comprehend* her reasons for entering Carmel; which seemed to them a mysterious and bizarre way of life that appeared to go against the very grain of human nature. Edith, sensing that the atmosphere of the house was extremely tense and highly inflammable, neither attempted to defend her decision nor engage in Catholic apologetics but simply tried to maintain her inner peace and convictions while praying that she would not flag or falter.

"I know that my mother is only somewhat pacified," she wrote to Dominican Sister Callista Kopf in Speyer, " because, inwardly, she still hopes I will not be able to manage to carry out what for her is the worst thing imaginable."[36]

Edith's last full day at home was her birthday, the Day of Atonement, and in what must have been an excruciating experience for them both, she accompanied her mother to the synagogue for

---

[36] Stein, *Self-Portrait in Letters*, p. 156.

services. By this time both mother and daughter had moved to a place of love and pain that was beyond words and that night, while Frau Stein could do nothing but silently weep, her daughter did nothing but hold her until she fell asleep. The next morning Edith left the house on the Michaelisstrasse for the last time and, emotionally and physically drained from the events of the past few weeks, she boarded the express train from Breslau to Cologne.

Novice in Cologne

Despite the fact that the desire for the religious life was such a powerful driving force in her life, Edith's entrance into Carmel was a relatively quiet and low-key event. Aside from her spiritual father Dom Raphael, the superiors of the Cologne Carmel had expressed not a few reservations in regards to their celebrated postulant before she actually entered the order. At forty-two, Edith was about twice the age of the average young woman seeking entrance into Carmel and, with most contemplative orders placing strict age limits on their candidates, this alone should have presented a major obstacle. Aside from the age question, the asceticism, the fasts, the manual labor and the subordination of intellectual work to spiritual matters made a few members of the community uncertain whether the brilliant, independent, middle-aged convert was equal to the rigors of convent life.

When Edith crossed the threshold into the heart of Carmel, however, it soon became increasingly clear, especially to Edith, that she had made the right decision with her life. Any hesitations, doubts or sense of qualified support harbored in the minds of those entrusted with her soul, melted away in the face of overwhelming proof that Edith was indeed home. Contrary to popular misconceptions the cloister is a hiding place for those who cannot face the world, if Edith were indeed misplaced in her choice she would have been able to pretend she would have been able to fool herself or her friends for only a short time.

The most patent evidence was the grace and ease with which Edith adapted herself to the life of a Carmelite novice which, even in the case of the most prepared aspirant to the religious life, is never quite what one expects. There is a sort of prototypical novice – regardless of gender – that Edith's age and maturity helped her to avoid becoming once ensconced in her cell. Novices, especially younger ones most susceptible to romantic preconceptions of the cloister, generally commence their religious life convinced of the immensity of their sacrifice for God. Dramatically jettisoning the world and all its false allurements, the novice can easily enter a pseudo-mystical cloud of unknowing – generally of their own making – until wiser heads and the realities of community life eventually shake them back into the less romantic but more pragmatic world.

While Edith did in later years confess to the difficulties she experienced in entering the cloister – especially with women half her age – this bit of honesty did not detract from the ultimate fact that she was able to grasp the rhythm of Carmelite life relatively quick. Up between 4:30 and 5:00 a.m., the sisters began the day with an hour of meditation before the first of Liturgy of the Hours – set times of prayer that punctuate the day – followed by the Eucharist and an alternation of work and prayer that concluded with supper, recreation and private time before retiring about 10:00 p.m.

While based on the balance and common sense that Saint Teresa abundantly possessed, the silence, the long periods of prayer, the mortifications and the inevitable stress arising from communal life, however, demanded a tremendous concentration of will from the novice in ways that pushed their spiritual endurance to the limit.

The rewards of life in the Carmel, however, were rich, and the love, support and friendship given by the nuns to one another on the same long path to God would endure to the deathbed and beyond. Had Edith been a twenty-year old girl in the full bloom of youth and bursting with rosy outlooks on life, she probably would have settled into religious life in a much different way once the golden glow of the novitiate wore off and faded away. As it was, Edith was a mature, intelligent woman of vast experience in the fullness of adulthood, but also someone who had already been living a life of solitary recollection and prayerful solitude for several

years to the astonishment of all who knew her. While she had
fasted and prayed and mortified herself at Speyer and Beuron and
Münster, however, it was on her own terms and at the discretion
of admiring directors. Now she had to practice those same virtues,
but in perfect obedience hidden under the same roof with other
women attempting to do the same with understandably different
degrees of success. Ultimately, this ego-deflating process was the
true test of her humility and her love of God over self that proved
to be the greatest measure of her devotion.

From the start, Edith formed a deep bond with many of her
fellow novices as well as with her superiors and sisters in the community. She joined in on all the fun and laughter that seems to be
part of every novitiate curriculum, and like all novices she found
herself capable of seeing humor in just about anything. Years of
intellectual work in the field of academia made a re-acquainting
with brooms and buckets a necessary part of her novitiate, and no
one laughed harder at her often humorous housework attempts than
Edith herself.

For all her ability to learn and desire to earn a place in the community, Edith did not, however, treat her Sisters in a condescend-
ing manner and play the brilliant philosopher tolerating the younger
or provincial girls in her class. Indeed, aside from her immediate
superiors, no one really knew about Edith's background in the world
of philosophy and education; a bit of intelligence Edith herself was
more than happy to keep on a need-to-know basis.

The fact that Edith was indeed where God wanted her to be was
not manifested in dramatic, glorious displays of religious virtuosity
but in quiet and very ordinary examples of love and forbearance.
Her sense of connection with the world and the problems of those
living outside the cloister did not end with her reception of the
Holy Habit and the making of vows but, on the contrary deepened
and grew with the passing of time.

From the time of her entry Edith expressed a desire, indeed a
need, to witness to the love of Christ by being present to anyone that
wrote or came to her for help and prayers. Unlike many sisters, who
found being called away from their cell and private prayer a cross,

Edith always welcomed the opportunity to speak with anyone who called her to the grille (the grated window through which the sisters spoke with people outside) in the speakroom of Carmel. Barely a year into her religious life, Edith was aware enough to know that to that relieving people's burdens with a few words of encouragement and support was just as much an apostolate of love as was her hidden life of prayer and mortification.

"When someone comes to us worn out and crushed and then takes away a bit of rest and comfort," Edith wrote to a fellow religious in 1934, "that makes me very happy."[37]

Peace and Challenges in the Cloister

One of the most profound outward signs of a genuine transformation at work in Edith's life was the noticeable change in the letters she continued to write to family and friends after her entrance into Carmel. While an inveterate letter writer her entire life, Edith penned her thoughts in a style that was markedly different before and after she took up the religious life in Cologne. While always warm, caring and solicitous to both dear friends and casual acquaintances both, Edith's letters as a laywoman have a straightforward, no-nonsense undertone about them that conveys the image of a solemn and highly intelligent woman engaged in the serious business of life. A professional in the world of academia and pedagogy, Edith's letters prior to Carmel were almost always addressed to other professionals in the field and left little room for light-hearted banter and chatty minutiae.

After 1933, when she entered the Cologne Carmel, Edith began not so much to write as paint her letters, filling them with a warm, gentle sense of childlike awe over every aspect of her new place in God's universe. Not the bubbly, overly effusive giddiness of the newlywed, but the deep, genuine sense of exultation and peace of someone who has found their life with a beloved spouse. In letters to old friends ranging from the Benedictine Sister Adelgundis

---

[37] Ibid., p. 167.

Jaegerschmid and the Ursuline Mother Petra Bruning to family members and former colleagues, Edith poured out heartfelt feelings and observations with a renewed sense of child-like enthusiasm and awe that Hatti Conrad-Martius found "absolutely charming."[38]

The first year in the convent flew by rapidly, and with great joy Edith approached the day of Clothing on April 15, 1934, at which time she would formally received the Carmelite Habit. In a time-honored ceremony of great beauty and symbolism – held in the monastery church in Cologne – Edith began the ceremony dressed in the white silks and veil of a bride on her wedding day. Having expressed a desire to take Christ as her Spouse, Edith's wedding silks were then exchanged for the brown wool tunic and white veil of the Carmelite novice.

A photograph of Edith taken on the Clothing day shows her radiant and joyful, her head modestly bowed and a shy smile crossing her lips, looking more like a girl than a mature woman of forty-two. Rounding out the ceremony was the taking of a new name to symbolize her rebirth into the religious life, which in Edith's case represented her devotion to Saint Teresa of Avila, Saint Benedict and the redemptive hope represented by the cross of Jesus. From that day on, Edith was to be known in the religious life as Sister Teresa Benedicta of the Cross – literally, in Latin, Teresa Blessed by the Cross.

Edith did, however, remain 'Edith' to her family, many of whom while not understanding her vocational direction, nevertheless wished her well with the choices she had made. Frau Stein, however, had remained distant and aloof to her daughter during Edith's first year in the convent and had come to imagine the worst possible scenarios regarding her daughter" new life. Things remained so tense, in fact, that the Clothing ceremony was kept from Frau Stein and in the end it was Rosa Stein who secured all necessary silk and materials for the wedding dress.[39]

---

[38] Herbstrith, *Edith Stein*, p. 74.
[39] Stein, *Self-Portrait in Letters*, p. 176.

A year and a week later, Edith pronounced her simple vows on Easter Sunday – April 21, 1935 – thus beginning the period of simple profession that lay between the end of the novitiate and the taking of solemn vows. Adapting to the rhythm and the flow of convent life, Edith was approached soon after by her superiors with a project that at first glimpse seemed to put her back to the point where she was several years earlier. This time, however, her efforts were to be directed solely towards the glorification of God and would be free from academic ambitions and desire of notoriety.

The Intellectual Work Resumes

Edith's superiors knew the magnitude of her mind and the breadth of her reputation in the world of philosophy and education and had no intention of letting either atrophy and wither away simply because she was now a religious. While Carmel has enriched the Church, indeed Western literature, with sublime works of great literary and theological beauty, the Order never placed the emphasis on academic pursuits as did the Benedictines, the Dominicans and the Jesuits. The purpose of life in Carmel is the wholehearted pursuit of the Hidden God in silence, solitude and prayerful love. Edith had freely jettisoned all of her academic pursuits when she entered the religious life and was perfectly content to live the remainder of her life without ever picking up a pen again.

Her talents, however, were seen by her superiors as gifts from God that needed to be used in His honor and at the prompting of the local Father Provincial of the Order, Edith once again turned her mental skills towards philosophical writings. *Act and Potency* was a philosophical work Edith had started years before as a quiet contribution to a *festschrift* – a collection of essays written in honor of an eminent scholar – in this case for Edmund Husserl but was eventually left as an orphan in the hands of Hatti Conrad-Martius. Dealing with the implications of exactly what the title said, act and potency, the work went through several revisions as Edith delved deeper and deeper into the Thomistic philosophy and Scholastic method she worked so hard to master.

Per the directives of Edith's superiors, *Act and Potency* underwent a total metamorphosis and was completely rewritten by the light of pure faith and infused knowledge. Expanded into questions of the very nature of Being, *Act and Potency* was re-christened with the more theologically-oriented title *Eternal and Finite Being* and, after a torturous regimen of revisions and redrafts, was sent off to find a publisher. While there was some initially positive response to the work, the idea of trying of getting the pedagogic work of a Jewish woman past the Reich censors made one large firm drop the whole project completely.[40]

Despite the setbacks in regards to her resuscitated literary career, Edith continued to write at a surprisingly brisk pace. Even though she had limited research resources available – journal subscriptions were costly and strict enclosure precluded access to adequate libraries – Edith managed to squeeze a considerable amount of her undoubtedly brilliant writing into the two meager hours per day allowed for manual labor.

Not only did Edith rework *Act and Potency*, she also wrote biographical sketches of Carmelite saints, did translations for various liturgical ceremonies and even got around to writing the Index for her previous translations of the works of Saint Thomas. Aside from these arduous, time-consuming tasks, Edith's renewed association with the academic and publishing worlds brought in a constant flow of requests for contributions to an endless array of anthologies, newspapers and philosophic journals. As Edith was now a vowed religious under obedience, all requests had to be discerned, approved by her superiors and then somehow worked into her already stretched schedule.

The problem with being an author in Carmel, even a great author like Edith Stein, is that any time given to research and writing means less time to share in the endless household chores and manual labor. A delicate balance was achieved – in the spirit of the eminently sensible Saint Teresa – by Edith's superiors who saw to

---

[40] Spiritu Sancto, *Edith Stein*, p. 175-176.

it that her intellectual work was complemented by equal time spent in the laundry, refectory and orchards.

Instead of feeling either superior or isolated by her return to the rarefied atmosphere of research and writing, Edith actually felt drawn closer to her sisters and the purpose of Carmel, with is total self-surrender despite the circumstance of the moment. Not losing her sense of humor over the whole situation, Edith would invariably walk into recreation on Sundays and with mock exasperation announce her delight at not having to write that day.[41]

Two Losses and a Joy

Despite the intense schedule of life in Carmel, compounded by the resumption of her philosophical and spiritual writings, one area in Edith's life remained an aching wasteland of emptiness and pain. Even though two years had passed since her entry into religious life, Frau Stein continued her policy of non-communication with her daughter. In her mind, as long as Edith did not take the Carmelite habit, she could consider her daughter as dabbling in a foolish little folly before ultimately coming back to her senses and her home. Once Frau Stein learned of Edith's clothing with the habit, a fait accompli of sorts was realized and her silence then became absolute.

Despite weekly letters sent from Edith, often with friendly postscripts jotted down by members of the community, the redoubtable matriarch simply refused to budge.

The immensity of Edith's joy can only be imagined when, shortly after her simple profession in 1935, she received a short note from her mother expressing her love and best wishes. The gulf of silence between mother and daughter had been an agony for Edith, but more so for the eighty-six year old woman still struggling to understand what had happened to her precious child. Sporadic encounters with a sister who was in Breslau overseeing the foundation of a new Carmel (which would come into existence for nearly forty-five

---

[41] Herbstrith, *Edith Stein*, p. 75.

years) had begun to dispel the hobgoblins Frau Stein had conjured in her mind regarding the mysteries of Carmelite life. Soon Edith's mother began adding postscripts to Rosa's frequent letters to her sister in Cologne.

While she remained outwardly joyful and placid as always, the deafening two year silence from Breslau had ripped Edith apart inside, and this reunion of sorts with her mother was a poignant as well as a portentous blessing for them both. Though neither knew it, the seemingly indestructible Auguste Stein, the rock of the family who was never been known to have been sick a day in her life, had a little over a year to live.

In the summer of 1936, the now eighty-seven year old woman was discovered to have a lump on her stomach that the doctors declared to be an inoperable cancer. Despite the growing pain and the obvious decline that soon set in, Frau Stein clung to life as tenaciously as ever and continued to communicate with her daughter in Carmel as long as she was able. With little her siblings could do but give tender care and loving nursing, Edith herself commended her mother entirely to God's mercy and by letter asked her many friends to do the same.

On the morning of September 14, 1936, Feast of the Holy Cross, Edith joined the community in the Choir for the private renewal of vows that the Carmelites did yearly on that particular feast day. When leaving the chapel, Edith remarked to a Sister how she felt the unmistakable and distinct presence of her mother standing beside her as she renewed her vows. Later that day a telegram arrived at the Cologne Carmel, informing Edith that her mother had died that morning during the time she was in the chapel.[42]

Through wars, death, joys, tragedies and uneventful stretches of time, Frau Stein had always been there as the one constant in Edith's life, and her death left a deep and sorrowful hurt in the daughter's heart. Being such a remarkable and beloved matriarch,

---

[42] Spiritu Sancto, *Edith Stein*, p. 168.

it was inevitable that the family began to go their own ways in her absence. The times also dictated the fragmenting fortunes of the Stein family and, with the dark clouds of Anti-Semitism having already darkened the life of Edith she harbored no illusions for hers or her family's safety when the clouds finally burst.

Edith's brother Arno would emigrate to America in 1938 and was followed a year later by her sister Erna and her husband Hans Biberstein. Else Gordon, Edith's sister, would join her son with her husband and children in Colombia while brother Paul and sister Friede would face grimmer prospects as the Nazis stepped up their persecution of Jews throughout Europe.

A ray of hope for Edith in the dark days following her mother's death was the baptism of her sister Rosa into the Catholic faith. Having held off as agreed until after their mother's death, Rosa, who was single and had acted as the housekeeper for the Stein home on the Michaelistrasse, was now free to pursue the calling of her heart. On the evening of December 24, 1936 a few friends gathered in Cologne's Hohenlind Church to witness the baptism of Rosa Stein, which was followed a few hours later by her first Holy Communion. Hospitalized with casts on her broken foot and hand, the result of a serious fall down a flight of darkened stairs in the convent, Edith joined her sister in spirit for the deeply moving ceremony for which they had both waited so long.

As a gift to her elder sister on the day of her re-birth in Christ, Edith wrote a lovely, extremely well-crafted poem that captured the joyful mystery of the event. Using metaphorical images of darkness, doors, water and light, Edith's poem of longing, love and fulfillment could have been penned by Saint John of the Cross in his Toledo prison cell. A baptism poem written during Advent, the expressions of love and hope in the face of overwhelming darkness she put into Rosa's mouth can also be seen in a much wider and more inclusive sense. Edith had sensed the imminent danger closing in on European Jewry since 1933, and the words she wrote quite possibly could have been intended not only for Rosa, but Edith and millions of her Jewish brothers and sisters throughout Europe. The poem concludes:

No human heart could ever conceive.
What you are preparing for those who love you.
Now I possess you and will never leave you.
For wherever the road of life leads me, you are beside me,
Nothing can ever divide me from your love.[43]

As the decade began drawing to a close, it was apparent that the Nazi harassment of Jewish citizens was metastasizing into a large cancer of hatred and intolerance throughout Germany. Edith's prescient observations in regards to the worsening political conditions, dating back to Hitler's accession to power in 1933, were eerily coming to pass and she shared her concerns for her people in letters and private conversations in the Carmel.

With several of her siblings beginning the long process of emigration, Edith herself gave some thought to leaving Germany for the safety of a Carmel in another country. Hoping to spare her sisters in the community punishments and reprisals for harboring a non-Aryan in the convent, Edith briefly contemplated transferring to a Carmel in Palestine. When informed that the quota of emigrating Jews had been reached there, however, the plan was quietly shelved. The fact was that it was a time of great danger and persecutions not only for the Jews but for Catholics as well. With anti-Catholic on the rise in Germany and with the Gestapo routinely searching and harassing religious houses and convents, it soon became clear to Edith that unless she contemplated moving to America like her brother Arno, there ultimately was no place she could flee with a guarantee of security.

In Spain, a bloody civil war between the Republican government and Loyalist rebels had been raging for several years with no end in sight. A brutal bloodbath waged for the very soul of the nation, the Spanish Civil War had seen horrendous atrocities committed by both sides against the civilian populace. The clergy in particular became targets of the largely anti-clerical Republican forces, and the blood of hundreds of priests, monks and religious enriched the soil of

---

[43] Ibid., p. 171-172.

ancient, Catholic Spain. The fate of numerous Spanish Carmelites had steeled Edith to the fact that evil times were being rapidly unleashed upon the land, and she was daily resolved to a life of total abandonment to whatever God's will asked of her.[44]

1937 saw the tercentenary, or 300th anniversary, of the Cologne Carmel. As part of the festivities, a commemorative booklet was put together including a history of the monastery as well as an endless array of facts, figures and biographical sketches pertaining to its presence in the city. Working closely with the Prioress, Edith assisted in this massive undertaking and in the course of her research she established ties with the Carmel in Echt, Holland, where the community had fled during Chancellor Bismarck's anti-Catholic *Kulturkampf* of the previous century. The ties she established with their sister community in Holland were fortuitous indeed, and the friendship would serve her well in the coming years.

The following year, 1938, was a momentous one for Edith that would shower down graces beyond her most fervent expectations. The prescribed three years had passed since Edith pronounced her simple vows, which meant that if she chose she could pronounce the indissoluble perpetual vows that would bind her forever to the religious life.

Technically, when the bishop exchanged her white novice's veil for the black one of the finally professed religious, Edith formally became a member of the Community with voting power and a voice in deciding the important decisions of the sisters life. In a deeper and more profound sense, Edith's perpetual vows represented an espousal, a union with Christ that would employ all the sublime and timeless language of traditional matrimony. In taking her final vows Edith would offer herself as a virgin to her Bridegroom and, having given herself in freedom for all eternity, would be adorned by Him with "treasures beyond price."

The language of union and self-offering, while always a magnificent mystery for any woman on the day of her final vows, was for Edith a consecration of great significance and portent. In accepting

---

[44] Herbstrith, *Edith Stein*, p. 77.

Christ as her Spouse, in cleaving to Him as His bride, she asked to share in the totality of His divine and human life, which embraces not only the light of salvation but the darkness of the Cross.

On April 21, 1938, Edith made her final vows in the Chapter Room of the Cologne Carmel following a ten-day retreat. On May 1, Sister Teresa Benedicta of the Cross received the black veil of sacrifice and consecration, while the auxiliary bishop of Cologne proclaimed "Come, bride of Christ, receive the crown which the Lord has prepared for you from all eternity."[45]

The second great event of 1938 that was an occasion of profound joy and gratitude for Edith was the deathbed return to God of Edith's old professor and mentor, Edmund Husserl. It had always pained Edith that the great man she admired so much had used his Christianity as little more than an abstract tool to make brilliant Phenomenological points. Though he admired and respected his former assistant's path to Christ by the heights of Carmel, the Master simply could not embrace the reality of a living and loving Triune God in his life the way Edith had.

By 1938 the Master was desperately ill – dying actually – and, forbidden by the Nazi's Nuremburg Laws to teach, write or speak to Aryans in any Reich institution, was in effect a fugitive from the Nazi's racial laws. Together with his wife Malwine, Husserl had fled to the Benedictine convent of Saint Lioba, where he was tended by his former pupil and friend of Edith, Sister Adelgundis Jaegerschmid, OSB. Edith, meanwhile, fervently prayed for her dying mentor who, despite his thoughtless and often cold-hearted refusal to help her professionally, had done so much to put her feet on the road to God.

Lying near death during Holy Week, Husserl had an intense mystical experience in which he began to almost physically struggle with forces of darkness and light that struggled for his soul. On April 27, 1938, six days after Edith had pronounced her final vows, Husserl once again gave a lucidly detailed account to Sister Adelgundis of an immense experience of God that he was having. Saying that he

---

[45] Spiritu Sancto, *Edith Stein*, p. 179-180.

was seeing something magnificent, he told her to write down what he had to say. When Sister Adelgundis returned to his bedside with pencil and paper, the Master was dead.[46]

For the second time in as many years, Edith had lost a powerful and much revered force in her life. As it was with her mother, the death of Husserl was accompanied by an inexplicable mystical sense of presence and spiritual phenomena that not only helped ease the sorrow of the loss but reaffirmed the Lord's promise of life everlasting. Edith had prayed fervently for Husserl during his last illness as she had for Frau Stein during hers, and the deep spiritual sensations that accompanied both deaths convinced Edith that these two precious souls had entered into the loving presence of God. Nevertheless, another link with her past was severed and gone and, begging prayers from these souls, Edith turned to face the uncertainty of the dark days ahead.

Flight to Holland

Late 1938 had seen the sporadic, spontaneous violence towards Jews in Germany transformed into open and organized warfare. With the so called "night of broken glass" or Kristallnacht of November 9, so called because of the orgy of window smashing and looting of Jewish shops and homes, the Nazi police and civilians received official approbation to attack Jews at will. In an ice-blooded demonstration of Nazi efficiency, SA chief Reinhard Heydrich proudly reported that within a few hours 815 Jewish shops and 171 private homes were destroyed, 119 synagogues were burned with another 76 razed and 20,000 Jews were arrested and sent to concentration camps.[47]

Those who had the means, got out of Germany as quickly as possible but those who could not began living with their necks in a noose that was beginning to slowly tighten.

---

[46] Herbstrith, *Edith Stein*, p. 78.

[47] Stefan Lorant, *Sieg Heil!: An Illustrated History of Germany from Bismarck to Hitler* (New York: W.W. Norton & Company, Inc., 1974), p. 282.

In the Cologne Carmel, it was apparent that not only was Edith at risk but the sisters themselves faced grave dangers and possible reprisals in harboring a non-Aryan among them. After much deliberation and soul searching on the part of Edith as well as her superiors, it was decided that the wisest thing to do was to send her to the safety of a Carmel outside Germany. It was not an easy decision to arrive at, for not only had Edith found a home and a family among her Sisters in the community, but she had already committed herself wholeheartedly to God's will; even if it meant sharing in the persecution of her Jewish brothers and sisters.

However, A letter from the Prioress of the Cologne Carmel to their sister community in Echt, Holland with the cryptic notation that Sister Benedicta needed a "change of air" was clearly understood without need of gloss or clarification. Plans were set into effect immediately to somehow get Edith across the border to the relative safety of neutral Holland. It was with a heavy-heart that the sisters set about preparing for Christmas of 1938, a pall that was relieved only by the unflagging strength and calm of Edith herself.

Passport photos would be necessary to validate Edith's documents, and she sat in the courtyard of the Carmel for a series of quickly snapped photographs. The resulting session gave us the best known and most widely-reproduced image of Edith Stein.

While her petite, modestly girlish looks had long given way to the maturity of middle age, something defying articulation emanates from her faraway yet surprisingly immediate look. Top lit by a bright shaft that creates deep contrasts of shadows and light, Edith appears untouched by the anxiety and uncertainty which was almost constantly present in her life during this time. Her head tilted slightly, her mouth set delicately halfway between resignation and musing, Edith's dark shadowed eyes seem to command the entire photograph with a look of utter peace and contentment. In spite of the promise of blood and fire from imminent war and the awful persecution of her people, Edith's eyes convey the fact that it is still God's world and that her conformity to His will is the source of all peace.

It was with great difficulty that Edith made it through her final Christmas at the Cologne Carmel with the final farewells still to come. On December 31, 1938 – New Year's Eve – the sisters gathered to bid farewell to their Sister Benedicta. The emotions felt were beyond the power of words, and Edith's goodbye proceeded along from Sister to Sister without incident until one in particular broke down in tears. It was all Edith needed and she too began to weep with the women who had been her family and her support for the past five years. Stopping to pray for a time before the statue of the Queen of Peace in the former Carmelite church of Maria vom Frieden in Cologne, Edith then got into the car of a layman who was close to the community, and he drove her across the border to her new world in Echt.[48]

Echt

The lengthy communications Edith had with the Echt Carmel during her research for Cologne's tercentenary had resulted in deep bonds, and the Dutch community welcomed the new Sister into their midst with warmth and affection.

Actually, since so many nuns had remained in Holland after fleeing Bismarck's anti-Catholic laws, the Echt Carmel had been transformed into a predominantly German house. The German language and customs used in the house made Edith feel at home immediately, but soon after her arrival changes were made that made Dutch the house tongue.[49]

Situated in a more rural setting rather than the bustle of a large city like Cologne, the Echt Carmel was somewhat more provincial in its work and in the makeup of the community. For Edith, the renowned philosopher and brilliant author, being among simpler nuns in a pastoral setting was neither a hindrance nor a burden, and she soon came to love her new Community of Sisters as they did her. As a tribute to her humility and her genuine sense of compassion, Edith quickly mastered the Dutch language so that any assimilating would be done by her and not the Echt Sisters.

---

[48] Spiritu Sancto, *Edith Stein*, p. 185.
[49] Graef, *Edith Stein*, p. 189.

Domestic needs as well as the endless work in the convent's orchards and fields kept Edith moving at a fast pace that did not allow for quieter activities like writing and research. Also, the fact that there were more elderly nuns than younger ones meant that Edith had to do the work of several nuns in order to keep the house running smoothly.

Even though she felt deep gratitude to God for allowing her to live in relative safety with a community of caring Sisters, a certain unsettling sense of impermanence seemed to follow Edith into Holland. Despite the enclosure, the realities of life and the worsening conditions of Jews in Europe in general crackled through the Carmel like an electric storm.

With brother Arno and sister Else safely out of Germany and Erna preparing to do the same with her husband Hans Biberstein, the fates of Frieda, Paul and Rosa remained an increasing source of anxiety for Edith that she daily took to her prayer. While never gloomy or fatalistic despite the ominous news trickling into the Carmel on a daily basis, Edith began to face questions regarding the very nature of suffering and sacrifice that God could possibly ask of her in the near or distant future. Instead of being passively carried along by the tide of political events, Edith decided to take a proactive stance in regards to her displaced, unsettled status in a way that would allow her to live life freely conforming to God's Divine plan.

On Passion Sunday, March 26 1939, Edith asked permission from her Prioress to make a freewill offering of herself to the Sacred Heart of Jesus. In a masterpiece of spiritual brevity, Edith made a simple petition in which she offered her life in atonement for the sins of the world and that the reign of the "Antichrist may perish, if possible without a new world war, and a new order may be established." Edith closed with a declaration of belief that the Lord would soon call many others to do the same. This offering of self-immolation and oblation, coming a mere seven months before Germany and the USSR invaded Poland and effectively began World War II, again shows Edith's prescient pragmatism in affairs of the world and of the soul.[50]

---

[50] Ibid., p. 188.

In the hands and heart of a less spiritually mature religious, such an offering of self during such a time of impending war and mass destruction could have been at best maudlin piety and at worst fatalistic despair. In the hands and heart of Edith Stein, however, who was being drawn deeper into the redemptive mystery of Christ's suffering on the cross, this self-offering became nothing more than a declaration of absolute, pure love. Neither a bargaining chip for her life or her family's nor a cocksure bit of spiritual bravado, Edith's offering is a loving, self-immolating gift to God in reparation for the coming suffering of millions.

Despite the disintegrating social conditions and the questionable nature of her own security, Edith once again displayed not only the soundness of her theology but the clarity of her common sense. She does not actively seek martyrdom any more than she asks to be spared pain and suffering; she simply begs to give her self in total freedom to whatever God in His infinite mercy and wisdom has prepared for her.

By the middle of 1939, with the grim pallor of imminent war coloring more and more the ebb and flow of daily life in Europe, Edith settled placidly into the never changing routine of Carmelite life. Her letters, which once poured out of her pen on a vast array of subjects, began to level off to a measured pace stream of peaceful, almost chatty communications to friends and fellow religious. Despite what must have been a tremendous amount of tension and uncertainty clouding the air for everyone, but for Jews in particular, the tone of profound calm in Edith's letters during this time point to a deeper reality at work.

In her letters Edith does not nervously wonder about what the next day might bring nor anxiously ponder escape plans should emergency situations arise. Instead, in letter after letter, Edith makes inquiries about the health of friends, offers birthday or religious anniversary greetings, asks prayers and gives thanks for even the smallest gift or act of kindness. Indeed, the prominent theme running through Edith's letters during this period is gratitude and concern for others.

In only one letter, written to her brother in law Hans Biberstein in New York on his birthday, does Edith engage in anything like speculation or nostalgia. Waxing poetically over the fate of the Steins left in Europe, Edith wonders aloud to Hans whether or not they will be around to see the historical events of the day pass into history.[51]

As to the rest of her letters, they are not the false heroics of the nervous whistler in the graveyard, but the calm reflections of a centered individual living with more and more of the self slowly submerging out of sight into the depths of the interior life.

The safety of her family, however, was an entirely different matter, and Edith remained in a constant state of concern for their safety and well-being. While Arno kept trying – ultimately unsuccessfully – to get his brother Paul and sister Friede out of Germany, Edith undertook a rescue attempt of sorts on behalf of her older sister Rosa.

The quiet, hard-working Rosa, who had the same pretty, dark-eyed looks of all the Stein women, had been having something of a rough time of it since her conversion to Catholicism in 1936. Having moved out of the Stein home in Breslau, Rosa took up residency with the Carmelites in Cologne where she acted as portress and liaison with the outside world. Moving with great difficulty to Belgium in 1939 with all her possessions, Rosa took lodgings with a woman who had advertised herself in Germany as a Secular Carmelite with hopes of beginning a community of Catholic laywomen. This began a nightmare situation for Rosa from which she had to be extracted by her younger sister with almost Herculean efforts.

Rosa discovered soon after her arrival that the woman was an unscrupulous swindler, who kept her unwitting "novice" in a state of near-enslavement with neither money nor knowledge of the native language. With the world collapsing into war around her Edith also took on the almost impossible task of finding Rosa and somehow getting her out of Belgium. Through friends she located her sister who, though she had to leave all her possessions behind, she managed to get to Holland by sending a pass and a few guilders. With the Community's permission, Rosa, who would be admitted into the Secular Order of Carmel in the summer of 1940, came to

---

[51] Stein, *Self-Portrait in Letters*, p. 315.

live at the Echt Carmel as a laywoman where she continued the role she had in Cologne as portress.[52]

A quiet, devout woman of genuine faith and simplicity, Rosa impressed the community with her material detachment and dedication to prayer. Like her sister, Rosa came to spend hours in silent meditation before the Blessed Sacrament and was soon loved and respected by the nuns as well as the townsfolk. Reunited with her sister, Edith felt a certain measure of relief and solidarity, especially since soon after Rosa arrived in the summer of 1940 the Nazis invaded Holland.

As the black cloud of war once again rained down death upon Europe, Edith and Rosa struggled against great odds to live lives of patient waiting and prayerful fortitude. With the German occupation of the Netherlands came all the attendant evils which the Nazis used in their widening reign of terror. The modus operandi of the SS and the Gestapo towards the Jews as they trailed in the wake of the frontline Wehrmacht and Luftwaffe was one of identification, isolation and ultimately, deportation to camps in what was rapidly becoming Reich territory throughout Europe.

As Hitler's victorious and apparently unstoppable forces rolled over nation after nation, it was becoming apparent that the Führer's lifelong obsession with destroying European Jewry was becoming more and more of a reality.

At the time of the German invasion, the Netherlands held one of the largest populations of observant as well as baptized Jews in Europe. A very old and vibrant community with a cultural and spiritual heritage hundreds of years old, the Dutch Jews enjoyed a warm and stable bond with their Christian neighbors that extended to foreign born Jews like Edith and Rosa Stein. Despite a groundswell of silent and often active support from their adopted countrymen, Edith and Rosa were soon in the path of the dreaded Gestapo with no place to hide.

Regardless of their spiritual status as Christians, the Stein sisters were classified primarily as Jews, and as such were forced to register

---

[52] Spiritu Sancto, *Edith Stein*, p. 189.

with the local Nazi officials in Maastricht. Adding to the humiliation of the identification process was the interrogations that all Dutch Jews, including Edith, were subjected to for often hours at a time. The sisters were also ordered to wear the yellow cloth Star of David, marking them as Jews, at all times when they were in public.[53]

During this time the newly elected prioress, Mother Antonia, directed Edith to forego some of the manual labor and once again take up her pen. With the 400th anniversary of the birth of Saint John of the Cross approaching in 1942, a book on the Mystical Doctor would give the Order a scholarly work but would also afford Edith an opportunity to be distracted from the gloomy state of affairs in which she was entwined. The book, which would translate from the German *Kreuzewissenschaft* as *The Science of the Cross*, would not only stand as one of Edith's greatest works but in dealing with the mystery of suffering and abandonment would stand in a way as her spiritual testament.

Although Edith had long been an ardent follower of Saint John of the Cross, in the last few years of her life she began to renew her spiritual acquaintance with him on a higher and more sublime level. Like all Discalced Carmelites, Edith had a great and abiding love for the works of 'Holy Father John' as she did for the Order's 'Holy Mother Teresa.' By the time she arrived at Echt, Edith had read just as much of Saint John of the Cross – *The Ascent of Mount Carmel, The Living Flame of Love, The Spiritual Canticle* and of course *The Dark Night of the Soul* – as the average Carmelite novice. When she began the journey of her final major work, however, Edith seemed to have established a profound link with the heart and soul of the Spanish friar's mind and heart.

While the poems bearing these aforementioned names are relatively short (*The Living Flame of Love* is only four stanzas long) it is John's commentaries on his own work that comprises the bulk of his *oeuvre*. The majority of John's starkly beautiful verse, crafted by a true artist who has been called the greatest poet in the Spanish language, arose primarily from direct experiences of isolation,

[53] Herbstrith, *Edith Stein*, p. 101.

suffering and the apparent withdrawal of God. Locked in a closet-like cell for nine months in 1577 when he attempted to reform the Carmelite friars of the Mitigated Rule, John began composing poetry in his mind to pass time and probably to save his sanity.

Centered on the soul's burning but natural desire for union with God, John's poems use themes of loss, search, memory, abandonment and the often searing purgation of the senses of all that is not God. John's God is a jealous God, but not in the wrathful, punishing sense of Genesis and Exodus. God's jealousy is the jealousy of a tender lover who wants to possess His beloved for himself with no attachments or false illusions in an eternal night of pure love.

The irony of John's poetry is that, despite the often sensuous beauty of his verse, his final analysis is that the beauty of God and the touch of that pure divine love is beyond sense, beyond thought and beyond the power of human speech to express. John's failure to express that experience of God's love is the glory of Spanish verse, and the "ah, I don't-know-what" in the dark of night he can only equate with knowing without knowing.

The ultimate visible manifestation of our Father-God's love for us is in the sacrifice of His son on the absurdly humiliating Cross on Calvary. The Cross, both as symbol and as theology, plays an integral role in John's work because it played a central role in his own often brutally painful life. Unlike the wisdom of the world, which sees suffering as a non-productive scourge unto itself, the wisdom of the Cross sees suffering not only as a means by which Christ shared in our humanity but also the way in which we can share a small portion of His eternal victory.

By 1941, already a fugitive from the Nazi terror closing in on her from all sides, Edith felt the first singeing heat of the flames that seemed to presage exactly the type of purgative suffering and darkness of which John spoke.

Science of the Cross

Kreuzeswissenschaft, which translates into *The Science of the Cross*, was Edith's classic study of Saint John of the Cross that probably comes closer to the heart of a mystery than any of her previous works. While the term "Science" may sound a bit cold or formal, the true meaning of the translation is probably more an 'understanding' of the Cross, or an 'essence-knowledge' of the Cross. While she was about to come to an experiential knowledge of the Cross quite soon, in the end the book became an exaltation of the Cross as a doorway through which we all must temporarily pass on our way to eternal, indescribable love.

Edith had become more and more fascinated with a famous ink drawing of the Crucified Christ made by the Saint himself – who, aside from a mystic writer and poet was an accomplished musician, artist and even amateur architect – and is today still preserved at the Carmelite Monastery of the Incarnacion in Avila, Spain.

In the drawing, Jesus hangs weighed down by our sins in perfect expiatory obedience to the Father's will. Despite the nails, driven into His hands like railroad spikes, Jesus is nevertheless in a state of tension and transformation. While His agony is not yet finished, Jesus has begun to pull away from the earthly instrument of His passion, while His legs bend as though ready to propel Himself into the waiting arms of the Father. Hovering for an instant between two worlds, John's drawing shows Jesus closer to His glory by virtue of the fact He has performed the greatest act of love in the history of the world.

It is the love symbolized by the Cross which John endeavored to reveal in his drawing, the same love that Edith revealed in *The Science of the Cross*. The time of the terrible utterance of Jesus from the Cross, "My God, my God, why have You forsaken me?" has passed into history. As the appearance of Jesus withdrawing from the Cross symbolizes the triumph of life over death, so does the apparent withdrawal of God from the soul presage a fullness of unifying love to be poured into the empty depths.

"The Cross is not an end in itself. It is raised up and points above itself. Nevertheless,
it is not only a sign, it is the strong weapon of Christ, the shepherd's staff with which

the divine David fights against the infernal Goliath, with which he
knocks at the gate of
heaven and opens it. Then the divine light streams out, embracing
all those who follow the crucified Lord."[54]

Waiting to be arrested any day by agents of the "infernal Goliath"
Hitler who was reaping a growing harvest of death and destruction,
Edith no longer looked to the written or spoken word as the deepest form of expression. Both John and Edith had known not only
suffering but persecution as well: John, kidnapped, beaten and
imprisoned for his attempts to renew the spirit of Carmel; Edith,
chased as a fugitive with her family from country to country in
constant fear of arrest and deportation simply because they were
Jewish.

Like John, the circumstances of Edith's passion were accepted in
freedom and transformed by faith into a sharing of Christ's
redemptive suffering on the Cross. While she could not choose the
time, place and manner of her suffering, Edith used The Science
of the Cross – as she used her private self-sacrificial offering – as a
way of reserving to herself the way in which her sacrifice would be
given meaning.

The Science of the Cross did indeed become a paean to Edith's
own embrace of the Cross, and not surprisingly it was completed
the week before her arrest.

The depth and beauty of Edith's final work did not mean that
she was living in some sort of ethereal cloud of unknowing, unre-
sponsive to fear or unconcerned about the future. On the contrary,
she was actively working with her superiors to find a means of
escape with Rosa into yet another country that would hopefully
stay neutral for the duration of the war. Roundups of Jews in the
Netherlands were beginning to increase in frequency and numbers,
and despite their technically Christian status, even baptized Jews
were not safe from the Gestapo and the collaborating Dutch Nazi

---

[54] Edith Stein, *The Science of the Cross*, Edited by Dr. L. Gelber, Translated
by Hilda Graef (Chicago: Henry Regnery Company, 1960), p. 11.

police. As she had in Cologne, Edith realized that by remaining in the Echt Carmel she placed not only herself but the entire community in jeopardy.

In 1941, when his mastery over the European continent appeared inevitable, Hitler began stepping up his bullying of all political, social and moral power structures in the conquered lands to bring them into line with his goal of complete nazification of ever facet of life. The Catholic Church was high on the Fuhrer's list of targets. Though he had allowed, even encouraged, verbal attacks on the Pope, the hierarchy and the morals of the clergy – primarily in speeches and in the pages of the semi-pornographic Nazi paper *Der Sturmer* – Hitler increased his attack on the Church in direct proportion to his military victories.

Thousands of priests, religious and lay leaders, beginning with the presbyterate and the intelligentsia of Poland, had been arrested, sent to concentration camps and even executed for opposing Nazism in thought, word or deed. The closing of Catholic schools and the silencing of the powerful Catholic press in conquered countries was followed by the widespread seizure of Church property. The Carmelites were not absolved from this oppression, and convents in Luxembourg and the cities of Putzchen, Aachen and Duren were seized and the sisters turned out in the streets. One pilfered convent was transformed by Party leaders into a Nazi youth dance hall.[55]

The Cologne Carmel had prepared for the invasion and seizure of their convent by collecting and destroying all incriminating letters and documents to, from, and regarding Sister Benedicta of the Cross. While it robbed the world of a literary treasure trove of Edith Stein's works, it did point out just how serious the situation had become for Catholic religious in Germany.

The Carmel in Echt then began secret negotiations with the Carmel of Le Pâquier in neutral Switzerland, where it was hoped Edith could retire with Rosa until the end of the war. While she was disposed with a full and open heart to wherever and whatever

---

[55] Spiritu Sancto, *Edith Stein*, p. 193.

God called her, she was much too sensible to think the Lord could be bought by dramatically and blindly throwing away her life and not only hers, but Rosa's and possibly those in the Echt community as well. In fact, a great consolation to her was a ver from Saint Matthew, which she printed out and pinned over her heart under her scapular, "If they persecute you in one town, take refuge in the next." (MT 10:23)[56]

Negotiations, however, were slow and the process of communications dragged on for months. Criticism has been leveled, perhaps much too unfairly, at the dilatory nature of Edith's superiors that has been seen by some as contributing to her fate. It must be remembered that the continent was engulfed in war, and that the Carmelites in occupied Holland, supported as best as possible by the Carmelites in Germany, were trying to establish secret communications with a group of Carmelites in yet another country.

Furthermore, a triangulated plan of escape was being formulated for the two Jewish women which, if discovered, could have had the direst consequences for all concerned. Complicating the matter further was the fact that as a vowed religious and cloistered contemplative, Edith needed the canonical approval of Rome before she could hopscotch around the Carmels of Europe. The fact that the plan got as far as it did was in itself quite miraculous.

Word finally came through from La Pâquier that a room was being held for Edith but that nor room could be found at the moment for Rosa. Edith, offered the chance to legally cross the border into a neutral country and safety, refused to even contemplate doing so without her sister.

On the political front, the tension in occupied Netherlands was heating up to a boiling point of dangerously high levels. Though the Dutch military was unable to defeat the overwhelmingly superior Nazi forces, as a people they resolved to put up a unified front of resistance against the Nazis that was both fierce and indomitable. The Dutch underground posed a formidable and elusive threat to the SS and the Gestapo, and ordinary citizens by the hundreds

---

[56] Ibid.

performed countless acts of heroism in the defense of their persecuted Jewish neighbors.

The Dutch Reformed and the Catholic Church were both extremely vocal in their condemnation of Nazi persecutions of the Jews, and the hierarchy of these two churches used all the means at their disposal to help the Jews survive the terror. While the clergy performed nobly in the field by aiding and sheltering them, the hierarchy used the greatest weapon in their spiritual arsonal – communications – to do their part in fighting the good fight.

In July, 1942, the Catholic Church and the Reformed Church jointly composed a telegram to Nazi Reichkommisar Arthur Seyss-Inquart denouncing the arrest and deportation of Dutch Jews. Demanding that these criminal actions cease immediately, the officials of the two churches threatened to make the denunciation public if they did not. The Nazi authorities responded with a compromise of sorts, in which they promised to leave alone all Christianized Jews in exchange for church silence in the future on the issue of observant Jews. While the Reformed Church found this agreeable and backed down, the pugnacious Archbishop of Utrecht, Monsignor De Jong, found the compromise offensive and went public with a nationally broadcast denunciation of the Nazis. Upping the protest into a pastoral letter – an official letter from a bishop on matters of faith and morals – Archbishop de Jong's denunciation of the Nazi arrests and deportations of Dutch Jews was read from the pulpit of every Catholic church in the Netherlands on July 26, 1942.[57]

Infuriated, Seyss-Inquart struck back swiftly and mercilessly to show what happens to any person or institution daring to speak out publicly against Nazi policy. Because "the bishops interfered," Seyss-Inquart ordered an immediate roundup of Jews – primarily Christian Jews – throughout the kingdom. The fate of Edith and Rosa Stein was sealed with any chance of escape now literally beyond all hope.

---

[57] Anthony Rhodes, *The Vatican in the Age of the Dictators: 1922-1945* (New York: Holt, Rinehart & Winston, 1973), p. 345.

"We're going for our people"

On Sunday, August 2, 1942, the timeless routine of Carmelite life flowed as placidly as always within the Echt cloister. Edith probably spent the day putting the finishing touches on *The Science of the Cross* or praying, as she had been observed doing more and more, in a cruciform manner in her cell. At five in the evening, as the sisters gathered in the Choir for their hour of meditation, the sound of loud knocking boomed through the silent convent.

Two Gestapo officers were at the door demanding to speak with the Superior in the matter of Edith and Rosa Stein. When told that the two women were to come with them immediately and that they had five minutes to pack, the Prioress' fear and disorientation quickly spread among the whole community. The Nazis had finally come for their Sister Benedicta.

Momentarily stunned by the naked impact of the blow, Edith quickly regained her composure and her complete grasp of the reality of the situation. The Prioress tried to reason with the two men and perhaps buy a few precious days in which the escape from Echt could be quickly facilitated. It was all in vain. With a handful of basic toiletries for the journey, Edith proceeded into the parlor to say farewell to the assembled Community and receive a blessing from her Prioress.

The initial fear and confusion of the moment simmered down to a heartbreaking moment of sadness and resignation. Outside the Carmel, among the gathered townsfolk who had grown fond of Rosa Stein, the feelings of sadness were thickened by a quiet but helpless rage.

In hoping to calm her sister, who was much more visibly shaken, Edith took her hand as they went outside the Carmel for the last time. Always a model of balance and integration, the bride of Christ remembered Israel as well as she prepared to enter the police truck. "Come Rosa," Edith said quietly, "we're going for our people."[58]

---

[58] Herbstrith, *Edith Stein*, p. 103.

From the Carmel, the sisters were taken to the police headquarters and then to the prison camp at Amersfoort. At Amersfoort
holding prison, the repercussions from the Archbishop's pastoral
letter were manifested almost from the minute of the sisters' arrival.
Within a few days, almost all the Protestant Jews were released
while the Catholic Jews remained. From there they were taken to
the notorious detention camp of Westerbork in northern Holland,
which was for many Dutch Jews a last stopping place before transport to the death camps in the east. After suffering the indignities
of prison reception and registration, Edith and Rosa settled into the
camp as best as they could under the terrible circumstances. Finding a few old friends among the Catholic Jews in the camp, now
separated from the Jews of Protestant denominations, Edith began
at once to seek out the spiritual nerve centers of the place and soon
was in prayer and rosary groups. Soon priests, nuns and religious
of other Orders arrived, which provided a great source of comfort
and solidarity for Edith and her sister. She also began to seek out
the neediest among the young, terror-stricken Jewish refugees and
assist them in emotional and material needs.

Many people, especially young wives and mothers, had become
senseless due to the surreal horror of the camp and the deprivation
of even basic necessities. Edith did what she could to feed, wash
and clothe the children as well as to offer friendship and support
to the adults and the elderly. Many accounts from survivors of the
camps attest to Edith's singular and memorable ministry of quiet
love during these terrible days when she moved closer to the mystical center of the Cross of Christ.

While the Sisters in Echt frantically tried to get word on the
sisters, Edith was able to actually get off a series of short notes that
became shorter and more cryptic in nature, reflecting a growing
sense of uncertainty in regards to the future but more importantly
commenting on her current situation. Telling the Prioress that her
prayer was actually flourishing, Edith also asked for a short list of
items for her and Rosa, including more toiletries, another Habit
and the next volume of the breviary. She also asked the Prioress to
redouble efforts in securing exit visas for Switzerland as quickly as

possible. Regardless of the outcome of the unfolding events, Edith remained, by her own admission, firmly in the presence of the Lord.

Early on August 7, Edith and Rosa were taken, along with several thousands of Dutch Jews by train from Westerbork south towards Germany. It was later that day, on a station platform in Schifferstadt, Germany, that a 'lady in dark clothes' was seen talking with a young woman who turned out to be a former student of the nun. After that, despite a surfeit of rumors and spurious testimonies by camp survivors, the exact details about the fates of Edith and Rosa Stein meld into the vast sea of human suffering behind the barbed wire of Auschwitz, Poland. According to the dates set by the Dutch Red Cross, Edith and Rosa died in the gas chambers with their fellow Jews shortly after arriving in Auschwitz on or around August 9, 1942 and their remains probably incinerated soon after. What is certain, however, is that Edith's spiritual journey to the Light of the East, to which the Lord had called her from all eternity, had just begun.

Edith's brother Paul and his wife Trude and her sister Frieda were all sent to Theresienstadt Concentration Camp in Germany. Frieda died there in 1942, Paul and his wife in 1943. On May 1, 1987, Edith Stein was beatified by Pope John Paul II in Cologne, Germany. On October 11, 1998 she was solemnly canonized in Rome's Saint Peter's Square by the Pope as a Saint of the Roman Catholic Church.

Bibliography

AHERN, PATRICK, *Maurice & Thérèse: The Story of a Love*. New York: Doubleday, 1998.

ALZIN, JOSSE, *A Dangerous Little Friar: Father Titus Brandsma, O.Carm*. Translated by the Earl of Wicklow. Dublin: Clonmore & Reynolds, 1957.

BOUSCAREN, T. LINCOLN, et al, *Canon Law: A Text and Commentary*, 4th ed., Milwaukee, WI: The Bruce Publishing Company, 1963.

CARROUGES, MICHEL, *Père Jacques*. Translated by Salvator Attanasio. New York: Macmillan, 1961.

CATHOLIC ENCYCLOPEDIA. Edited by Charles G. Herbermann. Vol. IV, New York: Robert Appleton Company, 1909.

de CAUSSADE, JEAN-PIERRE, *Self-Abandonment to Divine Providence*. Translated by Algar Thorold. Rockford, IL: Tan Books, 1987.

CHARLES DE FOUCAULD, Edited by Robert Ellsberg. Maryknoll, NY: Orbis Books, 1999.

CHRIST IN DACHAU, Westminster, MD: Newman Press, 1952.

THE COLLECTED WORKS OF SAINT JOHN OF THE CROSS, revised edition translated by Kieran Kavanaugh, OCD and Otilio Rodriguez, OCD. Washington, D.C.: ICS Publications, 1991.

ENCYCLOPEDIA OF THE HOLOCAUST, Vol. 4. New York: Macmillan Publishing Company, 1990.

ESSAYS ON TITUS BRANDSMA: CARMELITE EDUCATOR, JOURNALIST, MARTYR, edited by Redemptus Maria Valabek, O. Carm. Rome: Carmel in the World Paperbacks, 1985.

EVERETT, SUSANNE & PETER YOUNG, *The Two World Wars*. London: Bison Books, 1982.

De FABREGUES, JEAN, *Edith Stein: Philosopher, Carmelite Nun, Holocaust Martyr*. Boston: Saint Paul Books, 1993.

FORCEVILLE VAN ROSSUM, JOKE & KEES WAIJMAN, *Titus Brandsma: A Continuing Source of Inspiration*. Nijmegen, The Netherlands: The Foundation of Friends of Titus Brandsma.

FRIEDMAN, PHILIP, *Their Brother's Keepers*. New York: Crown Publishers, 1957.

GLUECKERT, LEOPOLD GEORGE, *Titus Brandsma: Friar Against Fascism*. Darien, IL: Carmelite Press, 1985.

GRAEF, HILDA, *The Scholar and the Cross: The Life and Works of Edith Stein*. Westminster, MD: Newman Press, 1955.

HARRIS, WHITNEY R., *Tyranny on Trial: The Evidence at Nuremburg*. Dallas, TX: Southern Methodist University Press, 1954.

HERBSTRITH, WALTRAUD, *Edith Stein: A Biography*. Translated by Father Bernard Bonowitz, OCSO. San Francisco: Harper & Row, 1985.

INTERNATIONALER KARL-LEISNER KREIS RUNDBRIEF, Nr. 34, Dezember 1996.

KREITMIR, KLAUS, "Ihr Mut Is Vorbild". Weltbild, Nr. 7 vom Marz 1996.

LAPIDE, PINCHAS E., *Three Popes and the Jews*. New York: Crown Publishers, 1967.

LEJEUNE, RENE, *Wie Gold im Feuer Gelautert*: Karl Leisner (1915-1945). Hauteville, Switzerland: Parvis-Verlag, 1991.

LORANT, STEFAN, *Sieg Heil! An Illustrated History of Germany From Bismarck to Hitler*. New York: W.W. Norton & Company, 1974.

MURPHY, FRANCIS J., *Père Jacques: Resplendent In Victory*. Washington, D.C.: ICS Publications, 1998.

NEUHASLER, DR. JOHANNES, *What Was It Like in the Concentration Camp at Dachau?* Munich: Trustees for the Monument of Atonement in the Concentration Camp at Dachau, 1965.

NEVER FORGET: CHRISTIAN AND JEWISH PERSPECTIVES ON EDITH STEIN, edited by Waltraud Herbstrith, OCD, translated by Susanne Batzdorff. Washington, D.C.: ICS Publications, 1998.

OESTERREICHER, JOHN M., *Walls Are Crumbling: Seven Jewish Philosophers Discover Christ*. New York: Devin-Adair Company, 1952.

PHILIPPE DE LA TRINITÉ, Le Père Jacques: Martyr de la Charité. Paris: Descleé de Brouwer, 1947.

PIES, OTTO, *The Victory of Father Karl*. New York: Farrar, Strauss & Cudahy, 1957.

PIUS XI, POPE, *The Church in Germany*. Washington, D.C.: National Catholic Welfare Conference, 1938.

PRESSER, DR. JACOB, *Ashes in the Wind: The Destruction of Dutch Jewry*, translated by Arnold Pomerans. Detroit: Wayne State University Press, 1988.

RHODES, ANTHONY, *The Power of Rome in the Twentieth Century: The Vatican in the Age of the Liberal Democracies, 1870-1922*. London: Sidgwick & Jackson, 1983.

RHODES, ANTHONY, *The Vatican in the Age of the Dictators: 1922-1945*. New York: Holt, Rinehart & Winston, 1973.

ROSENBERG, ALFRED, *The Memoirs of Alfred Rosenberg*, translated by Eric Posselt. Chicago: Ziff-Davis Publishing Company, 1949.

RUUSBROEC, JOHN, *The Spiritual Espousals and Other Writings*, translated by James A. Wiseman, OSB. New York: Paulist Press, 1985.

SPIRITU SANCTO, TERESIA, *Edith Stein*, translated by Cecily Hastings. New York: Sheed & Ward, 1952.

STEIN, EDITH, *Essays on Woman*, 2nd ed. rev., translated by Freda Mary Oben, PhD. Washington, D.C.: ICS Publications, 1996.

STEIN, EDITH, *The Hidden Life: Hagiographic Essays, Meditations, Spiritual Texts*, edited by L. Gelber and Michael Linssen, translated by Waltraut Stein. Washington, D.C.: ICS Publications, 1992.

STEIN, EDITH, *Life in a Jewish Family, 1891-1916*, translation by Josephine Koeppel, OCD. Washington, D.C.: ICS Publications, 1986.

STEIN, EDITH, *The Science of the Cross*, edited by Dr. L. Gelber, translated by Hilda Graef. Chicago: Henry Regnery Company, 1960.

STEIN, EDITH, *Self – Portrait in Letters, 1916-1942*, translated by Josephine Koeppel, OCD. Washington, D.C.: ICS Publications, 1993.